July

NO CHINESE
STRANGER

BOOKS BY JADE SNOW WONG

No Chinese Stranger

Fifth Chinese Daughter

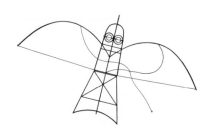

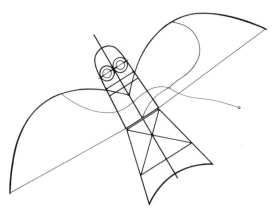

Jade Snow Wong

ILLUSTRATED BY DENG MING-DAO

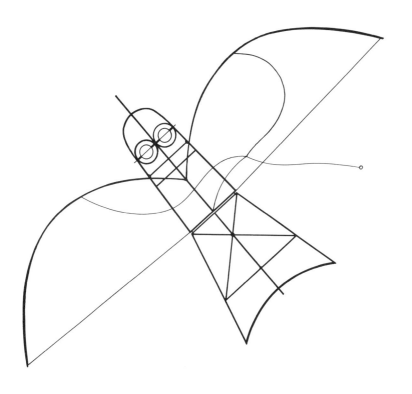

NO CHINESE STRANGER

HARPER & ROW, PUBLISHERS

New York, Evanston, San Francisco, London

PORTIONS OF THIS WORK ORIGINALLY APPEARED IN SOMEWHAT DIFFERENT FORM IN *Holiday* MAGAZINE.

FIRST EDITION

Designed by Janice Willcocks Stern

Library of Congress Cataloging in Publication Data

Wong, Jade Snow.
  No Chinese stranger.

  1. China—Description and travel—1949– I. Title.
DS711.W625   915.1'04'5   73–14301
ISBN 0–06–014732–6

75 76 77 78 79 10 9 8 7 6 5 4 3 2 1

FOR WOODY

WITHOUT HIM, THIS BOOK

WOULD NOT BE POSSIBLE

CONTENTS

INTRODUCTION

More than twenty-five years have passed since the publication of *Fifth Chinese Daughter*, the story of my growth and family training. During these more than two decades, the Chinatown of San Francisco where I was born has lost its tranquillity as fresh waves of immigrant Chinese have doubled its population to about 60,000 persons. They bring new talents, new dialects, and new problems.

My work in ceramics has expanded beyond its store window beginnings. Daddy's remaining years became my lasting benediction. My life has given life. I married Woody, also a Chinese-American, and we are the parents of two sons and two daughters who have the bodies of their Chinese race, the health and carriage of Americans, and values which combine the two heritages. This is our story.

The Chinese tradition which deems it unnecessary to sign works of art and unbecoming to talk at length using "I" or "me" prompted *Fifth Chinese Daughter* to be written in the third person. Following that form, I began Part I of this book in 1970. Some names are changed or omitted to protect privacy.

Part II describes the forging of my own life style, independent of my father's presence but bound by his precepts.

In June of 1971, my husband and I applied to the Chinese Embassy in Ottawa, Canada, for visas to travel to China. After Richard Nixon's visit, nine months later, our hopes increased. Through information from friends and relatives in Hong Kong, we believed that personal application at that gateway would expedite formalities, so there we flew in March of 1972.

A month of negotiation and nagging wait ensued before Peking granted our visas. During four weeks of travel in a land physically new to me, it was remarkable how very much I felt at home. Because of the radiance which enveloped me as I moved among the Chinese in the People's Republic of China, I discovered my comfortable bonds as one of them. Yet when I walk two familiar blocks between home and studio, in the freedom of the United States, I am conscious of being a minority in a "white" or Western world. Part III tells of my journey in China, where because of my father's discipline and education in my heritage, I did not feel a Chinese stranger.

When it was necessary to take temporary leave of ceramics, a visual art, to create this book with words instead, I was cheered and helped by Elizabeth Lawrence Kalashnikoff, who had edited *Fifth Chinese Daughter*. Ann Harris, now my editor at Harper & Row, has given me her sympathetic and analytical assistance. For their guidance, I shall always be grateful.

After I finished writing, my husband researched and sketched the chapter designs, which the artist completed, to enhance the format of this book.

Without the loyal support of loved ones and interested friends in San Francisco, who gave me the priceless gift of time, this book would have been a burden to bear rather than a joy to complete. My appreciative thanks include them too.

JADE SNOW WONG

父親大人

PART I

*"TO THE GREAT
PERSON OF FATHER"*

CHAPTER 1
THE UNSEEN REALITY

In 1950, just after Jade Snow and Woody were married, *Fifth Chinese Daughter* was published. When her parents heard that the book interested American readers and that the story was being translated into foreign languages, including Chinese, they were astonished. Hearing her daughter report, "My book is being dramatized nationally, on the radio," or "My book will be published in England," her puzzled mother could find nothing to say.

Her father would wonder aloud, "Why should so many people want to know about us?"

Jade Snow did not regard her life as remarkable, but curiosity ranging from idle questions to intense interest expressed by American friends and teachers made her aware that little had been written about Chinese family life. The request had come to her from a New York editor, and having been asked, she had to try.

When her parents, oldest brother, and sisters first learned that Jade Snow was working on an autobiography, they expressed their disapproval, for publicity was loathsome, and they doubted that this young family member could avoid disgracing them. Because she wished to continue living in peace with them, misgivings filled her through the period of writing. The magazine article which had attracted the Harper editor had antagonized her family, for the staff artist had depicted the Wongs in ill-fitting clothes, with unkempt hair and bare feet. It mattered little what text Jade Snow had written. American public reaction was of no interest to her family.

As Fifth Daughter, Jade Snow was not distinguished. First, Second, and Fourth Sisters had married. Third Sister had died in infancy. Sharing her tiny room was Younger Sister Jade Precious Stone, the Sixth and last daughter. A meticulous draftsman, she held an excellent position in an American engineering firm, was soon financially independent, and never found it necessary to marry.

Sons held separate numerical rank. Oldest Brother, who helped their father part time, was employed full-time as a civilian electrician for the U.S. Navy. He too had married and, according to custom, his wife lived in his parental household. Second Son, Jade Snow's younger brother, had served in the Army's occupation forces in Japan. With his G.I. Bill of Rights, he was now in college. Third Son was youngest, only six years old.

Spokesman for his family was Father Wong, who was now in his early seventies, with thinning grayish hair. He preferred old-fashioned collarless shirts, to which he could attach a fresh starched white collar with a shiny gold stud in the back, and he normally wore a vested suit and tie. On his feet were high black kid shoes, with laces which crisscrossed through numerous holes and were caught by hooks at the top. When he went out, a hat was always necessary—straw in the spring and summer, and a gray felt at other times. He was only slightly stooped and not very wrinkled, and his face was usually tanned, for he would pause in his work when the evening paper came and read it at the front door of his blue-jeans factory, facing the setting sun. Daddy, as Jade Snow called him in affectionate English, usually had a serious expression, but when they looked at each other, a fondness passed between them requiring no words.

Father Wong had been reared in Fragrant Mountains, Canton, by the nineteenth-century standards of China. When he immigrated to San Francisco in 1903, he carefully transferred those tastes and values to his new home. By denying individuals expression of their feelings as his family grew, he saved his household from human racket and kept authority comfortably unchallenged. In the intense life of a family trying to overcome acute poverty through thrift and hard work, in the somber atmosphere of a home where praise was never spontaneous—because "If a flower is fragrant, it will be noticed without comment"—there was no vocabulary for feelings of joy except on rare occasions of prayer.

To the devout Methodist Christian Father Wong, spoken prayer was the perefct way to express heartfelt gratitude to God for those mysterious life blessings which occasionally came unannounced. He used elaborate, respectful, formal Chinese prose, which bordered on the poetic, as if delivering a speech to a king (as God indeed was to him). The ears of his children, their heads bowed in silence, registered that fervor, and they heeded his hopes and feelings. But afterward, their lips discussed nothing. God was power; God rewarded. Father Wong's prayers to the Unseen Reality became associated with some of the most significant events in the life of his family.

Jade Snow had dedicated her book to her mother and father, and when she received the first royalty check, six months after publication, her immediate thought was to share it with them. It had been a long pull from factory piecework to this check. When she asked Woody for approval and permission, he said, "You don't have to ask me about anything which is right." In his acceptance of obligations to parents, a Chinese son was no different from a Chinese daughter.

She telephoned her father that they would come home that

night for dinner. He wondered why. She replied, "I have something for you."

He was suspicious. "What is the something?"

She was secretive. "A surprise—you must wait."

Dinner at home was always at exactly 6:00 P.M. She and Woody arrived with their gifts properly wrapped in red paper, as at New Year's. Daddy and Mama were both preparing dinner when she presented them. Father Wong opened his envelope at once, beamed in excitement, and gave his hundred-dollar bill an American kiss!

Mama continued to cook, ignoring her envelope on the stove top, but murmured, "Thank you." Later, she left the kitchen with it, making no additional comment.

Both parents had reacted typically, as suited each temperament.

Daddy always said grace before dinner. Sometimes it was routine, sometimes it was silent, sometimes it was to ask forgiveness for their sins. But tonight, it carried a different tone. As Jade Snow, her younger sister, two younger brothers, her husband, and her mother bowed together with their father, he said, "We are gathered here because of a book about which fellow villagers, merchants, and friends on the street have been congratulating me. For this book was written in America by a Chinese, not only a Chinese but a Chinese from San Francisco, not only a Chinese from San Francisco but a Wong, not only a Wong but a Wong from this house, not only a Wong from this house but a daughter, Jade Snow. Heavenly Father, this accomplishment was not mine but Yours! From Your many blessings, this girl, raised according to Your commandments, was able to do this work."

It was the first and only time the family heard what he thought of the book, and one of the few times a daughter was complimented in prayer. There was no further discussion, for that would have been bad taste. The prayer had rewarded Jade Snow in a way which the most flattering review from an astute critic could not.

Mama began to serve dinner, and family sounds filled the air. First, there was a soup of fresh vegetables, followed by her village specialty of black Chinese mushrooms simmered with bits of pork, sliced water chestnuts, and whole ginkgo nuts. The fish was deliciously different—chunks of halibut fillet had been crisply fried and assembled in a sweet and sour sauce accented with slivers of sweet pickled vegetables. Steamed red Chinese sausages came, sliced and juicy. There was dried salted fish, without which Father Wong considered a dinner incomplete. Jade Snow had brought another gift, a hot barbecued duck, which graced another platter. What a feast! Daddy produced a treasured bottle of French cognac to make the happy meal complete.

Though Mother Wong never indulged in spirits, she lingered with them over the rare celebration meal. She was barely five feet tall, in her fifties, and enjoyed good health. As she had for more than thirty years, she continued to work with her husband. Her specialty was to run the double-stitch machine for blue-jean seams, a physically demanding job because fabric parts were distributed in five-dozen-lot bundles which were heavy to lift. The Wong family had recently moved their living quarters from part of a basement factory which was in a redevelopment area targeted for a housing project, keeping the business manufacturing there until the building was razed. The rented new location east of Chinatown would accommodate a factory when that move might prove necessary, but in the meantime, Mama sewed alone, attending conveniently to domestic duties and her young son. Oldest Brother brought home the materials for her work.

Mama's daily dress was the Chinese "cheongsam," a straight-cut, side-fastened dress with little hem slits and a high collar. Only when San Francisco suffered through an occasional hot spell would she alternate with cooler Western styles. Like Chinese women all over the world, except within China today, she always wore pierced earrings and a pendant of pure jade, and she owned some solid gold adornments. Even a Chinese woman of modest means saved her pennies for a real gem. Jade was the precious talisman stone, also prized for its color, its clear cool green being a standout against black hair and golden skins. Costume jewelry was ignored as inferior.

Jade Snow remembered the dreadful depression years, when her mother would send her to one of the row of goldsmiths around the corner on Jackson Street with a 24-karat gold brooch or ring or chain to sell. The shopkeeper would weigh the precious metal on a little hand scale, click his beady abacus, and give her a few dollars in exchange.

The opportunities in California, the "Golden Mountains," had run out. Many Chinese, having made some money, repatriated to China, either with or to their families. "Second Uncle" on Daddy's side (actually his first cousin by American definition) retired with his family to Fragrant Mountains. "Third Uncle," a bachelor on Mother's side (actually her older brother), also departed for China. Chinatown apartment buildings showed numerous vacancies. Its streets were uncongested, for there were few residents and practically no automobiles. Among the families who did remain were the Wongs, in part because they lacked steamship fares. But they would not accept federal welfare even when their factory orders declined, and expenditures for food were doled out in dimes. Yet even without milk, they were never hungry. Rice, fish, or chicken, green vegetables, and unlimited tea for six or eight around the table could be managed for less than fifty cents.

Poverty was not new to her parents. Sometimes Mama talked of her childhood in Fragrant Mountains. Food had always been a problem. If they had rice, they were fortunate. If there was salt, or oil, second and third necessities, they were even more fortunate. Since water was impure, a beverage made with tea was the fourth basic necessity. Sometimes there were a few pennies to spare, and the child took a rice bowl (packaging being nonexistent) to purchase a few salted olives, a lump of brown sugar, a dollop of thick, red soy, or a wad of dried turnip root to make plain white rice palatable. Meat and fish were rarities. Green vegetables sometimes came their way as a gift from visiting relatives. Fresh scallions with some shrimp sauce constituted a delicious variation. In very hot weather, Grandmother would treat each child to a banana, but "juicy" fruits generally cost too much. Childhood sicknesses were frequent; fevered brows were soothed by home remedies, such as rice gruel simmered with citrus peels. Only during a few feast days or on a birthday might there be a chicken.

"Then my mother was so anxious to show her neighbors that we could afford a chicken, I would be sent to take a piece to each of a number of them," Mama recalled. "By the time I came home there would scarcely be any chicken left for me."

Since Grandfather Tong had already immigrated to San Francisco, it was Grandmother who determined the character of her family life. Her friendliness and generosity in sharing what little she had attracted cooperative houseguests even less fortunate than herself. Mother Wong recalled a regular visitor: with her bed roll and belongings packed on her back, the tiny lady would walk for hours on swollen feet to seek a change from living with an uncharitable nephew. Arriving at Grandmother Tong's, she would settle down for a few weeks to do mending and sewing. Because of her bound feet, she was clearly limited to sedentary chores.

In a simple economy, other abilities could be welcome in houseguests. Another sociable sometime visitor cleaned house with thoroughness and vigor, a task distasteful to Grandmother Tong.

The rarity of good food in childhood was also recalled by Father Wong: "As a thirteen-year-old boy, I was critically ill with a ravaging fever. My mother vowed to the gods that if I recovered she would make a sacrifice. I did, and in gratitude she distributed three whole barbecued pigs to the entire village. I tasted only one of the feet. Nothing I have tasted since then has duplicatd that flavor."

Despite the gloom of bad times in the United States, there was no doubt that her parents felt that they had improved their lot by immigrating here.

CHAPTER 2
FATHER TO DAUGHTER

His unusual prayer epitomized Daddy's surprised reaction. In expressing humble gratitude to God, he passed over that which he had initiated and contributed to the chain of events leading through the years to that evening. Had he not been a rugged individualist, his daughter's life might have been very different.

Father Wong had immigrated in the waning days of the Manchu Empire. He had been in his impressionable late teens when China lost Taiwan and Korea to Japan after the disastrous war of 1895.

10

Repeatedly through 1898, he witnessed China's disgraceful decline as one city after another was forced to become a Treaty Port for foreign trade (within which foreigners did pretty much as they liked) and territories were "leased" to European powers. He observed the unsuccessful Boxer Rebellion of 1900 when the Chinese tried to expel all foreigners, a failure for which reparations were demanded from China.

The populace was taxed to starvation; parents watched their sons conscripted into military service and sold their daughters into slavery. Warlords were in their heyday and raided without control. There was no future for Father Wong, who after five years of formal tutoring had apprenticed in his father's rice and lumber business. He was known to be an honest, thorough accountant. When he was offered a job auditing the books of the Sang Wo Sang firm's San Francisco branch, which supplied rice and staples in Chinatown, he asked his widowed mother, whom he adored, for permission to accept the opportunity. She objected strenuously. When he still insisted on leaving, she cursed her only son, "Go! Go! You wicked son, you will have the life to go, but not the life to return!"

In "Old Golden Mountains," a name for San Francisco which persisted after the Gold Rush, Father Wong found himself in an atmosphere of prejudice and persecution left over from decades of racial strife. Years before, railroad workers lured to California from Canton had finished the first transcontinental and other Western railroads, then drifted up and down the West Coast to start such small businesses as fruit farms, shrimp harvesting, or cigar rolling. But in many places they incurred the hatred and assaults of European immigrants seeking their own opportunities, who considered the Chinese heathens without souls. Mob violence murdered, persecuted, and drove Chinese out of communities from Wyoming to Washington, Oregon to California. The victims who survived pitchfork or fire attacks fled to San Francisco, but even here they were not safe. In 1876, celebrating the centennial of American independence, white mobs rioted through Chinatown, looting and destroying, until police cordons intervened and the Methodist Mission House opened its doors to the refugees. Its superintendent, Dr. Otis Gibson, a former missionary from China, stood up courageously against the mob, arguing that if

God had permitted Chinese to immigrate, it was also God's will for them to receive Christian treatment.

When a Chinese wandered outside of Chinatown, his end was likely to be brutal. A crab-fisherman was caught by ruffians, dragged under a pier, beaten, robbed, branded with a hot iron, and finally had his ears and tongue split. Pictures of San Francisco's Chinese showed them hurrying along with unsmiling faces, dressed in black Chinese coats, queues coiled under black-brimmed felts to avoid teasing.

The Chinese Exclusion Act of 1882 and later extensions had suspended the immigration of skilled and unskilled Chinese laborers. Only teachers, students, merchants, and travelers were exceptions. The California constitution prohibited the employment of Chinese in any branch of state, city, or county government.

Father Wong, who was admitted as a merchant, joined the predominantly male population huddled in Chinatown and living by its rigorous code. Peaceful community enterprises such as caring for the sick or providing burials for the dead were the duties of six geographical "Benevolent Associations," whose respective members spoke similar dialects and constituted the "Chinese Six Companies." Jade Snow's father was elected president of his Young Wo Association at a time when the post, by rotation, included presidency of the Six Companies and presidency of the board of directors of the new Chinese Hospital. Since Chinese were not allowed burial in white cemeteries, the Associations bought their own lands in Colma, south of the city. Ten years after interment, it was customary to exhume the bones from unsympathetic alien soil and return them for final rest to the land of their ancestors. Father Wong consistently volunteered for his Association's exhuming work, counting each bone and recovering any precious artifact, all to be wrapped in white cloth and sealed in metal containers for the voyage across the Pacific. No wonder Jade Snow's early memories were of a preoccupied family head.

Also carried over from China were family name clans (such as all the Chans in their clan, all the Wongs in theirs), irrespective of geographical origins. These clans gave Chinese their strongest individual identity, and they imposed standards of behavior. Sometimes a clan might embrace members bearing several names (such as the Louies, Fongs, Kwongs) knitted into one Association. Before provoking another person, a prudent man assessed the strength of his opponent's family name. An insult to one, when reported to the clan, aroused the defense of all. A disgrace by one shamed everyone bearing the surname.

Conservative Father Wong satisfied the traditional requirements, but he also departed from them. He began to study English at night classes sponsored by the Chinese Mission, where he also absorbed Christian theology. When he was gravely ill, missionaries visited him with Western medications, and he was convinced that God's will had saved his life. The Golden Rule and social conscience and action were a dramatic contrast to the "dog eat dog" philosophy of Chinese business practices. When a group of American missionary wives raided Chinatown to invite slave girls back to lives of human dignity, he was led to question the deplorable status of Chinese women who had been chattels without rights for thousands of years. With dedication and energy, he plunged into Christian leadership, and though tradition scorned revelation of faith, he was baptized in public.

He was untroubled when the unbelieving majority labeled him "Jesus' Little Boy" and opposed his turn to be chairman of the annual pilgrimage to Colma. How could a "Jesus Boy" be reverent about the souls of ancestors? He might even pollute the minds of impressionable younger people! Father Wong characteristically disdained to comment.

The 1906 earthquake and fire, which destroyed the general store where he worked, literally shook up his plans for a gainful occupation. Carrying a fifty-pound sack of rice and the set of books for which he was responsible, he fled with a group to a park at Steiner Street, over the hill from Chinatown. Then he and two other men hired a boat to take them to Oakland, where they found temporary housing.

Following this holocaust, Chinatown needed rebuilding. A beautiful new Methodist Church building was erected, and Father Wong took an active part in its affairs. With a handful of community leaders, he started the YMCA. Health lectures, team athletics and camp retreats were all innovations for which he worked, and he served on its board for thirty-seven years.

Father Wong was about ten years younger than Dr. Sun Yat Sen, who was born in a neighboring village. Dr. Sun campaigned abroad extensively for funds to finance his movement to forge a new China, and in the alley basement of San Francisco's Chee Kung Tong (Chinese Free Masons), Father Wong heard his compatriot speak of reforms necessary in their mother country: updating the quality of civil service examinations, reducing China's 95 percent illiteracy rate, eliminating for women the inhumanity of binding their feet, and for men, the humiliation of wearing the queues which signified their subjugation to Imperial authority.

To the excluded and rejected Chinese in America, Dr. Sun gave courage and the hope that the decadent empire in China would be replaced by a new strong government which would restore the immigrants' dignity and ensure their safety. He fired the imagination of an emerging group of Chinese graduates from American universities. Street rallies were held for the new cause, supported mostly by students and the working Chinese; the richer merchant class, allied to the Emperor's Dragon Flag, had too much to risk. An intermediate underground revolutionary party was formed. The Tung Meng Hui flourished in sworn alliance with several branches in China. In San Francisco, its flag was flown: five stripes of red, yellow, blue, white, and black, signifying the union of five races of China: Han, Manchu, Mongol, Uighur, and Tibetans. In the 1920s after the Empire had fallen, Jade Snow remembered seeing these colors flying over the rooftops of Chinatown and recalled her father's echoing Dr. Sun's three goals: Education of Character, Spirit, and Body.

When Second Uncle, who had owned a restaurant, left during the depression, he was typical of those whose ambition was to buy property in their native villages and enjoy lifelong rents, rather than stay in America and have their bones shipped back in a metal container. Having made money, they had no incentive to remain in California, where the 1913 Alien Land Act prevented noncitizens from owning real property; nor could a Chinese become a citizen by naturalization. These restrictions were not repealed until 1943. Before that year, if a female citizen married an alien Chinese she would lose her citizenship, and it was illegal for him to marry a white woman.

Yet despite these discriminatory laws, many others sank their roots here, Father Wong among them. Was he avoiding return to a land in political upheaval? Was he deliberately accepting his mother's prophecy? Perhaps he had found here a prize more meaningful than gold. Soon after the earthquake, he had sent for his wife, writing home to China, "In America I have learned how shamefully women in China have suffered. I will bleach the blackness of that disgrace by sending for my wife and two daughters. Here my wife will have opportunity to do honest work and my daughters will enjoy an education." Letters sent across the Pacific via slow vessel were respectfully studied by Father Wong's relatives, who quoted this passage over and over again in the fifty-five years that he remained in America. Great-grandfather Wong had only two sons: Father Wong was the only son of the older brother; hence, he was the family's senior patriarch whose authority extended to both shores.

Seeking a new occupation to support his arriving family, he began to manufacture blue denim garments, termed "donkey cloth" in Chinese because the heavy work was fit for a donkey. He leased the sewing equipment he couldn't afford to buy, and installed it in a basement where rent was cheapest. There his family followed the pattern of most Chinatown businesses—living and working at the same place. There was no thought that dim, cold, airless quarters were terrible conditions for living and working or that child labor was unhealthful. (Jade Snow could remember her family's blue-stained hands and the blue lint perpetually in their nostrils. Mama Wong so disliked denim that she always made corduroys for her sons to wear.) The only goal was that everyone in the family must work, save, and become educated.

Father Wong taught himself everything about the denim garment business, from cutting the yardage in five-dozen-layer lots to fixing machines when they broke down. (Factories with lightweight machines made dresses.) Jade Snow remembered Frank, a kindly Western mechanic who called regularly and showed her father how to make simple repairs. A Western jobber delivered the bolts of yardage and picked up finished garments for distribution to American retailers. Using an abacus, her father calculated costs to include thread, machine use, labor, and a narrow margin for profit. Workers were paid by piecework. Thread was a major cost, but what beautiful quality it used to be! Cotton six-cord was hard-finished, shiny like silk, tightly twisted to wear like iron.

Having provided the setup for family industry, the young father turned his attention to the education of his young. While public school took care of English, he had to be the watchdog of their Chinese training. Cantonese schools accepted only male students in the 1910s, so Father Wong tutored his eldest daughters each morning before breakfast.

By the time Jade Snow was six, in the late 1920s, the education of the young became a community problem. The Hip Wo Christian Academy was founded on a coeducational basis, and Father Wong served on its board for years. After Jade Snow began Commodore Stockton School, she spent three evening hours each weekday, and 9:00 A.M. to noon on Saturdays, at Hip Wo, learning poetry, calligraphy, philosophy, literature, history, correspondence, religion, and public speaking.

Father Wong continued to study Chinese classics all his life. He had a phenomenal memory for complex ideographs and could recite fluently lengthy lessons from his youth. Every evening after both schools, Jade Snow would sit by him as he worked at a sewing machine, singsonging her lessons above its hum. After Chinese lessons, she was dismissed to do American homework, feeling luckier than Chinese girls who knew no written Chinese because they didn't attend school, and luckier than Westerners who had no dual heritage to enrich their lives.

Jade Snow observed from birth that living, learning, and working were inseparable. Mama was the hardest-working seamstress in their factory, at her machine the minute housework was passably done, continuing there after the children had gone to bed, sewing and saving to have more than the four necessities. She accepted her life. "The path to virtue is narrow and difficult at first, but becomes broad and easy to those who walk it. The path to evil is wide and easy at first, but becomes narrow and difficult to those who walk it." Her children were therefore closely supervised, hearing her avowal, "A strict mother produces a worthy child, but a tender mother produces a weakling." Over and over, she admonished Jade Snow, "Face is given to you by others, but shame only you can bring to yourself."

Jade Snow never doubted that she too must work and save, but she had one other means to better herself which was denied to Mama: education. How to elevate herself from this factory-basement beginning was her responsibility and most important endeavor, for her father scorned mediocrity. He would not consider that excellence could be limited by economics.

Active as he was in the community, Father Wong was never too busy to supervise and discipline his children at home. To eliminate squabbling, he provided each child with his personal desk, study light, and scissors. As they grew older, each received a typewriter and sewing machine. For accurate identification, metal tools were filed with three notches, and wooden handles were burned with his company name (United Cooperation).

United   Cooperation

Table manners were indicative of a lady's background: how to hold a pair of chopsticks (with palm up, not down); how to hold a bowl of rice (one thumb on top, not resting in an open palm); how to pass something to elders (with both hands, never one); how to pour tea into the tiny, handleless porcelain cups (seven-eighths full so that the top edge would be cool enough to hold); how to eat from the center serving dish (only the piece in front of you—never pick around); and finally, not to talk at table.

There were other edicts: not to show up outside of one's room without being fully dressed; not to be late, ever; not to be too playful. In every way, every day, Jade Snow was molded to be trouble-free, unobtrusive, quiescent, cooperative. "It is clever to be obedient" were familiar words.

She was molded by being told, then by punishment if she was forgetful. Physical punishment was instant, unceremonious, and wordless. At the table, it came as a sudden whack on her hand from her father's chopsticks. Away from the table, it could be the elimination of a privilege, or a blow on her legs with a bundle of tied cane. Once when she screamed from its sting (she had been late getting home from the YWCA), her father reminded her of her good fortune. In China, he had been hung by his thumbs before being whipped by an uncle or a family friend called upon to do the job dispassionately.

Religious instruction was also a serious concern. Every Sunday prior to departure for church, Father Wong used his Chinese Bible to review the Sabbath lesson. Perhaps fifty to seventy adults attended services regularly, with greater crowds at Easter or Christmas. Father Wong was not only church treasurer for years, he stood through services as an usher. His faith in God's providence strengthened, and his wife and children absorbed his confidence. Chinatown contemporaries scoffed or ridiculed Christians as "do-gooders" who never shared their excitement in gambling. Even playing cards were not seen in the Wong family.

Though Father Wong's interest in the "Y" began altruistically, it became a personal satisfaction when he attended "Father and Son" banquets, another novelty to Chinatown. For at last, a son followed the first two daughters, and he remained the only boy in the family for fourteen years. This Chinese oldest son sandwiched between five girls was accorded lifelong luster. The best room was his alone, while his sisters were crowded three to a room. A Chinese scholar tutored him, and American lessons were learned in a private school. Nothing was too good for a male Wong, who would be responsible for that most important family ritual—the preservation of ancestral graves. Until he was born, their potential neglect was Father Wong's deepest emotional concern; now two male Wongs could be claimed for his family branch.

Perhaps his most precious tie with China was his hand-copied manual of their family tree. On page 1, black ink outlined the three keys to the locks of their home, followed by four pages of contour maps depicting ancestral burial grounds variously named "Three-Corner Pond," "Large Golden Pagoda," and so forth. By code the route was described leading through certain rice fields, to generations of graves which memorialized Wongs from the eleventh generation—those who had migrated to Fragrant Mountains—up to his father's, the sixteenth generation. The names of all male Wongs were recorded by generation together with family surnames of the women they had married, the dates of their births and deaths, and the names of sons born to each couple. No daughter's name held any place; someday her clan origin would be properly entered into her husband's family tree. This exclusion was no whim of Daddy's; it was Chinese law reaching back five hundred years before Christ, when Confucius codified already existing proper relationships and the practice of subjugating women.

As she grew out of childhood, Jade Snow felt that her father's religious conviction was not only derived from the strength of his faith; it was fortified by his belief in the Christian promise of eternal salvation, which suited a man who was a dynamic individualist. Contradicting a reactionary community where most residents either avoided criticism or, when involved in shady or potentially dangerous pursuits, joined strong "Tongs" for self-protection, her father did neither. He was genial, liked to speak in public, was well known to the man on the street, but he had few intimate friends. Cousins and uncles sought his counsel, but he never sought theirs. He contributed to causes and individuals when he could scarcely provide for his own dependents, but he never asked for help. Publicly he worked in the spirit of the Testaments, confident that his soul would merit accommodation in heaven. Privately he sacrificed for his son in the spirit of Confucius, so that his physical bones would be honored on earth.

CHAPTER 3

A TIME OF BEGINNINGS

If in those early years Jade Snow had a healthy fear of Daddy's thunder and strength, she also respected his individualism, and she grew up into womanhood handling her own affairs with a spirit of independence which expressed itself in an occupation concerned with art. Her book was an unplanned by-product. After her graduation from Mills College and four years before her marriage, she had started a small business in hand-thrown pottery. Lacking capital, she persuaded a Grant Avenue gift shop merchant to permit her to work at her potter's wheel in one of his two windows. Her finished pottery was displayed in a section of his showroom.

Nearly her father's age, Mr. Fong, the proprietor, was a stranger, and she had approached him wholly because of his location and available space. By usual Chinese standards, Jade Snow should have found a middleman to negotiate terms. But she was unconventional and less patient than most Chinese, so she just walked in "cold" and asked. Not being a Christian, he didn't believe in going one step out of his way to do a kindness. Yet by Chinese custom, if a stranger appealed to him, a request became his responsibility. He could have rejected a middleman but not her. Though noncommittal, he was occasionally helpful, and he taught her about shopkeeping and packing breakables.

Mr. Fong was a widower and lived alone behind the store. Occasionally his only son came home on Army leave, and he would walk to his father sitting by the cash register at the rear of the store, addressing him, "Father."

Mr. Fong, remaining seated, watching his store, never looking at young Fong, would ask without expression, "Have you eaten?"

Sometimes the answer was, "Yes, I have." No further conversation followed. If it was, "No, I haven't," Father Fong asked, "Would you like to eat?" To this question the answer was, "No." There was never the bustle of preparing a celebration meal.

The son would pick up his father's Chinese newspaper, open it, and read it while standing at the rear of the store, a few feet from his father. Silence prevailed. Then young Fong would fold up the paper and leave.

After he had departed, Father Fong would pick up the paper and remark, "This is the trouble with the younger generation. They cannot leave the paper the way they found it." As he criticized, the father carefully rearranged the paper so that every corner was even, and folded it as smoothly as it had been delivered.

This taciturn exchange was not surprising, and perhaps was even briefer because they spoke in the presence of a nonfamily female. To ask, "Have you eaten?" is the practical Chinese way of saying, "How are you?" The person replying usually answers affirmatively, for not to have eaten would indicate a lack of time, appetite, or funds. A friend also returns the question, "Have *you* eaten?" And if one runs into a friend while marketing, one always hears, "Buy more good things to go with your rice." No one is being personal; concern over food has been historically of first importance for working Chinese.

After Jade Snow began working in Mr. Fong's window, which confined her clay spatters, her activity revealed for the first time to Chinatown residents an art which had distinguished Chinese culture. Ironically, it was not until she was at college that she became fascinated with Tang and Sung Dynasty achievements in clay, a thousand years ago.

Her ability to master pottery made her father happy, for Grandfather Wong believed that a person who could work with his hands would never starve. When Father Wong was young, Grandfather made him learn how to hand-pierce and stitch slipper soles, and how to knot Chinese button heads, both indispensable in clothing. But to Mother Wong, the merits of making pottery escaped her—to see her college-educated daughter up to her elbows in clay, and more clay flying around as she worked in public view, was strangely unladylike. As for Chinatown merchants, they laughed openly at her, "Here comes the girl who plays with mud. How many bowls could you sell today?" Probably they thought: Here is a college graduate foolish enough to dirty her hands.

It has been the traditional belief from Asia to the Middle East, with Japan the exception, that scholars do not soil their hands and that a person studied literature in order to escape hard work. (This attitude is still prevalent in most Asian countries outside of the People's Republic of China and Japan.)

From the first, the local Chinese were not Jade Snow's patrons. The thinness and whiteness of porcelains imported from China and ornate decorations which came into vogue during the late Ching Dynasty satisfied their tastes. They could not understand why "silly Americans" paid dollars for a hand-thrown bowl utilizing crude California colored clays, not much different from the inexpensive peasant ware of China. That the Jade Snow Wong bowl went back to an older tradition of understated beauty was not apparent. They could see only that she wouldn't apply a dragon or a hundred flowers.

Many years later when Jade Snow met another atypical artist, a scholar and calligrapher born and educated in China, he was to say to her, "I shudder if the majority of people look at my brush work and say it is pretty, for then I know it is ordinary and I have failed. If they say they do not understand it, or even that it is ugly, I am happy, for I have succeeded."

However, there were enough numbers of the American public who bought Jade Snow's pottery to support her modestly. The store window was a temporary experiment which proved what she needed to know. In the meantime, her aging father, who was fearful that their home and factory might be in a redevelopment area, made a down payment with lifetime savings to purchase a small white wooden building with six rentable apartments at the perimeter of Chinatown. Jade Snow agreed to rent the two tiny empty ground-floor storefronts which he did not yet need, one for a display room, with supplies and packing center at its rear, the other for the potter's wheel, kiln, glazing booth, compressor, and other equipment. Now, instead of paying Mr. Fong a commission on gross sales, she had bills to pay. Instead of sitting in a window, she worked with doors thrown open to the street.

Creativeness was 90 percent hard work and 10 percent inspiration. It was learning from errors, either from her lack of foresight or because of the errors of others. The first firing in an unfamiliar new gas kiln brought crushing disappointment when the wares blew up into tiny pieces. In another firing, glaze results were uneven black and dark green, for the chemical supply house had mistakenly labeled five pounds of black copper oxide as black iron oxide. One morning there was a personal catastrophe. Unaware of a slow leak all night from the partially opened gas cock, she lit a match at the kiln. An explosion injured both hands, which took weeks to heal.

The day-to-day work of potterymaking tested her deepest discipline. A "wedged" ball of clay (prepared by kneading) would be "thrown" (shaped) on the potter's wheel, then dried overnight and trimmed, sometimes decorated with Chinese brush or bamboo tools. It took about a hundred thoroughly dried pieces to fill a kiln for the first firing that transformed fragile mud walls into hard bisque ware. Glazes, like clays the results of countless experiments, were then applied to each piece. A second twelve-hour firing followed, with the temperatures raised hour by hour up to the final maturing point of somewhere around 2,000 degrees Fahrenheit. Then the kiln was turned off for twenty-four hours of cooling. Breakage was a potential hazard at every stage; each step might measure short in technical and artistic accomplishment. A piece she worked on diligently could disappoint. Another made casually had been enhanced successively until it delighted. One piece in ten might be of exhibition quality, half might be salable, and the others would be flawed "seconds" she would discard.

Yet Jade Snow never wavered from her belief that if moments in time could result in a thing of beauty that others could share, those moments were immeasurably satisfying. She owned two perfect Sung tea bowls. Without copying, she tried to make her pottery "stand up" in strength and grace to that standard.

It became routine to work past midnight without days off. Hand work could not be rushed; failures had to be replaced, and a host of other unanticipated business chores suddenly manifested themselves. She had kept comparable hours when she worked all through college to meet her expenses. Again, the hope of reaching valued goals was her spur. If she should fail, then she could accept what tradition dictated for most Chinese daughters—to be a wife, daughter-in-law, and mother. But unlike her college, the American business world was not dedicated to helping her. Because she was pioneering in a new venture, her identity was a liability. Her brains and hands were her only assets. How could she convert that liability? How could she differ from other struggling potters?

To enlarge her production base, she experimented with enamels on copper forms conceived in the fluid shapes of her pottery, layering jewel tones for brilliant effects. They differed from the earth tints of clay and attracted a new clientele. With another kiln and new equipment, she made functional forms, believing that fine things should become part of the user's everyday life. The best results were submitted to exhibitions. Some juries rejected them, some accepted, and others awarded prizes.

To reach a market larger than San Francisco, she wrote to store buyers around the country, and, encouraged, she called on them. Traveling to strange cities far across the United States, as a rare Oriental woman alone in hotel dining rooms, she developed strong nerves against curious stares. That trip produced orders. Stipulated delivery and cancellation dates made it necessary to hire first one and then more helpers who had to be trained, checked, kept busy and happy.

The strains increased. So did the bills, and she borrowed in small amounts from her sympathetic father, who said, "A hundred dollars is easy to come by, but the first thousand is very, very tricky. Look at the ideograph for hundred—solidly square. Look at it for thousand—pointed, slippery. The ancients knew

(hundred)　　(Thousand)

this long ago." When hundreds were not enough, tactful Western friends offered help. Oldest Brother, noticing her worries and struggles, sniffed scornfully, "You'll be out of business in a year."

She had learned to accept family criticism in silence, but she was too deeply involved to give up. Money was a worry, but creating was exciting and satisfying. These were lonely years. Jade Snow's single-minded pursuit did not allow her pleasant interludes with friends. To start a kiln at dawn, then watch till its critical maturing moment, which could happen any time between early evening and midnight or later (when gas pressure was low, it took until the next dawn), kept her from social engagements.

Then, gradually, signs indicated that she was working in the right direction. The first was a letter from the Metropolitan Museum of Art in New York, where the Eleventh Ceramic National Syracuse Show had been sent.* The curator wrote, "We think the green, gold, and ivory enamel bowl a skillful piece of workmanship and are anxious to add it to our collections." They referred to a ten-inch shallow bowl which Jade Snow had made.

---

* An annual show sponsored by the Syracuse Museum of Fine Arts. Entries accepted at regional centers were shipped to Syracuse, New York, for final selection and awards. The exhibition was then circulated for a year to various museums.

A reviewer in *Art Digest* wrote, "In plain enamels without applied design, Jade Snow Wong of San Francisco seemed to this critic to top the list."

Recognition brought further recognition. National decorating magazines featured her enamels, and in the same year, 1947, the Museum of Modern Art installed an exhibit by Mies Van der Rohe which displayed 100 objects of fine design costing less than $100. A note introducing this exhibit read, "Every so often the Museum of Modern Art selects and exhibits soundly designed objects available to American purchasers in the belief that this will encourage more people to use beautiful things in their everyday life. . . ." Two of Jade Snow's enamels, a dinner plate in Chinese red and a dessert plate in grayish gold, were included in the exhibition, which subsequently went to Europe.

So it did not seem unusual to receive an interviewer from *Mademoiselle*, but it was indeed unexpected to receive one of the magazine's ten awards for 1948 to women outstanding in ten different fields. They invited Jade Snow to fly to New York to claim her silver medal.

The more deeply one delves into a field, the more one realizes limitations. When Bernard Leach, the famous English potter, accepted an invitation from Mills College to teach a special course, Jade Snow attended. Another summer, Charles Merritt came from Alfred University's staff to give a course in precise glaze chemistry. Again, she commuted to Oakland. She became friends with these two unusual teachers. Both agreed that in potterymaking, one never found a final answer. A mass-produced bathtub may be a technical triumph; yet a chemically balanced glaze on a pot can be aesthetically dull. Some of the most pleasing glaze effects could never be duplicated, for they were the combination of scrapings from the glaze booth. Like the waves of the sea, no two pieces of pottery art can be identical.

After three years of downs, then ups, the business promised to survive. Debts had been cleared. A small staff could handle routine duties. A steady clientele of San Franciscans came to her out-of-the-way shop. A beginning had been made, and it was then that she started seriously on a second activity—the book in fulfillment of her promise to Harper.

There was to be still a third beginning.

CHAPTER 4
THE SECOND MALE TO FOLLOW

Mother Wong's sewing machine was along the general pathway between kitchen and bedrooms. While operating it, without turning her head she knew who was coming from behind. One day, just when Jade Snow was most distracted about her commitments, she was passing Mama's machine and was stopped by Mama's voice: "Jade Snow, it is fine for you to have an interesting career when you are young, but it is not a natural or complete life for a woman. As you mature, you should have a husband to care for you in sickness, and when you are older, your children should relieve your loneliness. You know our saying, that in a lifetime a female follows three males: 'When young, she follows her father; when older she follows her husband; and when old she follows her son.' "

Her mother had not engaged in preliminaries or turned her head.

Jade Snow assured her that she wasn't antimarriage (she had turned down more than one parentally arranged match), but she would only marry someone right for her. Woody Ong, the someone right, had returned to Chinatown after fighting for the U.S. Army in China in World War II, and was startled by the sight of her in the store window.

Their families had been friends for many years. Jade Snow's older sisters, who used to work at the YWCA, had known his mother when she brought her little sons to the Y's public bath. (In the 1920s, hot running water was not available in most of Chinatown's apartments; 15 cents paid for a bath.) His petite and pretty mother, who had married at sixteen, laughed and played with them, and joked that she "grew up with my sons." Since Chinese boys do not stay home with their mother, who indulged all of them as Jade Snow's father had indulged his eldest son, Woody and his six brothers (Third Son, born after Woody, had died in childhood) spent much of their time at the YMCA gymnasium a couple of blocks away, swimming and playing basketball. The playground across the street provided tennis courts. His relationship with his mother, his freedom of movement, his proficiency in sports, and familiarity with a host of Chinatown young men of his generation differed from Jade Snow's experiences, even though they both grew up in the same time and place.

Like her family, the Ongs had been no less strained by the depression. The family had to move, cramming active boys into a small apartment which was also their father's informal office. Woody's easygoing, good-looking father was an employment agent for Chinese workers, and agent for the Greyhound Bus and Dollar Steamship lines. There was not much call for either of these services in a period of unemployment and the repatriation of many Chinese to their native land.

Woody's mother recalled that there was no money to buy the customary fifty-pound sack of rice for nine hungry mouths. Not to have rice, one of life's four necessities, was starvation. "With an old car we bought for twenty-five dollars, we depended on Oldest Son and Father selling and delivering bread—at five cents a loaf, people staved off hunger from day to day—to homes and factories. Our markup was only one cent. When demand was brisk, we delivered a hundred and fifty loaves, but gas cost fifty-three cents. I could only buy twenty-five cents' worth of rice at a time." At Portsmouth Square Woody shined shoes for a nickel a pair. During summers, he went to the Sacramento Valley to pick fruit in the hundred-degree heat for fifteen cents an hour, only to be assessed most of it for his room and board.

Jade Snow knew several of the Ong boys through school and community activities when she was in junior college. Then World War II broke out and six of the seven brothers were pressed into military service; five drafted into the Army, and the youngest in the Navy. Through the war years, she heard of them occasionally when she and Mrs. Ong ran into each other near Grant Avenue as each went between home and work. Sometimes they stopped to talk, for the mother missed her sons. Busy working people seldom had time to socialize at parties, and a major part of Chinatown's gossip, business, and visiting was done on street corners. Grant Avenue with its series of "village stores" and restaurants is the communications center of Chinatown.

At home now, Jade Snow learned, were only the elderly father bedridden by a stroke, an aged aunt, and the mother herself. They occupied a dark flat conveniently located behind Grant Avenue. In her spare hours each day, after caring for two invalids, Woody's mother went to sew at a factory. She endured her changing load of problems with the help and sympathy of a constant stream of relatives passing through San Francisco on military leave, or old friends of her husband. (Perhaps the custom of informal visiting in Chinatown prevents a notoriously high suicide rate from being even higher. In old-fashioned stores in those days, old men sat in the back, sipping tea and sharing companionship, even if they sat in silence.) Woody's mother welcomed those visitors to her table. A marvelous cook, she spared no effort in concocting delicious dishes, and the appreciative friends reported news, ran errands, brought gifts; at times they contributed gratefully to a kitchen "pot."

On one of these street chats, Jade Snow heard from the joyful mother that, one by one, her sons would be coming home. No longer would she go out to sew again. "I have seven bank accounts in my seven sons," she declared proudly. Miraculously, six brothers who served on the seas, in the air, on land, from Europe to Asia, were all returning safely. Sadly, they were returning after their father's death, and soon afterward, Auntie also died.

Thus prepared, Jade Snow was not surprised when Woody hailed her one day as she passed a restaurant and invited her to join him in a cup of coffee. He caught up on her family news and what she had been doing for the past several years. In turn, he said that he had decided against returning to his former Chinatown banking job. His mother had cherished a dream that her grown sons would work together, and they were starting a family grocery business, prepared to put in seven days a week. Their uncle, the succeeding patriarch after their father's death, was the quiet benefactor who raised financial backing. Oldest Brother would continue working at the YMCA. Brothers who were younger would continue with their college educations and, like many of their contemporaries, would utilize their G.I. Bill of Rights.

Jade Snow's younger brother also returned from Army duties and awaited entry to the University of California. He sought interim work as a carpenter, but the union would not admit a Chinese, so he helped Father Wong around the factory and accepted unemployment benefits from his G.I. Bill. He was bitter about their father's lack of financial success after years of hard labor, and blamed the Western jobber for excessive profit-taking—browbeating Father Wong to lower his labor contract costs but selling the finished jeans at prevailing wholesale price levels. When the jobber patronizingly asked Younger Brother why he wanted a college degree when he could take over his father's business, Younger Brother declared angrily, "So I can kick around people like you, who have been kicking around people like my father!" When Younger Brother entered U.C. and listed his major as Industrial Management, his counselor took him aside. "Don't you realize that American industry doesn't want a Chinese face up front? Major in something which will let you work unseen."

Older Chinese-American G.I.'s utilized their Bill of Rights for business loans. Others who were non-English-speaking and non-citizens had won the right to citizenship through their war service, and traveled to Hong Kong for brides. After the War Brides Act of 1945, six thousand Chinese women were admitted. As the ratio of married women to men increased, a third generation of youngsters began to appear.

For two years, while Jade Snow coped with her ceramics business and Woody with his grocery business, their paths crossed infrequently. When the older boys reestablished themselves, they pooled funds to lavish overdue gifts on the mother whom they adored and provided every comfort to delight her the rest of her life. Shy about entering stores outside of Chinatown to choose Western appliances, Woody's mother asked Jade Snow to help her with language and decisions. Woody, the treasurer, came to pay for purchases and arrange their delivery. One day, he telephoned about a more serious matter. His mother was having "female problems"; it was a realm beyond the power of the brothers. Would Jade Snow help to find a competent doctor?

It was not the first request of this type she had had. Most of Chinatown's needs were met within its geographical boundaries. In the 1940s, few non-English-speaking elders ventured outside their community except to shop (as Woody's mother had) or for medical appointments with Western specialists. Jade Snow had learned to interpret medical phrases into Cantonese and vice versa in order to help her parents and their friends.

Woody's mother had given birth to all her sons at home, sometimes even before assistance arrived. But the obstetrician had always been called, for otherwise there would not be any signed birth certificate, the precious proof of citizenship. In the hands of a competent gynecologist recommended by friends, Mrs. Ong now learned that an operation was necessary. It was a Chinese superstition that one entered a Western hospital only when death was imminent. Not long before, hospitals would not even admit Chinese patients. Her natural fear was compounded by her inability to understand instructions in English or to make her wants known.

After the preliminaries were attended to at the admissions desk, and the tiny, nervous figure was enveloped in the white bedcovers, Jade Snow surprised herself by asking impulsively, "May I pray with you?" At unexpected moments, she was her father's daughter. It was the first time such an offer had come to her lips. That this sick woman was not a Christian didn't matter. In low tones, she appealed for God's compassion so that the patient would function well again. When they both opened their eyes, Jade Snow perceived a degree of peace on the other woman's face.

Accompanying each other daily in postsurgery visits, Jade Snow and Woody were brought together by this family emergency. Each grew in awareness of the other, and devotion flowered. Another year passed. While Jade Snow was convinced that her work was right for her, Woody was convinced that notwithstanding family loyalty, the grocery business wasn't for him.

"I don't have the temperament to argue with a Chinese housewife over the price of a loaf of bread, and I don't like the constant loading and unloading in that business," he declared. "It's repetitive and back-breaking."

Would it be possible for him to join her business? He had a degree in banking and had worked with his hands in a dental laboratory. To Jade Snow, it seemed ideal to have a man she loved at her side, whose knowledge would complement hers. The business had to be diversified to support another person—jewelrymaking and silversmithing would be natural extensions. That summer of 1950, Woody enrolled in the Mills College Resident Summer Session to take an intensive program in pottery and these arts.

In the meantime, Kathryn Uhl was finishing illustrations for Jade Snow's book manuscript. Even using family snapshots, she often required authentication for Chinatown scenes. Woody supplied the details. When news came that publication would be in early fall, they decided that they should marry before then. One day Woody phoned: "How about a wedding ring?"

"I'd like you to make it, of course," replied Jade Snow. "You know I don't like diamonds."

"How about gold?" he asked.

"That's fine—something not too thin, as I shall be wearing it while I work. Chinese pure gold would be perfect."

"Well, listen. Go to a jeweler and measure your finger size. Then go to Wildberg Brothers on Market Street and order some ten-gauge square gold wire. How much? Well, better double whatever is your size, as I'm sure to mess up the first one. I've never made a wedding ring before. Oh, yes, I need some gold solder too."

The finished ring was unlike any in the world. Woody did not ruin the first ring, so he made a second loop which he attached to the first one with two connecting links. "One bridge for you, and one for me," he explained. Then with sudden inspiration, he added, "And I'll insert a link for each child we'll have—there's lots of room!"

To the ring, Woody added another wedding present: a new spinning rod and reel. His hobby was fresh-water fishing, and they planned their honeymoon: with Woody's mahogany boat strapped to their car top, they would drive and fish through the nine Western states.

It was time to tell Father Wong, who was pleased. Recalling long years ago when he had delivered pants parts to Woody's mother so that she could work at home while supervising her children, he reminded them that Jade Snow was frequently a small passenger in a red wheelbarrow used to transport heavy goods and finished jeans.

"You were six years older than my daughter—maybe she was four or five and you were ten or eleven. Even then, you were enough charmed with her to buy her her first ice cream cone!"

Woody's mother welcomed her. Because she loved her sons with fierce devotion and unquestioning loyalty, she would naturally be critical of their wives, but she longed for the feminine companionship and confidences sons could not give her. In token of her acceptance, she gave Jade Snow an unusual and beautiful pair of old jade and pearl earrings to convert to a ring, and a matching jade for a pin to be worn in her knot of black hair; Woody made settings for both of these. When she presented these precious adornments, Mother Ong counseled, "To have an enduring marriage, you must let your husband have his way, no matter what he says or does. If he should be wrong, he will know this later, but you do not argue with him at the moment."

This precept was not easy to accept at first, but it became fundamental to a harmonious household and a long marriage.

What kind of a wedding should they have? Jade Snow shuddered to think of the procedures dictated by Chinatown custom: a formal Western-style church ceremony, followed by an enormous lengthy banquet at a Chinese restaurant. Chinese tradition requires the groom's family to pay all bills, while the cost of an American wedding was borne by the bride's family. To compromise, parents of Chinese-American young people sometimes shared costs. "Face" was so important that some went into debt to present an impressive show.

Neither Jade Snow nor Woody cared for show, so they made their own kind of arrangements. Because Jade Snow found at Mills the warmth of welcome and a feeling of coming home, it was natural to choose newly built Reinhardt House, the alumnae headquarters, for their wedding. George Hedley, who would perform the marriage rites, had been born of missionary parents in Tientsin, China. He had also been Jade Snow's economics professor and Woody's tennis mate during summer session. The former dean, in whose house she had lived at Mills, and the dean's husband would be honor attendants. With a Western service and Western attendants, the reception should be Western too. Through his friends in the grocery business, Woody spent weeks looking for the right vintage French champagne. For this unprecedented occasion, the Board of Governors passed a "first for weddings"—wine could be served in Reinhardt House.

They thought about guests. To avoid offending their parents' many friends and distant relatives, they decided that members of their immediate families should witness the simple wedding, and only personal friends would be invited to the reception. When they began discussing names, the hundred or so guests represented such a wide circle of Western friends that Jade Snow and Woody realized for the first time that by their occupation and interests, they had become minorities in their Chinese community. That these friends had the white faces of Westerners (who represented to the average Chinese immigrant a stereotype of untrustworthy power) was less significant to them than the human quality they shared with valued friends of whatever race—that particular warmth which is instantly reciprocal. Additionally, these friends gave generously and kindly of themselves, qualities which Chinatown's population could rarely allow itself in its hectic efforts to make ends meet.

They also possessed another American characteristic strikingly different from the Chinese—they were frankly outspoken. Jade Snow had first noticed this trait in her college professors. Later in life outside of Chinatown, in business as in everyday life, in board rooms or living rooms, she found the air crisply cleared by Americans who spoke out and didn't live by the Chinese rules, "If you do not speak, no one will think you are dumb," and "Think three times before you open your mouth." Perhaps their well-bred silence has miscast Chinese into the cliché of inscrutability. Repressing speech was a polite way of ignoring social problems or reducing personal ones. A wife's noisy rages were muffled, and in large families, disturbing chatter was eliminated. Only fathers, with the prerogative of the senior male, had the right to raise a storm before their voiceless audience.

To the afternoon wedding came all of Jade Snow's family and all of Woody's family too. Only Norman, the seventh son, was missing. After the war and a year at Stanford, he had left for Canton to attend Ling Nan University (then known as the best in Canton) to follow through his interest in Chinese studies. Two years had now passed since the Communist takeover, and he had not returned.

It was a memorable day above days. Most members of their families were visiting the beautiful campus setting for the first time. At first, they were shy among so many Western guests, but after mingling with them, they relaxed as the happy afternoon wore on. To Jade Snow, a single high point of the day stood out clearly. When Dr. Hedley asked formally who was giving Jade Snow away, Father Wong stepped forward and replied in clear English, "Her mother and I do." Thus, this daughter was entrusted to the care of the "second male to follow."

CHAPTER 5
OUTSIDE—FOREVER FREE

Their home life began simply in one of the vacant apartments above their studio. Jade Snow and her youngest brother had renovated four tiny dark rooms while Woody was at summer session. They painted, laid new floor tiles, replaced kitchen fixtures, and bought minimum furniture. Most of their time, the newlyweds would be working downstairs.

The apartment-studio was two blocks from Daddy's factory. At least twice a week he would visit her, and if he saw a customer, he would never intrude. When invited, he had a ready smile and offered a warm handshake. His long fingers were work-roughened and scarred here and there from accidents. Dignity and pride were subdued with humility. As he waited while Jade Snow translated English and Chinese, he never felt awkward. The knowledge of his heritage gave him confidence to meet anyone.

If his daughter had trouble with her potter's wheel, for which he had installed the motor, he would get on his knees to examine and diagnose.

On Jade Snow's first wedding anniversary, she was in bed with a persistent cold. Her father came to visit and perceived that she needed cheering up. He excused himself briefly and returned with a fresh squab. He washed it, then disjointed and salted it. With the flat of a Chinese cleaver, he broke the fibers of a fresh piece of ginger root, which he rubbed on the bird's skin. He washed a small amount of rice and cooked it with the squab on top. The delicate blended flavors coaxed her appetite and made a great anniversary lunch. When his fifth daughter expressed her appreciation, he, who could not express his emotion except in prayer, said matter-of-factly, "Chicken is not good for colds."

Being near her family and Chinatown, living upstairs and working downstairs, her routine didn't have to relinquish family ties or neglect Youngest Brother, who was still attached to her and came after school for help with American homework before walking on to Chinese lessons, just as his sisters and brothers had done before him. Tirelessly, Father Wong devoted himself to tutor this apt and obedient pupil so that he had a top record and annually won Chinese scholarship awards.

Another boy, slightly older than Youngest Brother, had attached himself to Woody since grocery store days. Because he didn't attend Chinese school, Woody gave him a part-time job. Jade Snow would feed both boys with a fast hot meal, usually lamb chops, their favorite food. Neither Youngest Brother nor Woody's young friend could communicate with his parents in English. Subjects of daily interest in the American world, such as sports, did not interest older Chinatown folks, even though their sons could speak to them in Cantonese. It was natural for Jade Snow and Woody to become the boys' close friends and advisers.

The parents of Woody's young friend worked at sewing factories, the father as a cutter and the mother as a seamstress. Jade Snow sometimes saw her carrying heavy bags of groceries up a hill with cable car tracks, to cook for her family of hungry boys. After dinner, like many other seamstresses, she would return to the factory while the oldest daughter did the dishes. This left Woody's friend, being a boy, free to roam. Chinatown was a tranquil community; its residents came and went freely at all hours, and delinquency or crime that could be statistically documented was rare. After school, young people somehow found more or less constructive activities—at a store, a club, one of the Y's, a church, a playground, or some other organization—in order not to trouble their parents and to stay out of crowded, unattractive tenements. The older generation's authority was unchallenged; in those days their young made the accommodation to community limitations.

But Woody's friend was a defiant boy, and had he been born twenty years later his life might have been shaped by very different forces. Woody described to Jade Snow their first meeting. "Day after day, this kid came to our store and hung around the slot machines, hours at a time. A six- or seven-year-old has no business there, so I shooed him off. But the little toughie planted his feet apart in front of me, hands on his hips, and dared me, 'Make me!' I could have lifted him and thrown him out, but I decided to make it easy on myself. So I told him if he wanted to stick around, he had to help mark prices and restock the canned goods. I was sure that because of the prospect of being put to work, he would disappear forever."

But to his surprise the child did as he was told. Thus began a lifelong friendship with Woody and Jade Snow. On later vacations or fishing trips, Youngest Brother and this friend accompanied them like sons.

In this first year of marriage, they often walked the three blocks to Chinatown for a restaurant lunch, after which they would purchase groceries for that night's late Chinese dinner at home. The division of their studio work was natural. Financial records and bank deposits, mechanical problems, chemical formulas, checking kiln action, packing, pickup, and deliveries naturally fell into Woody's hands while Jade Snow stayed close to home, working on designs, supervising staff schedules, and keeping house. True to tradition, once Woody had locked the studio door and come upstairs, he was home as a Chinese husband, expecting their house to be immaculate and to be waited upon and indulged. They could consult with each other on just about every subject without disagreement. Kindness, devotion, protection with strength new to her, and extravagant gifts were privileges that gladdened Jade Snow's heart, while her husband's physical comfort and mental relaxation were her responsibility. Theirs was the pattern of most Chinese marriages.

Woody's upbringing differed in one respect from the Wong boys, who had been taught never to engage in the vulgarity of fistfights. Jade Snow remembered Younger Brother in his junior high school days returning home after his morning paper route, his eyes swollen shut, because white boys had beaten him and robbed him of his receipts. To spare their mother, she and Jade Precious Stone had locked themselves with him in their bathroom to attend to his wounds, but Mama had hammered hysterically at the door. Though the Wong boys tried to avoid physical fights, sometimes they were victimized when they could not escape or were outnumbered.

Woody and his brothers had grown up sparring with each other, and he trained at the YMCA. Their parents expected them to scrap. Not being Christians, the Golden Rule didn't apply. Instead their rule was, "When provoked, get the jump first and you have beaten your opponent psychologically. Then finish him physically." Chinatown stories of their exploits had lodged in Jade Snow's mind. Anyone who picked on one of the brothers had to reckon with the return of all of them to retaliate. Then Woody would train the injured brother to perfect his fighting technique.

Soon after their marriage, this All-American method of using fists was demonstrated at their front door. The bell rang at about 2:00 A.M., and Kenny, their pet Schnauzer, barked furiously. Woody went to investigate. She could hear rough words. In a trice, he came back, laid down his glasses, and went outside again. Jade Snow heard the sickening thuds of body blows and cracking bones, followed by a resounding crash. She waited in horrified suspense. Woody came back, took off his white silk robe, still spotless, and climbed back into bed.

She wondered: Should I ask him what happened and keep him awake, or should I keep still?

She kept still until the next morning, when she went outside and found that the entire stair handrail had been broken off, while Woody was calmly hosing blood stains from the gray steps. When he began nailing the rail in place, she asked what happened.

"This white drunk came to the door and asked where I kept the girls. When I told him to mind his own business, he said, 'Shut up, or I'll put you to sleep.' So I answered, 'Let's see who's going to put whom to sleep.' You can guess that I let him have it with both fists. He fell down the steps backward."

When the boys showed up that afternoon, they asked for a blow-by-blow account, wishing that they could have seen the action. Though Youngest Brother was never a fighter, Woody's friend grew up learning from Woody to "handle his dukes," and his proficiency later led him in and out of a number of scraps.

New experiences added dimension to her life, but new responsibilities, though willingly assumed, added to a work load which by degrees drained her energies. The doctors told her that it had been too taxing to work days, nights, and weekends in their effort to build up their business. "We doctors used to work out of our homes too," said one of them, "but now we believe in a change of environment from work to home."

When Jade Snow hunted for new quarters outside of Chinatown, she ran headlong into her first real problem with rejection because of her race. White-skinned managers or real estate agents never asked her about education or occupation; one look at her Oriental features and they told her the vacant apartment had just been rented.

Through a sympathetic Western friend, they found a landlady who was willing to lease them a flat in Tiburon. It was a twenty-five-minute drive across the Golden Gate Bridge to a rustic area. With the roomy, furnished, two-bedroom flat came a terraced garden and a wide sundeck that overlooked a gorgeous Bay view. The country was welcome quiet each evening and the complete change from work which the doctor had prescribed. For the first time in their lives, they awoke to sunshine and bird trills, instead of a light well and the rattling of the scavenger collector. They went to bed seeing the moon, the stars, the mellow lights strung across the Golden Gate Bridge, and they justified the extravagant lease as temporary health insurance.

By now, Jade Snow's parental household had dwindled down to her father, mother, and youngest brother. World War II and the ensuing peace produced profound social changes. Her brother in his twenties married, with the traditional Chinatown banquet ceremonies, and moved to Los Angeles, where the aircraft industry offered him employment in production engineering. He succeeded despite his academic adviser's pessimism, and thus began with others the diffusion of young Chinese into white suburbs. Having enjoyed rapid promotions, her younger sister could now afford her apartment. Oldest Brother established his own home.

Jade Snow was eager to have her family visit her in their new Western-style home, but her parents had to have a reason for change from routine. Since it was just after Thanksgiving, when Jade Snow and Woody had realized a successful two-day sale of studio "seconds" and rejected experiments, during which Daddy Wong had voluntarily come and stood up during most of these two days to guard against shoplifting, a celebration was in order.

Mama Wong murmured about lacking time. Daddy declared, "I can't sleep in a soft bed." Then both decided, "It will be too much trouble."

"Come on," Woody inveigled. "There's some wonderful perch fishing at Tiburon, where you have never been."

That was exactly the right reason. Youngest Brother was off to find his fishing tackle. Mama liked to fish, and she was intrigued.

"Bring some extra blankets and enough things for a weekend," Jade Snow suggested.

On the following Saturday, Jade Snow brought three pots to their favorite Chinese restaurant to hold a specially ordered dinner. She shopped for additional provisions, including Chinese white flowering broccoli, a large roasting chicken, sides of spareribs, double lamb chops, and a puffy Boston cream pie. The last two items would be exotic treats for her parents. A Sunday barbecue would also be a novelty. That evening, they collected the pots, from which good smells drifted out, and filled cartons with the groceries. Then they picked up their family, expectantly ready with overnight bags.

It began to rain, and gale winds howled so fiercely that the single-span Golden Gate Bridge swayed dangerously from side to side. It was suddenly closed off. All lights were extinguished.

Their car had to wait in a long line until the storm subsided. Both parents began murmuring at their foolishness in consenting to this visit and wondered why a usually sensible daughter and a practical son-in-law would leave the convenience of Chinatown for a daily trek to the wilderness.

More than two hours of suspense later, when the winds finally relented, they continued the drive. Tired, cold, hungry, they suffered the oppressive silence which follows when gay chatter is exhausted. Turning from the main highway into the long Tiburon Peninsula spur road, they found themselves in complete darkness because the power lines had snapped. They reached home at 9:30 P.M. It offered no lights, the refrigerator was dead, and the electric range was useless.

Host and hostess rushed around to find candles. Woody coaxed up flames in the living room fireplace to warm the restaurant-cooked contents of the pots. Daddy and Mama remained politely silent while Youngest Brother brightly declared that he had material for class news reporting without having to search through the newspaper. One end of the living room was furnished with an informal dining table flanked by benches. Woody insisted that Father Wong should take his place at head of the table, and this deference touched and pleased him. But the introduction to suburban living was dismal.

The next morning, everything looked brighter. When Jade Snow arose, Daddy and Mama were already dressed, enjoying the gorgeously clear Bay view with that sparkle possible only after high winds and cleansing rains. Daddy was pacing back and forth in excitement because Angel Island faced them across narrow Raccoon Straights. In clear view were "China Cove," a boat landing, and a small cluster of buildings, details Jade Snow had seen and dismissed, since Angel Island was no longer inhabited for lack of fresh water.

Suddenly, her father commanded, "Get on your knees and thank God!"

His daughter looked at him in wonder. Was this for a new and better day? Was it for the view he had never seen in Chinatown?

Daddy followed his own order. "We will all get on our knees to thank God." As they bowed heads, his feelings were poured out in prayer: "King of ten thousand kings, we have deep thoughts as we gather here and face Angel Island. Thirty-one years ago, Mama was detained there at United States immigration quarantine facilities. As a prisoner, she looked from her window to this very spot. In isolation, she was terrified. She could not understand a word of English. How could she foretell that some day we would be gathered here together in happiness, where my son-in-law placed me at the head of the table, and declared me to be master of the home? We are filled with gratitude to You for Your blessings. Sometimes we wonder if we can accomplish more than what we seem to have power to do. But You in Your wisdom provide for us better than we know how to wish.

"As we thank You, we humbly seek Your further blessings. For my youngest son, I ask wisdom as he grows up. On behalf of my second son, I ask steadfastness in purpose, for he is tossed back and forth in indecision concerning his future career. For my daughter, Jade Precious Stone, who has many personal problems, I ask for peace of mind. For my daughter, Jade Snow, who has accomplished much in her work, I ask You to give her continuous guidance. In her marriage, bless her with offspring so that she may also know the happiness which only comes with a family. For my beloved wife, who has worked so hard so faithfully, give her leisure in a new home for which we are searching.

"Thank You again for Your generous gifts. Our children born here can only have one view of those buildings on Angel Island: from the outside, forever free.

"We dare not address You in our own name, but in the name of Your Son who died for us. Amen."

"Amen," the family echoed.

Jade Snow's mother had landed before the 1924 Immigration Act which prohibited the entry of Chinese alien women for five years, another device to limit Chinese growth. Because authorities considered Chinese guilty until proven innocent, some immigrants waited three months on Angel Island while their qualifications were debated. Their mail was censored, their quarters cramped, their food poor. On walls inside that dilapidated detention barracks were many lamentations of past Chinese prisoners, carved or chiseled in the careful script of scholars. No ordinary laborer could have composed such moving poetry. One example in two stanzas, four lines of seven words each, if translated literally, expressed:

Wooden house detained me scores of days
Because rules in ink involve me
A pity that it's useless for a hero to be violent
Only await the word for the whip to spur him back to the old country

From now I leave this house for a long distance
All of my village gentlemen, rejoice with me
Never mind that everything here is Western style
Even if walls were jade, they have become a cage

Not until years after her father's death did Jade Snow learn from her mother additional reasons for his command to drop to her knees and thank God. Each time Daddy saved a thousand dollars (that slippery word!), he sponsored a nephew to come from China, enabling him to make a better living here. All but one entered successfully. This nephew, detained at Angel Island, become so nervous that he had answered incorrectly the date of his grandfather's birth. Consequently, he was returned to China, one of many who, like that poet, were never to see San Francisco. For him, Daddy had spent that thousand dollars without benefit.

CHAPTER 6
MAJOR MOVES

In 1951 surprising news came from a Chicago corporation, where Jade Snow and her husband were invited at company expense to meet the chairman of the board, and the president who had initiated the correspondence. In minutes, they knew that it was the chairman who planned, while the president was his yes-man. Their astonished eyes saw a display of their own enameled products, purchased from Marshall Field. The board chairman appraised them as coolly as he had their handwork. Actually, he directed twenty-seven other international corporations that manufactured fine quality kitchen ware and utensils.

The chairman explained, "I like to control my products from start to finish. If I need wooden handles, I will acquire the company which makes the best handles." Jade Snow and Woody were awestruck and she wondered aloud, "How can two people like us fit into your scheme of things?"

The chairman motioned toward his president: "His company has been concerned with white enameled cooking utensils, no longer popular in the United States, though used in poorer countries. We think that if we can mass-produce your beautiful colors, such cooking ware would find new acceptance in a higher-priced market. We have a huge factory with idle enameling facilities."

To the young couple, he emphasized, "Money can always be arranged. *Ideas* are the most important factor to expansion, but they are rare, and they are what I am always searching for." He was almost two decades ahead of new American trends in kitchen wares. When Jade Snow seemed puzzled that with his huge industrial empire, he should still manifest driving energy to organize more factories from Mexico to Brussels, he told her simply, "What I want most in life is a sense of accomplishment."

The meeting was brief. He departed, leaving his president to work out a proposal. Under contract terms, Jade Snow and Woody were to spend four months each year for three years in the company's Midwest factories. The compensation was staggeringly handsome. Their name was to be used nationally in promoting the new enameled products.

Back home, the Chicago proposition seemed like a dream, but the contract arrived to prove its reality. Jade Snow sensed that she and Woody should have advice from sources more sophisticated about American big business. She appealed to two good friends, who in turn invited legal colleagues to join them for a conference. Jade Snow arranged with the owner of their favorite restaurant to cook a special Chinese menu on its closed Monday. Their leisurely luncheon and a long discussion lasted into late afternoon. Although great sums of money would come to the young couple, they were advised against accepting the contract, for the use of their name should always remain their exclusive privilege. Who could know after three years what kind of public image corporate promotion might have developed? If unfavorable, they would have to live with it the rest of their lives. One of the advisers told them, "You have a million-dollar reputation standing for quality, and you should use this asset for yourselves."

Reluctant to reject what appeared to be "easy money," Jade Snow then went to her father, relating only the offer, not what the attorneys had recommended.

Daddy looked thoughtfully at his daughter. There was no elation about riches to this man who had been poor most of his life. Then he chose his words. "I would like to ask you some questions. No matter how rich you are, can you wear two suits of clothes at one time?"

His daughter admitted she couldn't.

He continued, "Can you sleep in a bed longer than seven feet?"

She acknowledged she didn't need a larger bed.

Then he asked, "Can you eat more than three meals a day?"

"Well, not really." She was perceiving his point.

He thought again, and added softly, "Someone is offering an attractive soft white ball of cotton for you to caress. Be careful, Jade Snow, be careful! Inside this fluffy ball may be a sharp needle."

Her old-fashioned Chinese father taught Jade Snow a lesson in moderation which she was never to forget. She recalled a Chinese truism, "Empty-handed I arrived. Empty-handed I shall depart." She had interpreted it creatively, to make some significant mark on life between two empty-handed events. Now Daddy's words emphasized the simplicity of physical requirements between those events and warned her to beware of limitless self-created material desires. Evaluate them carefully. Look for the needle. "The heart of man never tires of having enough," was another familiar saying.

Though he expressed it in an entirely different way, her father underscored the advice of her Western friends. With Woody's agreement, they declined the contract. Yet, to borrow her father's oft-repeated maxim, "God has His purpose." This maxim rang out happily during good fortune, and was repeated for reassurance in times of stress.

Soon after marriage, Woody had sought to borrow expansion funds as part of his G.I. Bill of Rights. But the bank's loan officer had shaken his head. "I can't give you a dollar, for a bank is not in a position to run a business. Without your wife and you, your business is worth nothing." Now the friend who at the lunch meeting had remarked on their million-dollar reputation urged the pair to expand. He would make a loan, using expensive new machinery as collateral. It was a real act of faith, for the equipment would be worth little if repossessed.

Jade Snow and Woody roamed all over San Francisco until they found an empty former spaghetti factory at the edge of Old Barbary Coast. They made extensive improvements and brought the facilities up to code requirements. Their neighbors were a Chinese sausage factory, a Basque boarding house, a seamen's flophouse, Sunshine Biscuits, and Tea Garden Preserves. Some of their best friends and customers worried that in such inelegant surroundings their business would surely die. As Oldest Brother observed the thousands of dollars being poured into remodeling, he cautioned Woody, "You know, Jade Snow's business can be here today and gone tomorrow." But within ten years, all their original neighbors had moved. In their stead were the wholesale decorators' showrooms and art galleries known as the Jackson Square area, now designated a San Francisco architectural "landmark." Wholesale and retail buyers and tourists came their way.

Customers found the working ceramic studio with its personal atmosphere refreshingly different from its exclusive neighbors. "How did you have the foresight to move here?" they asked. Jade Snow would smile and mentally echo her father's maxim, "Thank God, He had a purpose."

They were to use these premises for twenty years before another move. At five-year intervals, they paid rent increases to avoid the headache of relocation, for they found that first move trying to nerves and backs. Do they keep this, or do they not? If they do not, should they give it away or throw it away? If they give it away, to whom would they give it? The numerous decisions were exhausting. What they kept had to be transported.

Jade Snow loaded boxes of smaller articles into their car while Woody moved the enameling equipment with a borrowed truck. On one of her shuttle runs, she drove past her father walking to his home three blocks away from their new studio location. He was carrying his usual homemade large brown corduroy shopping bag full of groceries. When she offered him a ride, he told her at once, "I have found a home!" And he added with finality, "I have also bought it."

(She had dissuaded him from several unsound prospects.)

"Is this really so?" His daughter was incredulous, happy as he, for as indicated in the prayer at Tiburon, she knew that her parents longed to live their remaining years separate from a rented sewing factory.

Her Daddy was as excited as she had ever seen him except for the moment when he learned that his last-born child was a son. "It is at the foot of Telegraph Hill, walking distance to Chinatown. The first important point is that your youngest brother can conveniently attend Chinese and American schools. The second is that we have sunshine and good air. The third is that it is near a park and shops. I was working with an Italian agent who told me the price had been reduced by two thousand dollars. The bank gave it a favorable appraisal. By evening, I brought your mother to look at the building, but she didn't like it."

"Then why did you buy it?" Jade Snow wondered.

Her father explained, "Next morning I returned and asked the downstairs tenant to let me in through the back stairs. I made a scale drawing of the floor plan and showed it to your mother. She liked the room arrangement and consented to return for a better look, then changed her mind. The upper flat is suitable for three bedrooms, a kitchen-family room, with a sun porch for storage, washer, and clothesline. There is a view of Russian Hill to the west. The lower three-room apartment is suitable for your brother, who is graduating from college and wants some privacy with his friends. There is a rear garden, and a basement with a front entrance to the street. I can install a few sewing machines and tailoring tables." Daddy could not forget that factory! But he was never again to operate a business at home; Mama put a stop to it.

Jade Snow and Woody moved by day and worked late nights. She was trimming and decorating pottery for her first one-woman show, due to open in the Oriental Gallery of the Chicago Art Institute, then to be circulated to various other museums on a year's tour of the United States. Using knowledge from his summer ceramics course, Woody was experimenting with hundreds of new glaze combinations practical for their city kiln. (In the Orient, pottery was fired with wood fuel in hill tunnels for days on end.) His most pleasing results would grace her new forms; she was accomplishing a new range in her craft with Woody's help.

At 9:00 P.M., she suddenly realized that she hadn't bought dinner groceries. "I'll take you out to dinner," Woody suggested. Approaching Chinatown, they saw Daddy. Woody asked, "Why don't we ask him to join us for late supper?"

She objected, "He's never had late supper at a restaurant with me. I don't think he will come."

Woody was not discouraged. "Let me try."

Hailing his father-in-law, he called, "Let us give you a ride home." Daddy was carrying a briefcase full of books he had been using at citizenship classes. When he climbed into the car, Woody remarked, "It is good news that you have bought a home today, and we want to celebrate together. Won't you join us for midnight supper at a restaurant?"

Daddy politely demurred, "I'm still full of home dinner."

Woody ignored the reason. "Which restaurant do you like best?"

His father-in-law, unaccustomed to someone else's firm handling, was captivated. "Well, I know that you often go to Tao Yuan. Just some won-ton soup is all I want, so any place will do."

Woody decided, "I feel like the cooking at Tao Yuan tonight."

Jade Snow entered first with her father, while Woody went to get a celebration bottle. When they passed the cashier, whom Daddy recognized, he asked that surprised gentleman, "How is your brother Hing in China?" Then Daddy called each waiter by name; searching for the chef, he marched into the kitchen as his insignificant daughter trailed behind. He had a delighted audience at that late, uncrowded hour. The staff regarded him as a respected senior member from their native village.

They were shown to a family booth, its old-fashioned, round, marble-topped table framed in teak. From the Chinese menu, Daddy read aloud, "Shark's Fin Soup, Chicken Steamed with Mushrooms, Silken Squash with Fish Fillet, Bitter Melon with Frogs' Legs. . . ." (He paused here and said he would like that.) "Barbecued Squab. . . ." (He hesitated, but went on without comment, so she made a mental note.) "Long Green Beans with Roast Pork, Steamed Sliced Pork, Bamboo Shoots with Duck, Sweet and Sour Pineapple with Boned Ducks' Feet. . . ." (He hesitated again; again she noted.) At the end of the reading, he decided with contentment, "Bitter Melon and Frogs' Legs."

(Chinese foods encompass extremes in flavors and variety in colors and textures. The astringency of summer season bitter melon mated agreeably with the delicacy of frogs' legs in a garlic sauce.)

She seconded the order to the waiter, adding, "And Pineapple Boneless Ducks' Feet." (Seemingly worthless ducks' feet, when boned, presented a chewy texture; a sweet and sour sauce suited it well.)

Now Woody joined them. "How about the Barbecued Squab, and my favorite Bean Cakes with Beef? Be sure it's beef, not pork."

"No soup?" Jade Snow questioned.

"Just a simple melon soup, maybe," her father ventured.

They agreed. "Just a simple melon soup it will be."

Woody remembered, "But you wanted won-ton soup."

Daddy protested, "We have ordered quite enough already."

"This is a celebration," Woody reminded, and won-ton was added too.

When the food arrived, Daddy bowed his head in silent grace. Jade Snow found choice pieces with her chopsticks and placed them into Daddy's bowl. The frogs' legs satisfied his expectations. She whispered to her husband, "Let's order a repeat of the ducks' feet for Mama—I know it will be a treat."

Her father overheard. "Your mother will probably be in bed." But they dismissed that; it was a dream come true, to be able to provide novel treats for frugal parents who never impulsively dined at a restaurant. When the take-home box came, Daddy carefully laid on top some of the choice pieces Jade Snow had served him, for he had saved them for his wife.

It was very late when they reached their father's home. Younger Brother was still up, but Mama was in pajamas, her hair in curlers. When Woody proposed, "Let's all go to see this new place," there was no objection; Mama went to get dressed. Daddy miraculously produced five flashlights, one for each of them. As they approached the new home, Mama cautioned, "Do not make noise, as a family lives in the lower apartment."

Woody was surprised. "But don't they know you are the new owner?"

Mama was positive. "They have sleeping babies." So they subdued their sounds.

As they examined the freshly painted interiors, her father related, "I could have resold this house this week with a thousand-dollar profit."

To their astonishment, their noncommittal mother, who had scrimped for years counting every minute and saving every penny, burst into tears. "What is a thousand dollars compared to the dream of a lifetime?"

Daddy comforted her, "I was only saying I could, but did I say I would?"

When they drove their family home, Daddy was the last to leave their car. He turned to Jade Snow, asking quietly, "Do you think I made a good choice?"

His daughter reassured him. "It looked like a sound building, very suitable for you, and I am glad you own it." It stirred her that her father had sought her approval.

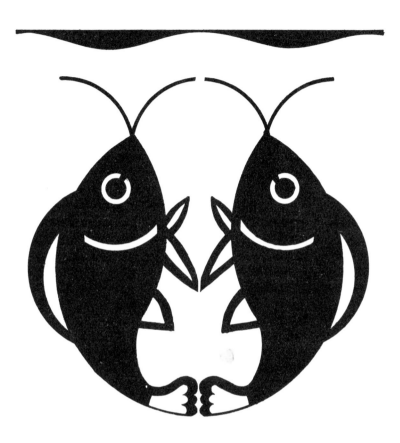

CHAPTER 7
HONG KONG AND OTHER WONGS

The State Department negotiated for rights to translate *Fifth Chinese Daughter* into a number of Asiatic languages. Two years later, foreign editions were being published and in Hong Kong, the Chinese text was scheduled for a printing of fifteen thousand copies.

As agreed, the 150,000-word Chinese manuscript was forwarded to Jade Snow, and she brought this version to her father. It had been nearly fifteen years since they had pored together over Chinese textbooks, and Jade Snow enjoyed the familiarity of listening to Daddy as he read explanations from his two enormous unabridged dictionary volumes.

As long as Jade Snow could remember, thrifty Daddy never invested in scratch paper: he used backs of envelopes or margins of the newspaper. As they worked on the manuscript, he might suggest a change in words, which he would write on a newspaper margin, then consider it carefully before correcting or leaving the translator's text alone. Sometimes it was content, not nuance, that was in question; and this brought uncomfortable moments for them both. The paragraphs about Daddy's indulging his sons or his refusal to support her through college—these too were read aloud in Chinese. Deliberate silence replaced discussion. The Chinese habit of not expressing inner feelings was most convenient.

When Daddy came to touchy points about family conflict, he looked at her sternly. "Did this really happen?"

Jade Snow was respectfully subdued, but firm. "Yes, it did," she answered softly. "I have not put in this book anything which did not happen, and much which did was better not recorded."

When their work was done, Daddy chose not to give her his opinion.

San Francisco's Chinatown had been public in its approval of the American text, for they gave Daddy a Father's Day present by selecting him as "Father of the Year" in 1952.

The story of a Chinese female who was able to educate herself and establish a career in the United States created an unexpected impact on foreign readers. Capitalizing on their interest, the State Department wanted to produce the author in the flesh. It would be good for the image of the United States and inspiring to Asians searching for identities in a new postwar era. Jade Snow's tour could be funded as part of the Leaders' and Specialists' Exchange Program. She was invited to commence speaking to Tokyo audiences and work onward through forty-five more Asiatic stops to terminate in Karachi. At first, two months were asked of her, but when her availability was announced, many more United States foreign service posts than anticipated wanted to be included in her itinerary, and at least four months of traveling would be necessary.

It was another complex decision. Should she leave a recently expanded and indebted business? Should she do so alone? If her husband accompanied her, it would be at his own expense. She would be paid a moderate salary, but the pathetically low per diem allowance fixed by Congress was not adequate even for herself. Yet Jade Snow could not refuse to contribute toward East-West understanding. She felt a moral obligation to interpret what she knew of the United States to fellow Asians. Her goals and dreams had been to utilize her dual heritage. Despite these financially unattractive terms, there would be the joy at last of seeing the Orient—that mysterious other half of the world about which she had heard all her life.

She resolved not to go alone. It would have made financial sense for Woody to stay with the business, but it would not have made marriage sense, which was more important. Besides (taking a cue from the corporate board chairman), their ideas and creative assets should be increased by the arts they would find in the Orient. Jade Snow could never have fulfilled this mission if they were working for that corporation. She could hear Daddy's "Thank God, it was His purpose."

Woody researched the technicalities of importing: invoice procedures, certificates of origin and antiquity, customs duties, F.O.B. and C.I.F. terms, letters of credit, were all to become familiar to him. They hoped to earn his expenses by bringing back to San Francisco unusual handicrafts from the Orient. That kind business "angel" who had underwritten their store expansion guaranteed another generous amount for letters of credit. Jade Snow and Woody were sent to see his bank's commercial loan officer, who briefed them and admonished, "Now this bank is not in the importing business. If a letter of credit says to pay so much in favor of a certain company, F.O.B. Kobe, we will pay them even though the boxes at Kobe could be filled with sand!"

Jade Snow was the first American of Chinese descent to be sent on the State Department program, and it was uncertain how she would be received at a time when anti-American feelings were strong in Asia. Eminent Americans on similar missions had been ridiculed in their parents' European homelands. Despite these doubts, Jade Snow was not briefed in Washington, D.C., prior to departure. Instead, she was to report after her trip. Long reading lists were sent, and she studied the economic and social backgrounds of the countries she would visit: Japan, the Philippines, Hong Kong, Malaya, Thailand, Burma, India, and Pakistan.

It was indescribably exciting to prepare for a first international journey. Jade Snow anticipated the climactic moment—meeting for the first time in Hong Kong and Macau all those cousins whose names had been in household conversations for thirty years. They were unhappy that China itself was barred to them, for in Fragrant Mountains there remained Second Uncle's widow.

Second Uncle had left behind in San Francisco his widowed daughter-in-law and grandchildren, a girl and three boys. His daughter and son-in-law, who with their large family had accompanied him back to China, returned to San Francisco after Japanese hostilities broke out in China. Since Jade Snow and Second Uncle's children were of the same generation, Jade Snow called them (and the children of her other uncles and aunts) "sisters" and "brothers." In the absence of Second Uncle, his three half-orphaned male grandchildren enjoyed her father's protective interest, and he constantly brought them gifts of food at a time when his own wife was finding it difficult to make ends meet. Their names were entered into the Family Manual.

Fifth Uncle had been the only other brother to come to the United States. He was a gentle widower, father of Cousin Kee, and both were shirtmakers. He was one of the many men living alone in Chinatown and sometimes came to visit the Wongs. Jade Snow recalled his sympathetic listening to her mother's woes while she sewed and he balanced her and her sister on his knees. But by the time they were grown, he had died.

Ninth Uncle's widow lived with her two grown sons in Portuguese Macau, about 35 miles from Fragrant Mountains. As the only male Wongs nearby, those brothers made annual pilgrimages to the home village to visit family graves with proper offerings, customarily at "Ching Ming," two weeks after the first day of spring. As long as Jade Snow could remember, Daddy's bedside wall was hung with oval colored portraits of her paternal grandparents and photographs of their funeral processions and of huge horseshoe-shaped raised grave platforms. He did not rise or retire without being reminded of his past. A son's bones owed their existence to ancestral bones.

There was also practical reason for the pilgrimages. Unvisited graves became overgrown with weeds or strewn with rubbish, invitations to grave robbers or to herders to let their water buffalo trample unrestrained. Annually, a remittance went to the sons of Ninth Uncle for the cost of offerings to the beloved dead. Each year, a report came from Macau of mission accomplished.

Just as the bank loan officer had cautioned Jade Snow and Woody about import frauds, so Daddy cautioned them about human frauds. He invited the departing couple for a farewell dinner, and read aloud the letters he was sending to their relatives. To those whom he had vowed to "cleanse as snow the disgrace of retarded Wong women," * he wrote, "My small fifth daughter Jade Snow will be arriving in your city on State business."

To his daughter and son-in-law he showed photographs of all their relatives. There was another branch of the family in Hong Kong, a daughter of his only sister, and her son who was in the pharmacy business. Here was also a sister to the Second, Fifth, and Ninth Uncles—Seventh Auntie, who lived with her only son, who was in the banking business. "Do not trust anyone in Hong Kong. You are to call on each of these relatives to whom I have written. They have not been told where to look for you. So if any other person comes to you, claiming to be a friend or relative, do not pay any attention."

Mama Wong added one of her rare comments: "Although your features are Chinese, you have the look of 'Innocents from the Golden Mountains' and you will be the target of 'little hands' [pickpockets]. Why, I have heard of robbers working in pairs. One will sneak up behind a woman and lift her, while his partner snatches her good American shoes from her feet!"

Jade Snow giggled and pooh-poohed Daddy first. How preposterous that a stranger would claim ties! Whatever for? Daddy looked at her reprovingly. "You do not know the confidence games in China, which has been a lawless country for too long; fraud was not prosecuted."

Then they pooh-poohed Mama. Woody promised her that he would watchfully walk behind her daughter, ready for rescue. "I will give chase if necessary," Woody laughingly assured her. Pri-

* "Snow" can be an active verb. To "snow disgrace" is to right a wrong.

vately, Jade Snow and her husband agreed that their parents had left China too long ago. Things would not be so decadent in modern times.

Father Wong prayed for God's benediction on their long journey, for wisdom in Jade Snow not to say or do anything to detract from the purpose of the United States, for strength in Woody sufficient to take care of both. Father Wong's appeal comforted them. His prayers, whether brief or silent, moving with poetic gratitude or humble with need, regularly brought the reality of God into their everyday lives.

Still, reassurance of the Almighty could not stop her apprehensions. What would fellow Chinese who had known their world only on the other shore of the Pacific think of her combination of cultures? Would they accept her and what she could tell them of the lives of Chinese in the United States? Or would they mistrust her as a facsimile of themselves who had taken on foreign ways? Would she prove to be a "bamboo node," as overseas Chinese are often dismissed in China? (This was a poetic simile for stupidity: as water cannot pass through a bamboo node, so knowledge did not penetrate the brains of overseas Chinese.)

Hong Kong, a distance from her parents' childhood home, was still part of the magic land of China, that China where "fruit is sweeter and flowers are more fragrant." As their plane approached, her mind combined anticipation with suspicious caution, while her body was exhausted from thirteen days of lecturing in Japan and a forced diversion to Manila because of bad weather. For the third time, their stratocruiser circled again around the rocky and historically strategic piece of land, the clouds parted at last, and they could see brilliant turquoise water below. Countless peaks rose from countless islands, and between barren areas she saw strips of narrow farmlands. The harbors were thick with ships. Gray military vessels and sleek large steamers lay next to tiny tubs of ancient design. The junk fleet at Aberdeen, several hundred strong, was tied up at leisure, in anticipation of Chinese New Year.

Jade Snow and Woody were relieved to land, but no less comforted than a swarm of Chinese reporters who had already been disappointed twice. In a waiting room, press representatives surrounded the pair. Perhaps it seemed like a larger crowd than usual because they had brought Chinese interpreters! They had indeed prepared for a bamboo node!

Amused, Jade Snow spoke in Cantonese. With delighted surprise, the reporters waved away interpreters. Misconception number one had been dispelled. Newspaper articles subsequently marveled, "A Chinese, born and educated in the United States, speaks Cantonese without an accent; in fact, speaks like one of ourselves!" Jade Snow found another reward for her father's strict supervision during those ten tedious years of Chinese lessons suffered when other children were playing.

Sing Tao, the major evening paper, ran the Chinese translation of her book as a daily serial. She was interviewed on the government network Radio Rediffusion. Questions revealed great curiosity about whether Chinese abroad were like themselves, or how they differed. How was she educated? What did she eat at home? What was the formula to accommodate traditional Chinese requirements to the need for adjustment to a changing and quite different Western world? Young people in Hong Kong under British rule had a similar problem: to what extent should or could one remain Chinese—or was it either/or?

Because of the publicity, true to her parents' prediction, miscellaneous strangers called at her hotel room, wanting advice, wanting assistance, wanting money. Mostly money. Even though few major events had been scheduled for her by the kind consul general in charge of her program, Jade Snow's time was consumed by total strangers with fantastic tales.

A pair of fat gentlemen said they used to be Kuo Min Tang (Nationalist) Army generals, but had been stranded in Hong Kong before they could get to Taiwan. An adolescent girl aspired to work her way through college as Jade Snow had, but college students here didn't do housework. A bearded professor from Yunnan Province asked for financing so that he could write a book on China's glorious past. Peddlers arrived with hideous squatting Buddha vases, which they hoped Woody would import in huge quantities. A clerk who was a Ph.D. told of the lack of cultural work in commercial Hong Kong, wherein resided the world's record collection of unemployed ex-college presidents.

One person actually claimed a blood relationship. Another said that his father had been in business with Jade Snow's father, who still owed their family money. Without appointment, early in the morning, late at night, any time, Jade Snow might answer her door and find a stranger pushing his way in.

Contrasting with their boldness, her cousins appeared shy and awed by her publicity. Obeying her father's instructions, Jade Snow presented each with a red-paper-wrapped gift of Hong Kong currency. Jade Snow called first on Seventh Auntie. She remembered her younger sister, Eighth Auntie, who had lived in San Francisco. Eighth Auntie had been a frail, tiny widow with dainty bound feet, and she spoke in slow, gentle gasps. She had had prominent cheekbones, had worn tiny glasses and a beautiful embroidered black band which kept her thin hair in place. She had been blessed with filial children who worked to increase slim family resources. Seventh Auntie was strikingly similar in physical appearance and manner. Also a widow, just as thin, just as sweetly genial, she lived with her son in a typical Hong Kong residential neighborhood apartment, one of many tall concrete buildings, with balconies to relieve the occupants during tropical, humid summers, and also to allow the drying of clothes strung on the long horizontal bamboo poles which Jade Snow had first seen in Japan. Every balcony looked prepared for invasion, for at the edges they bristled with spikes and barbed wire.

Not a tree or living plant graced the scene. Street-level fronts were crowded with narrow stores or huge theaters. At Seventh Auntie's address, the elevator brought Jade Snow and Woody to a cheerless dark hallway where all doors were securely closed. Admittance was gained only after a peephole inspection. Seventh Auntie was of better than average financial circumstances, for she employed a housekeeper. A live-in maid in the Orient is easily accommodated. She could roll out a mat in the kitchen at night.

A home-cooked feast honored the visiting pair. Jade Snow especially enjoyed black mushrooms cooked with fresh white ginkgo nuts—which reminded her of her mother's cooking.

"How is my brother? How is my sister-in-law?" Seventh Auntie welcomed them and longed for family news. Also a devout Christian, she was pleased to hear that Daddy had been the Methodist Church representative at a united Easter service with speakers from eight Protestant churches in Chinatown.

Her son, perhaps in his thirties, spoke to them bilingually and anxiously offered his services. They regretted that there wasn't time for further visiting.

The other Hong Kong family was Daddy's niece and great-nephew, an alert and quick young man working for a wholesale druggist. Courteously, he accepted an assignment to secure a list of purchases for Jade Snow's parents, including ginger root treated with lemon juice, a liniment, a cold remedy, and some old tea. Mother and son insisted on inviting Jade Snow and her husband to an elaborate Chinese restaurant banquet, a compliment which really distressed them, for a table of ten places would cost several hundred Hong Kong dollars.

One other branch of the family, that of Ninth Uncle, remained to be visited in Macau. The consul general accompanied them on the slow five-hour boat ride and tactfully left them for a private visit with Ninth Auntie and her two sons. The older one, who spoke with authority as head of the family, was a construction foreman. The younger one was about the age of Jade Snow's younger brother, and between them there sprang an instant liking. He was mild-mannered and quite artistic, for he presented her with a meticulously composed landscape he had painted, mounted on long scroll form. Jade Snow's heart ached for their mother, a tiny woman who spoke in the broad accent of Fragrant Mountain dialect. She spent her days handpicking the seams of black fabric gloves to supplement family earnings. The family of three lived in two dark rooms, sharing the flat's kitchen and bathroom facilities with another family.

"May we invite you to a restaurant dinner?" her aunt asked. Hastily, Jade Snow refused. She had a good excuse. "The consul general is waiting for us to return to Hong Kong; we came only to visit you. Let us talk a little instead."

Addressing the older son, who had made the recent visit to family graves, she asked, "How are things with the Communists?" It was three years since their takeover, and terrible tortures of peace-loving old folks had been rumored.

Buoyant Older Son answered in ringing tones, "The widow of Second Uncle remains there. While she used to enjoy the collection of rents, she now weaves baskets. However, her life isn't difficult. When I stayed with her, she was granted leave from work, and could purchase an extra chicken to entertain me."

He waved his arms. "Now come with me. The markets of Macau are famous, especially for seafoods and the rich oyster sauce (a thick, flavorsome sauce made with ground oysters and used in place of soy for certain dishes). Everyone who comes here brings back to Hong Kong imported Port and local oyster sauce. Come, come, I have borrowed the company car."

Jade Snow and Woody asked the family to pose for a colored picture which she would show Daddy upon her return. She had taken pictures of all the relatives for this reason. As they waved goodbye, both residents and visitors were suddenly touched with sadness. When and where would they see each other again, if ever? As if she could read this niece's mind, her aunt lamented, "I could not invite you to dinner, which you say you will enjoy another time. After a lifetime I am seeing you; another time I will surely be leaning on a cane!"

There wasn't much time to explore Macau, with its stone-paved streets, brightly painted pastel buildings smacking of Mediterranean flavor, and dimly lit noisy casinos. But back in Hong Kong, between speeches to various art, civic, and women's groups, she wandered with Woody.

She had noticed men and women alike carrying heavy twin loads balanced on either end of a stout bamboo pole slung across their shoulders; they loped along with the peculiar gait that such carriers affected. When a black-trousered figure carrying two huge baskets of long white Chinese cabbages stopped to rest and mop his sweating brow, she said to Woody, "I must talk to him." Woody sighed; he had grown tolerant of impulsiveness from a wife who would never leave well enough alone. When they got to him, Woody said dryly, "He's a she." And indeed she was, a happy peasant with bare feet, brown smiling face, resting in the shade among her cabbages. (Both men and women wore similar black cotton coats and trousers.)

"How much does your load weigh?" Jade Snow asked.

"About eighty gun," she replied. (A gun, or catty, is about 1½ pounds.)

"Isn't this heavy for you?"

"No, I have carried one hundred and ten gun."

Jade Snow recalled the California labor code which stipulated that women must not lift more than 25 pounds.

"How much does your cabbage bring you?" Jade Snow persisted.

"Oh, about ten cents or a little more per gun," she estimated.

Why, that was less than 2 cents in U.S. money! The whole load, if she could sell it, would be worth $8.00 Hong Kong or less than American $1.50. What about the labor in growing 80 pounds of cabbage? Woody and Jade Snow were both silent a long time after leaving the cabbage vendor.

Another memorable walk came on Chinese New Year's Eve, which was February 13 that year. They were among thousands who were shopping at specially set-up flower stands. For the Chinese, the new "agricultural" or lunar year was most important. Food omens rooted in old tradition must be purchased and rituals diligently observed in each household or business. Flowers which were purchased when in bud ideally should open for their owners without dropping, as a propitious sign of luck during the coming year. They saw whole plum trees, fifteen feet tall, with a price tag of $600 Hong Kong (a hundred U.S. dollars), suitable for meeting rooms in large organizations. Jade Snow's favorite flowers were delicately fragrant "water fairies" or narcissus, which were blooming from bulbs set into brown pottery bowls of water.

"All right," said Woody, "Happy Valentine!" and he bought two bowls for her. They were fooled by merchants more clever than they, after all, for the next morning, they found some of the blossoms had withered. Was it bad luck? No, just bad inspection. The flower vendor had stuck extra cut blossoms into slits in the bulbs, in order to make them look fuller!

Chinese New Year meant a three-day holiday. All businesses were closed. Mah-jong tiles clicked everywhere as the gambling instincts of the Chinese were given full range. Firecrackers which began at midnight continued around the clock. Not only evil spirits were chased away—a few human spirits must have wearied of the din!

The respite gave them a chance to drive through New Territories, which stretch along 27 miles of curving hills and border on the water's edge. Here was rural China. Water buffaloes were at the plow. They saw old graves and old gray stone houses with doorways plastered with red paper to ward off evil. They heard the percussion that accompanied the village lion dance, performed here as in San Francisco's Chinatown. Jade Snow was fascinated with the freshly lacquered and marvelously arranged long black shining hair on the Hakka women. She had never seen this before. Children everywhere were dressed in the bright reds and pinks of New Year outfits. Rural folk were whole-hearted celebrants of old customs.

As easily as she fitted into Hong Kong, and however lavish a life she might enjoy, Jade Snow concluded that she could never live there permanently. The acquisition of money was a mania, from the beggar on the street to the business tycoon. Contributions were made for charities, but the spirit of giving was negated as wives vied with each other in comparing whose husbands gave more. Between people there was little charity. A few women her age who had been educated in the United States, living here where their husbands worked, lamented the lack of adult education classes. Because help was cheap, wives were forced to be idle. Jade Snow had to come to this corner of China to affirm that her father was right; she could never have obtained her education, or learned her art, or started a career, had she been born on that side of the Pacific.

CHAPTER 8
HONOR TO A FEMALE

During these days, Jade Snow often thought of her father. How she wished that he could have shared the reunion with their relatives and enjoyed Hong Kong as a tourist. She wished for his presence most of all when an invitation arrived from the Wong Family Association. Accomplishment by one Wong glorifies all Wongs, so it should not have surprised her when one of the strangers knocking at her hotel room door turned out to be a Wong Family Association representative. He presented his credentials and drew forth two gold-engraved red invitations to a banquet honoring Jade Snow. Though she had married into another family, she had been born a "Wong"; in Chinese she retained her birth name, with *shee*, the equivalent of "Mrs.," added upon marriage. Woody had a separate invitation.

Those red invitations seemed to symbolize all that her parents had aspired to for their children. Jade Snow accepted in humility, but pleaded that she would have no time, in her full remaining schedule, to prepare a new speech.

The representative smiled smoothly. "It is your presence which is desired."

At one of the most renowned banquet restaurants of Hong Kong, posted Chinese characters in the lobby indicated the location of the dinner (the higher up the floor location, the more elegant). Climbing stairs, Jade Snow caught intriguing glimpses of how well-to-do Chinese spent their leisure hours. Small parties ate in private rooms where they would play mah-jong most of the night while groups of musicians amused them.

In the room reserved for the Wongs, they found thirty-four key members who had come by invitation. They were all male, but in consideration for Jade Snow, one older female had been included. This Mrs. Wong proved to be a friendly guide to protocol.

First, Jade Snow bowed respectfully and individually to her fellow Wongs. She had worn a new Hong Kong tailored gown of red satin brocade. The Wongs were also in their festive best. Most were dressed in dark blue or brown silk robes with long flowing sleeves, casually turned back to show exquisite linings of light fur. This was the correct winter garb for February in unheated interiors, even though the dahlias were blooming outside. Jade Snow was led to a table with a red satin banner, a black ink pad, and a Chinese brush. Each guest was invited to sign his name on the banner; each signed only his middle and first names, for of course, all were Wongs. Woody was the only person to enter three ideographs with his different surname. They watched interestedly to see Jade Snow's skill in calligraphy, which would be an accurate measure of her education in Chinese. How far away this was from her first attempt with this written art at the age of four, when her father had held her hand in his, and then later when he had rolled up a ball of newspaper, about the size of a walnut, to shape her fingers in the correct curvature for holding the brush!

After a group photograph, they were seated around a conference table. The master of ceremonies rose to introduce the president of the Wong Association, who offered a formal, flowery, affectionate discourse praising Jade Snow for bringing recognition to all the Wongs as an educated, artistic, and intelligent person. She was hailed as *their* "Fifth Daughter." All faces turned expectantly as he called upon her to respond. Her protest of being wholly unprepared was accepted as correct, courteous modesty. The faces looked just as expectant, and a respectful silence descended. She could not ignore them.

A formal Chinese address required clichés of exaggerated politeness to express "guest airs," embroideries of speech which dragged on with minuscule meaning. Jade Snow decided not to wander in that direction, but as a shy Chinese woman, she could say simply, directly, and briefly what was in her heart.

At the moment, what was in her heart was her father, who had toiled for this unforeseeable moment. Aloud, she regretted that the Wong whom she would most wish to be there was not, a Wong who had instilled in her the necessity of always doing her best for the name.

"From the time I could understand words, he has taught me to honor the name of 'Wong.' How rewarding it would be if he could see now that I have not disgraced either him or the Wongs."

There was a bustle of activity as the conference table was removed and three dining tables were set, twelve places to each. The center table was occupied by Jade Snow, her husband, the special lady guest, and various Wongs. Mrs. Wong told her that they were wealthy merchants in the most strategic positions of Hong Kong business life. Each of the cards they presented proudly listed numerous connections in the paper, metal, and tobacco trades, or as local managers for international Western corporations such as American Express or Canadian Pacific.

An impressive array of foods began to arrive. The opening course of eggs, spinach, oysters, and a dried, finely shredded brown sea vegetable carried a special connotation for New Year as the names of the ingredients had the same sounds as "good deeds" and "prosperity." Sharks' fin soup, without which any first-class banquet was incomplete, was decorated with orange crab roe. Attractive hostesses spooned this delicacy into silver cups. A beautiful combination was juicy, white, boned chicken with pink aromatic Yunnam ham, and bright green Chinese broccoli. The height of lavishness followed, one whole roast suckling pig for each table. Each had been boned, carved into bite-size pieces, then rearranged carefully with shiny brown skin refitted into the look of a whole pig. Paper-thin pancakes served with the pig enabled each guest to roll tiny sandwiches, into which coarse white sugar was sprinkled, a crunchy delicious Cantonese combination more unusual than Peking duck. Duck tonight was tender, steamed with its head on, and that head was pointed straight at Jade Snow because she was guest of honor. Chinese spirits were freely poured. Each course had been different from anything Jade Snow had tasted in San Francisco.

Jade Snow's kind friend reminded her to make the gesture of thanking the Wong family, and with filled cups of tea, the two women went to each table to toast their hosts, who rose as one to return her compliment.

While Chinese home meals do not include a dessert course, at formal feasts the meat and soup courses are followed with a sweet. When they returned to their places they found cups of sweet almond soup. Made from fresh untoasted almonds slowly ground in a stone mill, it had been cooked until it was like a runny, translucent pudding. It was accompanied by thumb-size sponge cakes, fresh water chestnuts, and sections of sweet Teochow kum (similar to a large tangerine) arranged with larger sections of pale yellow pomelo.

There was an extended pause when all had finished eating. The food had stopped arriving; the speeches, as at all banquets, were dispensed with before dinner. Jade Snow wondered how long they were supposed to make conversation. Her companion hinted helpfully, "No one can leave until you, the guest of honor, make the first move."

Relieved, Jade Snow rose. Immediately, so did the others. She shook hands with each Wong, to thank them individually again. Her friend whispered, "This has been one of the most elaborate dinners I have ever attended in Hong Kong. I was at the one they gave for the Duchess of Kent. The Wongs set a more bountiful table for you!"

Months later, when she had completed her travels, she wondered how she could adequately convey her gratitude to the Association. Perhaps the most handsome enameled copper bowl she could execute would be appropriate, even though the art standard in Hong Kong emphasized decorations different from Jade Snow's creed in ceramics. Would they understand something she made? Yet she must express herself in her own way.

She created a bowl fourteen inches in diameter and five inches deep, fired at 1,500 degrees with jewelry enamels. Its interior was glowing Chinese red, contrasting with an outside color of quiet black and gold. Underneath, its copper base was polished, ideal for an inscription. Jade Snow sought her father's advice on Chinese words which could be appropriate in addition to her customary signature in English. It was a simple request, she thought.

Her father replied carefully, "First, I must come to see your bowl." Time elapsed before he came, examined the bowl, made no comment, and left.

More weeks went by without a word. Her mother informed her, "Your father is deep in thought about your message to the Wongs. With his magnifying glass, he looks up each word in his dictionary volumes to be sure it is correct, both in written form and in symbolism."

One day her father telephoned. "Are you going to be there for a while? I am coming with the information for the bowl."

When he arrived, then sat down at a table, it was a signal that what he had to say was of some length and importance.

"After I had completed the wording of your inscription, I took it to consult with the learned pastor of our church, for he had graduated from Ling Nan,* and he said, 'I will be glad to look at your inscription, but of course, I would not have the audacity to correct you.'"

Her father looked at her and added, "He was merely being polite, you know.

"Sometime later the pastor notified me that he had taken my words to consult with Mr. Leong, the teacher of the most ad-

---

* The same university Woody's brother Norman had left San Francisco to attend.

vanced class at Hip Wo School. Mr. Leong has made a few corrections and has vastly improved upon my original."

Her father spread out some papers and began to explain. Jade Snow felt again the joy of learning from her father's reservoir of wisdom. First, there was a letter which her father had carefully written by Chinese brush. It was brief:

"To the worthy elders of the Hong Kong Wong Family Association, respectfully submitted to those who may read this.

"Last spring, the affairs of state made a path for me to pass through your esteemed Hong Kong. I am blessed to have returned home safely. As fast as the blinking of the eyes, many months have passed, for my inferior business affairs are as many as the quills of a porcupine. I am sad and apologetic to have failed to inquire about your welfare. Please overlook this bad shortcoming. Now I have made a coarse bowl, which is a gift to you in remembrance. I beg you to accept it, and ask for your magnanimity in forgiveness. With best wishes for good fortune to all of you—in the fall of 1954—Jade Snow Wong, Wah-Jom Ong,* in bowed respect."

Her father folded the letter, carefully replaced it in its envelope, and opened another paper. The words before them were no simple inscription of "To . . ." and "From . . ." but a beautifully composed lyric poem, in ten lines of exactly four words each, in formality and subtlety deeper than everyday usage. A free translation approximates the meaning:

> My head has been lifted in aspiration toward your glory
> My heart turned in longing, as a sunflower follows the sun
> Because of state affairs, I passed through Hong Kong
> At last my ambition was realized.
> Your magnificent treatment and huge banquet overwhelmed
> me with shame
> The food was of exquisite rarity, served with highest
> ceremony
> And as we were filled with spirits, we were also filled
> with high morality.
> Like the ancients who carved inscriptions on the arms of
> a chair to commemorate affection of magnitude

* Pronunciation of Woody's Chinese name.

In clean spirit this bowl was made
In order to thank you respectfully.

Jade Snow was impressed by the effort that had prepared this poem, and she wondered how she could transfer these intricate, scholarly words onto the copper underside of the enameled bowl. Engraving with a vibrating tool was not simple, even when the quality of the handwriting did not matter. To reproduce the forty words of the poem, and thirty-two other words of salutation, dating, and signature within a circle eight inches in diameter, in a "hand" to equal the sentiment, for an audience across the Pacific who most certainly would be critical, was a challenge she had not encountered in years of craftsmanship.

She was apprehensive. "How can I do justice to these fine words with my poor hand? The Chinese brush flows on absorbent paper; my tool must dig into metal!"

Her father said three words: "Take your time."

The painstaking task took hours. When completed, she rushed over to her father's home, asking him to check on the correct reproduction of each word. Secretly, like a child who has completed a neat page of difficult homework, she hoped for his approval. Her father held the bowl under the bright kitchen light and read the inscription aloud. Youngest Brother came in to listen. Her mother remained busy at the sink, back to them. These affairs of the world were not her province.

"Is everything correct?" Jade Snow asked.

"It is correct." No other adjective was offered in front of her mother and brother.

"Well, then, I have to leave. Woody is double-parked outside." Clutching the bowl, she made her way downstairs. Her father followed her down to the front door. There he added gently, "Your words were well written." For her ears alone, he saved his praise.

Nineteen years later, she heard a story from her mother which explained her mother's and father's lack of comment in the kitchen. During the mid-1930s when China's Nationalist forces were embroiled in dual battle against the Communist party and the invading Japanese, overseas Chinese were asked for financial support. Daddy was made treasurer of the drive for War Relief funds. The community cooperated in a dramatic sacrifice: fast for one day and give up the equivalent in money to help fill the rice bowls of China. Daddy made an accurate accounting of the proceeds and turned them over to the consul general, a Wong, who invited his friends to a restaurant banquet and drank merrily. Daddy reproached him: "Our people gave up food for their brethren in China. You as a leader should do likewise."

The criticism incensed the consul, who reported to the Wong Association that their member had insulted him without observing rank. Jade Snow's mother recalled the dreadful aftermath. "Consecutively without end, representatives of the Wong Association called at our factory-home. They declared that your father had disgraced the Wongs and should be expelled as a traitor. They threatened to beat him and extorted blackmail. We were so poor that all we could manage was five dollars to each one. But they kept on coming, until by nightfall nine groups had been paid off.

"But though your father paid them, he would not accept the judgment. 'If I am to be expelled for having dishonored the name of *Wong*, then print it in newspaper headlines. Let the community judge who is wrong!' He had some friends who promised to write to the headquarters in Hong Kong with the true facts.

"From that day forth, he never returned to the Wong Association. He left me a letter which I kept in the safe deposit box; in case he met a violent end, I was instructed to take the letter to his Young Wo Association to exonerate his name in a public reading."

Jade Snow wondered why her father had never mentioned his distress, and her mother sighed. "Such unpleasant episodes should not be discussed. His temper was bad, so he could not refrain from criticizing. But he was a true Christian; he forgave. He never talked about anyone's bad points, nor did he mention his own good ones."

The letter stayed in the safe deposit box until his natural death. Her father never dreamed when he agitated to emancipate Chinese women that someday his daughter would vindicate that report to the male Hong Kong Wongs.

CHAPTER 9
NEW FRIENDS IN SOUTHEAST ASIA

Jade Snow had found in Hong Kong the truth of her parents' predictions and the truth of their legends as well, and she had had almost overwhelming personal acceptance. But Singapore was to fulfill the State Department's apprehensiveness and her anticipation that she might be regarded as a Chinese who would be intolerable because she had taken on "foreign ways."

The tall young Cultural Affairs officer from the United States Information Service had trained only a year at Cornell before being sent over to handle the tangled, hostile relations in this British colony. Meeting them at the airport, he told them that the *Young Malayan* magazine had serialized the English version of her book, and added, "In Malaya, Jade Snow Wong has become a legend like Franklin D. Roosevelt." He had scheduled an early morning press conference even though they had been flying all night. Having discharged his duty, he disappeared. He would have been of greater service if he had not greeted them with an overstatement which lulled his charges into expecting a friendly reception. Reality proved otherwise.

The Chinese reporters distrusted Americans; their questions tried to determine if she were Chinese "truly" (and therefore one of their kind), or Chinese in "face" only (and really an American). Controversy was raging over the right of Chinese Singaporians to build their own university, independent of British authority and Malay sultans. Not having been briefed, Jade Snow began by asking questions. The press thought this questioning attitude superior; they were enraged that she was not sympathetically Chinese. They misquoted and denounced her. Singapore was certainly not another Hong Kong!

What was underneath the bitterness of the Chinese on this island? In those days Singapore was part of Malaya, where easygoing Malays worked at agriculture, and educated ones held government positions. An Indian minority was composed of merchants or laborers brought in by the British to undertake road construction, garbage collection, and other urban work neither Chinese nor Malays would do. Banking, mining, and business wealth, the economic backbone of the country, were Chinese controlled. Architecture in the countryside was Malay; in the city it was Chinese.

The three races seldom mingled. Polynesian Malays, once conquered by Arab traders, had been converted to Islam and had not intermarried with arriving Chinese immigrants who enjoyed the pork Moslems abhorred. Tamil Indians eschewing beef clung to their Hindu faith. The isolation of the Chinese in Malaya has been special, for elsewhere in Asia, Chinese and Japanese, Filipinos, Portuguese, Thais, and Burmans have intermarried for generations.

Chinese immigrants began coming almost five hundred years

ago to explore the incalculable wealth lying within the jungles. After they dredged for tin, the soil was drained and rubber plantations were established. They coaxed fabulous yields from virginal lands, while the British Commonwealth accrued strategic materials. Eventually, the Chinese equaled the native Malays in number, but only the Malays had citizenship rights.

The situation reminded Jade Snow of the Chinese in early California history, who, in striving for financial independence, also served economic interests of greater magnitude than their own. But California Chinese, also a minority who did not intermarry, continued to be marginal workers for the next hundred years. The Malayan Chinese, over a longer period and in increasing numbers, had acquired the power of wealth although they continued to feel like second-class citizens. Later, a huge exodus transferred much of this wealth to Singapore, which became a separate government in 1965.

During World War II, these separate interests had already reached revolutionary fervor. When England gave up Malaya to the invading Japanese, the Chinese dug into the jungle. After the war, the British invited them to surrender their guns for a forty-dollar bounty. But many of the infuriated guerrillas kept their weapons to continue fighting for the "free" Malaya they wanted. At the time Jade Snow visited Singapore, the jungles still hid five thousand "Communist bandits." Truckloads of British and Malay soldiers returned daily from fighting them. The Federation of the Nine Malay States was in a state of emergency.

Chinese students at Raffles University told her of their frustrations. From childhood, their parents had urged them to be well-educated Chinese who would complete their university work in nearby China. Thus, the Communist takeover of China in 1949 imposed a terrible dilemma. Since they had no local citizenship, they could return to China to claim citizenship by ancestry, but this would require acceptance of Communism. These were the reasons they were agitating for their own college in Singapore.

Two different Chinese in Singapore supplied this data to Jade Snow and Woody. They and others they met in later travels became their first adult Chinese lifelong friends. They saw one another again and again, in the Orient, or San Francisco, or New York. They embodied the expected Chinese characteristics which made them comfortably familiar, but they were also outspoken, confident nonconformists.

The State Department had authorized 50 pounds of overweight baggage so that some of Jade Snow's ceramics could accompany her. An exhibit was set up at the Chinese Chamber of Commerce, and Professor Chang came to look. Surprisingly for a stranger, he presented Jade Snow with a stone chop (a signature seal), which he had carved for her use to press on pottery clay. (The ability to carve chops is a skill of many Chinese artists.) He volunteered to show them around the city's Chinese section, where he shunned huge banquet halls for little specialty shops. They were led to wonders such as spare-rib soup, poached chicken served cold with thinly sliced cucumbers and hot chili sauce, or oversize Fukien noodles with tiny oysters. Professor Chang was a running conversationalist who could tell their fortunes (Woody would live to be seventy-seven, and Jade Snow would not have many children) as readily as he told of his own past. In his home in Canton, he had kept a menagerie, including peacocks, horses, and tigers, as models for his paintings. He also owned an aquarium of fish. He was famed for his paintings of tigers, whose eyes seemed to follow the viewer as he moved.

"I knew those tigers well," he explained. "I fed them beef with opium. They were tamed enough to play with."

He had comfortable opinions of himself, without sounding conceited. "Other people have to spend money when they travel, but I make money." Or, "I work one year and loaf for two, during which time I just read, sleep, and think. I seldom leave my house."

He had correspondingly humble opinions of others, also without seeming conceited. "Everyone in Singapore knows me, but I choose to know only the superior ones." And, "Most of the people are kept too confused to think here, but what sort of person am I? I happen to have a head *and* a brain."

Yet years later, when they met each other in Hong Kong where he was exhibiting in the City Hall, he could just as easily poohpooh himself. Noting Woody's premature gray hair, while Woody remarked that he, the older man, was not gray, the professor smiled. "You use your brains, but I do not use mine."

Practicing medicine without a license, he prescribed ground

celery and dried mussel soup for Woody to lower his blood pressure. "Raw turnip juice and seaweed soup are also good," he added. Whatever the subject, the professor had a ready answer.

On the Singapore visit, they became such good instant friends that they were entertained in the bosom of the family, in the huge, all-purpose, airy, light room which was the professor's painting studio and study. He had written down an elaborate menu including one chicken cooked in three separate styles, juicy abalone slices, crisp roast duck, and giant shrimp. His wife prepared their lunch according to his order. Typical of many Oriental homes, she served but did not join them. The best part of the lunch, homemade Chinese soup without that crutch, monosodium glutamate, was what Jade Snow and Woody always missed when they traveled. Mrs. Chang used distinctively flavored lotus root, which colored the clear broth a delicate brown, familiar to all palates reared on Chinese cooking.

After lunch, Professor Chang entertained them with his latest collection of pictures and colored slides taken in Borneo. The women's breasts were bare, their earlobes stretched down to their shoulders by heavy earrings, their short sarong lengths decorated with handsome silver girdles. Their faces were pretty, gentle, and innocently unaffected. But the men looked quite fierce. They were lean, tattooed, and decked with feathers. Every home displayed a few skulls, covered with cobwebs.

They looked at the smiling face of a sensitive man with taste, who had been educated in Peking, whose standard of Chinese feminine virtue paralleled that of Jade Snow's parents. "What makes you want to go to Borneo?" they wondered. "Aren't you afraid?"

"No, I always bring showy and inexpensive jewelry to give them and they will not harm me. I live with the natives who take care of me and prevent me from worrying. I bring paintings to sell to their Chinese businessmen who have no opportunity to acquire art."

Jade Snow and Woody could only shake their heads at a man whose sense of adventure prompted him to leave an attentive, adoring wife, eight children, and his home, to rough it for months in aborigine country. Yet, given the urban neuroticism of Singapore, perhaps this was the professor's way of finding the personal balance necessary for creativeness, that elusive magic known as "calling one's soul one's own." How many human beings have the courage and opportunity to stake out lives this free? The practice was not unlike that of Chinatown Chinese who divided their lives between Canton and San Francisco. How many other husbands were so fortunate in having a sacrificing wife? With pride and devotion, she had her work, and he had his.

Singapore also introduced Jade Snow to an energetic, articulate Chinese woman who would never have considered playing a secondary role to a Chinese man. Tautly intelligent, Han Suyin took bilingual aim with words and struck bull's-eyes in rapid succession. *Love Is a Many-Splendoured Thing* had just been published; Jade Snow heard it discussed all through her Asian tour. She had not expected that she would participate with its author in a radio interview. As they were introduced (off the air) Jade Snow murmured small talk of having heard much about her book. The author's crisp reply was disconcerting: "Oh, yes. No doubt you also heard speculations from missionary wives who believe I would climb into bed with any man!"

She continued, "I am an Eurasian born of a Belgian mother. It has always been tough for me to fit in Chinese society. There were only two Eurasian students at Yenching University in Peking when I attended it, and the other one committed suicide."

She had trained in Europe to become a doctor. A restless traveler, she had now settled in Singapore where she felt needed. Earnings from her books financed a clinic-pharmacy located near settlement houses for the poor. In its small, neat rooms, she supervised a staff of five other assistant doctors and nurses, while she pursued a relentless schedule. "When I go into the jungle, the bandits do not bother me. I need only produce my needles and ask if they need an injection, and they disappear! But today, I was working in the clinic collapsing lungs," and she named a tremendous number which indicated a high TB rate.

Warm and honest, impatient with superficiality, she was instantly liked and admired by the San Francisco visitors. She explained the press antagonism Jade Snow had encountered. "You are an artist, so you must believe in natural beauty and the goodness of people. I am a doctor, so I expect their ills. If you had been ugly, or cross-eyed, or at least homelier than your pictures, they might have found you acceptable. They resent your good health, your balance, your independent honesty." Jade Snow realized that these were the American qualities of her heritage.

The following week in Kuala Lumpur (K.L. for short), the capital of Malaya, she found a surprising welcome. Leading citizens of K.L. had organized the first art exhibition in the city's history with Chinese ceramics on loan from private collectors to compliment Jade Snow's pieces. Although Malaya had been labeled a cultural desert, this exhibition drew a huge response. Chinese schoolchildren came in scheduled groups, and Jade Snow stood by each day to explain in Cantonese the greatness of their ceramic heritage, encouraging them to create an art of their own. "In this land of your birth, as I did in San Francisco, you can make your own beauty." Traditionally, illiterate craftsmen didn't consider themselves artists, and Jade Snow wanted to free the youngsters from such preconceptions.

They made another lifelong Chinese friend here: a gentle hostess who with her Cambridge-educated attorney husband honored Jade Snow and Woody with a cocktail buffet-dinner outdoors, providing sit-down facilities for hundreds of guests, from a Malay sultan to Chinese schoolteachers. Their hostess had heard that Woody liked barbecued duck. Miraculously, there was enough duck that night for all guests.

She was revealingly direct. "We Chinese here have made it through thrift and hard work. Our ancestors who came a hundred years ago had only three pairs of work pants between a husband and wife, but their descendants now own tin mines and rubber plantations."

"Three pairs of pants between husband and wife" echoed in Jade Snow's mind. From the 1500s to the 1900s, from Malaya to San Francisco, immigrant peasant-type Chinese men and women have worked side by side. As with the black-trousered cabbage vendor in Hong Kong, it was not discernible who wore which pants. Perhaps it was the fact of having to plunge in and get the job done, as her own and Woody's mothers had to do, which was responsible for the strength, endurance, and authority of working Chinese women. The hard-headed man in public, privately head of his household, nevertheless delegated to his wife her realm of authority.

According to her K.L. hostess, descendants did not grow soft. "Times were hard under the Japanese occupation. We buried our silver, but they found it with detectors, so we lost all our valuables and the valuables of friends who had buried theirs with ours. Sweet potatoes and tapioca were our diet, and we grew them ourselves." However, priceless porcelains were not detectable, and these graced their home again.

Though naturally they conversed with each other in Cantonese, the hostess was not shy about talking to other guests in English. Jade Snow thought of her mother, who after more than thirty years in the United States still depended on her children to interpret English. San Francisco's Chinese women had been more isolated than the Malayan Chinese.

She recalled Woody's mother's explaining why she hadn't learned to speak English. Opportunity to do so had been offered by an English tutor at the YWCA where she had brought her boys to bathe.

"In an early lesson, I had trouble pronouncing *the faucet* . . . *th* and hard *t* ending. The teacher opened her mouth wide and asked me to stare at her teeth and tongue position. Then I had to open mine, repeating, 'the faucet, the faucet . . .' after her. How impolite to be so personal and appear so stupid! I stopped my lessons thereafter."

Jade Snow's father also had difficulty with English phonics, and she could remember early years of listening to him practice his lesson over and over,

> Goosey, goosey, gander,
> Where do you wander?
> Upstairs? Downstairs?
> In my lady's chamber.

Their K.L. hostess was so friendly, taking Jade Snow and Woody under her wing, entertaining them with anecdotes about important guests, that Jade Snow impulsively remarked, "I wish I had you for a sister," and the compliment was accepted.

"Sister" was delighted with the party. She scarcely tasted anything herself, epitomizing the placid Chinese matriarch and attentive hostess, helping guests to choice tidbits while her husband strode around, conversing with notable political figures. She was educated, and one of the few of her class to travel from Canton to K.L. for marriage with an immigrant descendant. Reared in a large household that included concubines, who in that era were part of the life style of a wealthy man, she told Jade Snow and Woody fascinating bits of her girlhood, as the thirteenth child born to a man with government rank. It seemed that concubines were not so bad; some of the children loved them better than their natural mother.

Not long afterward, "Sister" was widowed, and she became an international traveler who eventually arrived in San Francisco for a visit and met each of their mothers. It was Woody's mother who noted her hands. "They have not had to work hard a day. Beautiful, smooth, and flexible—they are the hands of a wealthy person born to high class." Jade Snow knew she was wondering: So why should she bother to know working people like us? Jade Snow had known wealthy Americans who "bothered" with her, so had not thought it peculiar for a Chinese to do so. The reason might have been the respect accorded to self-accomplishment in Malaya.

Back in 1953, Jade Snow and Woody reluctantly left "Sister" in K.L., continuing upward through Malaya to Ipoh, Malaya's wealthy tin center, which was so small that there was no United States Consulate. American affairs were supervised by a Methodist missionary who was also president of the Rotary Club. This community leader met the visitors at the airport and announced that the Rotarians were honoring her at dinner. "We have made this invitational banquet formal, so we will expect you to dress accordingly," he informed the couple, as Woody's white shirt clung to the perspiration on his back.

It was to be the only time on this tour that formal attire was *de rigueur*, and though Woody had been prepared with both a white linen suit for day receptions and a black tuxedo for nights, he hated its accompanying starched shirt. He grumbled as he dressed. It was 95 degrees in the shade, with a humidity of 90 percent, in a town so small that their hotel accommodation and the formal dinner were in the only large semipublic building, which was the railroad station.

After her speech, none of the Rotarians' many questions was

so startling as that from an uninvited East Indian who had wandered in from his train. He was not trained in Chinese courtesy, nor did he feel part of the invited throng, and he asked, "From your speech, Miss Wong, do you imply that there is no prejudice in the United States?"

There was a sudden silence. It was the first time she had been asked this publicly. She talked about prejudice where she had found it in employment and housing; but she emphasized that in the United States racial prejudice had never stopped her from getting where or what she wanted, and that the dimensions which her ancestral culture had added to her life offset occasional disadvantages.

"Fear of prejudice and the excuse it offers for personal failure are chronically more damaging to a person of a minority race than to expect the reality of encountering and dealing with prejudice."

Government resentment against the Chinese which existed in Malaya was not unique, as Jade Snow found later in Bangkok. There Chinese schools could teach their language only ten hours a week, and were taxed heavily. The Chinese were also strategic in Thailand's economy. It wasn't easy to get rid of them, since most Thais had some Chinese blood; there was a familiar anecdote about the time the king irritably asked all those with Chinese blood in his court to step to one side, and the entire court moved to one side!

Jade Snow met some of the local Chinese-Thais. One was the publisher of her book, who had arranged an autographing party at his firm. Another was charming Mr. Thonglaw, who began his career by supplying wild animals and birds of Thailand to zoos of the Western world. Forwarding those animals led him into the shipping business.

"Animals mated and multiplied abroad. Zoos traded with each other, and soon they needed no more from me. The shipping business led me to the travel business after the war."

Thonglaw had graying hair, was probably in his late fifties, and proudly claimed a Chinese grandfather from Fukien. "I am a quarter Chinese," he declared, instantly binding himself to them. Like their Macau cousin, he insisted on bringing them to Bangkok's Chinatown to choose the best local products to ship home;

in this case, dried birds' nest soup. Passing street vendors, he impulsively bought Jade Snow unexpected treats: juicy tropical fruits and an armful of fragrant tuberoses.

This man combined the friendly charm of the Thais with the dignity of his Chinese heritage. A grandfather as proud of his family as any Chinese, he reminded Jade Snow of her father. Despite government prejudice against the pure Chinese minority, Thonglaw easily and proudly identified with both his Chinese and his Thai heritage, perhaps because this blend wasn't unusual in his social situation.

On this journey, Jade Snow had discovered manifold problems of other Chinese. In Bangkok she perceived the adjustment of those descended from Chinese and native unions. In San Francisco, older Chinese had not accepted occasional Asian-Western blends. She remembered the "toughness" which Han Suyin had to develop against social pressure in China if she were not to become suicidal. In Hawaii, the great exception, where all racial blends are socially and politically acceptable, the older Chinese and Japanese still clung to their special festivals and customs and preferred their offspring to "marry our own." Jade Snow's mother used to say, "It's all right to have white friends, but when it comes to marriage, it makes for fewer problems when a Chinese marries a Chinese."

Yet, Jade Snow had found that being "pure Chinese" did not guarantee Chinese social acceptance either. She had been ridiculed in her family and by the community when her occupation deviated from the traditional. What is a "pure Chinese"? Even the five-color flag of rebellion symbolized five races of China (the Cantonese being in the Han majority). An individual attains his unique self-image from his goals, his work, and his experiences, which in America to a great extent are consequences of his own choice, whether he is "pure Chinese," part-Chinese, or non-Chinese. Neither being all-Chinese nor being part-Chinese can excuse individual failure.

After almost two months of working travel, which daily called for adjustments to emergencies, strange environments, and psychological crises, the worst defect of the State Department assignment became clear—there was no overall coordination. When she was still in K.L., Jade Snow had written to Washington via diplomatic pouch but received no reply. Every local American representative squeezed his bit out of her, assuming that she could go on indefinitely. As she worked deeper into the enervating tropics, rebellion began to rage through her body. When a coughing, aching, feverish woman arrived in Bangkok to carry through a jammed program, the end was not in sight. Though Woody pleaded against it, she rose at 4:30 A.M. to leave for an excursion 400 miles north to Chiangmai, the opium-growing center of Thailand. How many husbands would have humored such determined wives? It seemed far-fetched that Americanism had to be disseminated there, and as it turned out, she was not to be the one to do it. Her voice disappeared as she arrived at the consul's office. Woody sought out the best available doctor, a Thai who had trained at Johns Hopkins. Diagnosing her problem as overwork bordering on a nervous breakdown, he confined her to bed rest for a week at the local Presbyterian McCormick Hospital.

Since the town lacked a telephone system, the vice-consul rode around in a jeep to announce by bull horn the cancellation of her appearance.

Ward F (for foreigners) had no other patient, so Woody was welcome to share her front corner room, which was open to the outdoors on three sides. To the east were the hospital grounds; to the south, fields of grazing water buffaloes; to the north, the main road where traffic passed: groups of Buddhist monks in their saffron-colored robes, young men with girlfriends perched on the same bicycles, or graceful women on foot, shaded under red parasols. Walls of the ward were dark teak from nearby forests, and provided cool, peaceful respite from weeks of heat and crowds.

Restless Woody found diversions. He borrowed a bicycle to visit the leper colony. Then he called on relatives of the royal family who were local weavers. He reported giving advice to both lepers and royalty on their handicraft production.

Enjoying their meals on the outdoor porch, they noticed an interesting family. Three Chinese Shan State tribesmen and a woman, all clad in black coats, black balloon trousers, red sashes, and small brown felt hats, came and lived for three days under huge trees in front of the hospital. They were hill aborigines whose two-year-old boy had climbed a tree and got caught in an animal snare. He had developed an infection, so the family walked three days and two nights, by turns carrying their beloved child. Even they knew of Western medicine and the excellent care here. Jade Snow and Woody watched for daily progress. As the boy felt better, the family took turns walking with him on their backs. The day he recovered, they joyfully carried him off. A few minutes later, the procession reappeared, marching to their tree shelter again. They had overlooked their drinking cup in the excitement!

When she was nearly well, she took a tour of the hospital. Scattered units housed different departments. The gentle, tiny nurses complained of the long distances between buildings, for during monsoon months, footpaths were under water. Within a distinctive one-story building, faintly reminiscent of a Buddhist temple, were four beds, temporarily unoccupied, reserved exclusively for Buddhist priests, who could never be in a building with women patients above them; after all, the lowliest of objects were a woman's feet, and a priest could never rest with those above his head!

After a week, Jade Snow was well enough to leave, but the doctor warned her not to work more than six hours a day while in the tropics. Ironically, a consular representative who saw her off at the airport reported that they had just received a cable advising that her schedule be lightened, a message which had originated three weeks ago in K.L. and had gone bureaucratically through the various embassy desks in Bangkok before being forwarded to Chiangmai.

Upon returning to Bangkok, they found that tight hotel space had been canceled upon their delay. The nervous young embassy representative who met them complained, "You were assigned to me like a hot potato!" He got rid of this potato when the Austin Flegels offered their home. (He was chief of the U.S. Mutual Security Agency for Thailand.) For the next few days, after required public engagements, Jade Snow and Woody celebrated their pleasant circumstances by sitting with Mr. Flegel on his front porch which faced a canal (or *klong*), where they could see unabashed Thai life. A young man with his red sarong rolled up short was scrubbing the varnish seller's white boat, and a young woman who had been bathing at the basket weaver's landing changed deftly from her wet sarong to a dry one. "I have watched them change a hundred times," Mr. Flegel remarked, "but never have been able to see a thing!"

When Jade Snow discussed with her host the slowness of progress she perceived during her travels in Asia, he produced a poem by Rudyard Kipling which he said he read whenever he became discouraged:

Now it is not well for the white man to hurry
    the Asian brown,
For the white man riles and the Asian smiles and it
    weareth the white man down.

And the end of the fight is a tombstone white
    with the name of the late deceased,
And the epitaph drear: "A Fool lies here
    who tried to hustle the East."

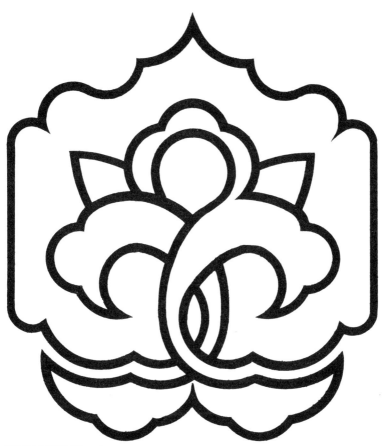

CHAPTER 10
RIDDLES IN RANGOON

Jade Snow arrived in Rangoon with a mental impression—a result of her reading—of successive political coups, for after the British withdrew, Burma's several states had competed to obtain control of the Union. U.S. Embassy representatives cautioned her about the local Chinese community. With the exception of a handful of tycoons, they were small merchants living in a Chinese tenement house section. It was "conceded" that 80 percent were Communists using books from Communist China. Burmese politics were tangled—

there were several Communist groups, and they could not get along with one another.

The Burmese government remained neutral in world politics. At the time of Jade Snow's visit, Burma was provoked by the United States stipulation that she should not send rice to the People's Republic of China; she ordered the United States to withdraw its entire economic assistance program. There was another reason for irritation. By that spring of 1953, some Kuo Min Tang (KMT) troops from Generalissimo Chiang's army had been abandoned in upper Burma for more than three years, and they continued their guerrilla warfare against rural Burmans. Newspapers carried pictures of KMT marauders shot by the Burmans, and killed with them were three white men identified as United States "trainers" because of their address books with Washington, D.C., numbers. Anti-American hysteria was high.

In this complicated situation Jade Snow's speeches would be sponsored by the Burma-American Institute, which worked under a Burmese board of directors but was staffed by U.S. government employees. This sponsorship would take the "stigma" out of her State Department mission. She has been brought to Rangoon because 2,000 copies of her book's Burmese translation had sold out in one week. The Shumawa Company, local publisher of *Fifth Chinese Daughter*, honored its author in an outdoor garden restaurant where long tables had been set up to serve seventy or more guests simple fare: bowls of noodles with a curry sauce. But the guests were far from ordinary. Key members of the Burmese Women's Club invited her to become a guest member, the first American to have this honor. Other guests included those from the Prime Minister's Cabinet.

The Shumawa Company presented Jade Snow with two volumes of her book, bound in dark green leather and lettered in gold. This graphic accomplishment was not to be taken lightly in a city which had not yet solved its garbage collection problem. The highlight of the evening came when the personal representative of the foreign minister presented the volumes to their author, for this representative was U Thant.

Jade Snow's other appearance was at the Burma-American Institute. Because of British colonialization, educated Burmans spoke excellent English. But she was not to be introduced to the Chinese community because of its known Communist sympathies. After the first lecture, the unexpected happened. A young Chinese woman, introducing herself in Cantonese to Woody as a schoolteacher and, moreover, an "Ong," said that the Ong Association wished to honor him at a reception. Since Woody did not know the political leaning of the Rangoon Ongs, he declined politely, murmuring about a full schedule. Both Jade Snow and Woody were relieved that they worked that one out!

The next evening a member of the United States Embassy was hosting a cocktail party at his home where important members of the Burmese government would meet the visiting author. A large delegation of the Ong Association arrived uninvited to obtain official sanction for their reception. There was scarcely chance for reasoned discussion among the Americans. The object of Jade Snow's travels was to stimulate as much natural local response as possible. To refuse might damage feelings—was a Chinese American "too good" to accept a local invitation? The delegation pressed its point—they were willing to plan this reception for any day, any hour. So the Chinese Affairs officer (a Caucasian) gave reluctant permission.

The reception was after dinner the next evening. The couple drove to a dark and narrow street of the Chinese section and found the doors of the Ong Association thrown open, a blaze of light silhouetting the members gathered in the doorway. At least another hundred casual onlookers, including numerous small children, clustered outside. Their car had difficulty pulling up to the door.

They entered a small conference room on street level. A long table covered with a white cloth dominated the interior. Artificial flowers had been arranged stiffly in bright vases. The young Cantonese woman teacher introduced Jade Snow and Woody to the chairman, who launched into an elaborate welcome speech that said, in gist, "We are not worthy of this illustrious visit by this famous Ong couple." And, in gist, Woody's reply was, "But we are not worthy of this honor."

A banner was unfurled from its gold foil case. On a royal blue satin background bordered with red satin, three lines of ideographs had been brushed in gold: "Welcome Mr. Wah Jom of our family, who passes through Rangoon to study business; save this in remembrance." Four larger characters stood out in the center: "The Rukh journeys ten thousand miles." * The last line read: "From the Burma residents of the Ong Association, united in respectful giving."

Refreshments were served on the white tablecloth. They were English-style pastries and exceedingly sweet room-temperature Ovaltine. After a polite sampling, everyone gathered together by the doorway for the documentary photograph.

Determined not to be drawn into politics, Jade Snow neverthe-less noticed pictures of Chiang Kai-shek and Sun Yat Sun hanging side by side under a conspicuous KMT flag. The young school-teacher said their anti-Communist tuition-free Chinese school was in a decided minority. The teachers were paid only seventy dollars a month, but, she said evangelically, they believed in their "cause."

The next day, the Chinese papers published the Ong group pictures with an account of the reception. One face among them was identified as a KMT leader. How embarrassing, when in the same papers the press indignantly denounced the KMT guerrillas' latest inflictions!

In turn, the Wongs were incensed that the Ongs had stolen their thunder, and immediately invited Jade Snow and her hus-band to attend a reception at their headquarters. What could they do but accept?

The Wong Association owned a five-story building in a more prosperous section of town. Like the Ongs, the members were lined up in front to greet them, and as on other informal occasions, the men were in shirtsleeves with open collars. Up the stairs the party climbed, past four empty floors, the base for a magnificent penthouse room which had been added recently at considerable cost. Around the room hung pictures of members who had do-nated handsome sums to the building fund. Jade Snow looked around for the customary flag which would define political affili-ation, but saw none.

A chairman began the proceedings and called upon a young man. Dressed more formally than the others, in a Western sum-

---

* The Rukh is a legendary Chinese bird exceeding all others in size, with a "back like the Tai Mountain and wings like the clouds of the sky." In one flight it could travel 90,000 miles. So the maxim was an allegorical com-pliment covering the physical distance Woody had traveled and the potential success he was yet to achieve.

mer suit, he spoke Cantonese dialect from Toi-Shan as he read a formal resolution commemorating Jade Snow for her accomplishments. A banner of royal blue taffeta, bordered in red satin, with characters appliquéd in white fabric, was presented to husband and wife. Four words which constituted its main motto meant "New Stars of Artistry." The last line read: "Respectful gift of the Rangoon Wong Family Association."

Apologetically, the young man added, "Please excuse the simplicity of this little gift; we had only twenty-four hours between order and completion."

Refreshments were tall glasses of an orange-flavored drink, accompanied by large dishes of ice cream, a variety of sweet pastries, cakes, and hot tea. As Jade Snow cautiously sampled them (she had learned to be careful of uncooked foods in the tropics), the young man told her about himself. He too was a teacher. His large Chinese high school had eight hundred students. Tuition was also free.

Jade Snow casually asked, "How do you get your textbooks?" One of the major problems for San Francisco's Chinese schools was lack of adequate texts, because in the past they had depended on Shanghai for their source.

The young man answered, "From Toi-Shan."

Jade Snow was stunned. Toi-Shan was under Communist rule. Who was subsidizing this tuition-free school? she wondered uncomfortably. The chairman must have guessed at her change in mood, for he leaned over to whisper, "Remember, we are a family association, and therefore completely neutral. The politics of our members are their own concern."

The schoolteacher continued earnestly, "I am so anxious to read your book. I have been to the embassy many times, but they have only two American copies. One was being used by the Burmese translator, and the other has a long waiting list. How can I read a copy? I do not know Burmese. I would like to see the English edition and obtain a Chinese translation for my school."

Jade Snow could not answer. She had hoped the foreign translations would tell their readers the truth about Chinese in America. This Chinese and his students were eager to know the story, but the State Department had ignored them. She studied the faces of these Wongs whose politics were their own concern. Craftsmen and marginal businessmen with the look of hard work about them, they were not the comfortable V.I.P.'s of Hong Kong. Like her father, these were Chinese with a tough economic row to hoe who wished to perpetuate the Chinese way. How confusing and impossible for them, whose eyes were oriented toward China as their home, to forget its existence because it had become "The People's Republic"! Would an American who was in business abroad cease to think of the United States as home if he found that its government had radically changed?

And so, as always, she remembered her father. He had told her that the first legendary Wong parents had had thirty sons, and that every Wong today could trace his ancestry to one of the thirty branches. Whatever the politics of the moment, even a female reared in San Francisco could always find a family welcome halfway around the world from home from descendants of those thirty men.

Jade Snow's experiences with the Rangoon Ongs and Wongs strengthened her belief that Asians had been less interested in her as an American citizen than as a Chinese representative. She also had a cherished belief underscored—people could not be consigned to convenient mental slots. The no-no American word "Communist" might in reality prove to be a flesh-and-blood young man trying to make his social contribution. The man who most enthusiastically helped to install her exhibition in Kuala Lumpur had been the head of the Bank of China, a Communist bank. "Communist" was a catch-all, a scapegoat term.

At the same time, she wished she could also have told those Asian Communists of many Americans who did not fit their clichéd images either. By definition capitalists, these people quietly gave to or worked for charitable causes, and far from exploiting the masses, they endeavored to help them.

CHAPTER 11
AN INCH OF TIME: AN INCH OF GOLD

Jade Snow moved on toward the end of her four-month assignment. Despite a warning from the American consul general in
Calcutta which alerted her that other American "leaders and
specialists" had been booed by university students and grilled by
their press, she and Woody encountered friendly interest as they
moved across India for eighteen days. Strangers on the streets
would stop them, curious as to whether they were Burmans or
Thais. When they answered, "Neither, Chinese," the Indians

thought they were from China. Hearing, "No, from America," they looked bewildered.

The summer heat was now fierce—100 degrees in the shade. In Karachi, the last stop, the final speech had to be made in cooler evening air, outdoors in the garden of the USIS library.

To more than 650 people who came, Jade Snow gave her speech for the last time: "I am a craftsman who has spent most of her waking hours for the past seven years working with her hands. My materials are clay from the earth or chemicals for the alchemy of glazes. My tools are simple bamboo. My inspiration comes from the weeds in the fields or the colors of a sunset. I do not think of myself as a writer, and even less as a speaker, for these are fields concerned with words—and a craftsman has little need for words. . . .

"It is not possible for me to guess what questions are on the tip of your tongue. Perhaps if I tell you of my early childhood, which was not so different from that of many other children born of immigrants in America, Asian or otherwise, and how such a beginning could grow into the miracle of standing before you as a 'leader' from the United States, I could somehow tell you the truth concerning America as I have known it.

"I was born in San Francisco of parents who had come from Canton, China. While I was raised in old-world Chinese standards, when I ventured forth into American public schools, I found a new American world waiting for me. It promised independence, but the path between the two worlds was untried. For I was known as the second generation, whose first-generation parents, searching for economic security in the new world, had unwittingly created for their children completely new problems of adjustment. The first generation of a racial group comes to America with a mature philosophy from their old world. . . . They may not care and may not have to consider the values they find in the new American world. But the second generation, exposed in their growing-up years to American new-world values in the schools they attend, or the books they read, or the movies they see, must decide about their own degree of acceptance of both old world and new. Sometimes their decisions are wisely thought out, and sometimes they are wild ones of rebellion, but nevertheless they must make a choice in defining their place within or between their two worlds.

"What are the important emphases for a young girl raised in the old-world Chinese home in San Francisco? Her parents speak only in the Cantonese tongue, and they shape her into their ideal of a good Chinese daughter as the mother herself was raised in a Chinese village forty or so years ago. . . . Their standard of Chinese womanhood, established by a great nation, was to confine her within the doctrines of Confucius and to raise her in the expectation that her highest reward was to be a matriarch of a large, respectful family. All this was for her own good, for in the China they knew, no one dreamed of being unmarried. So little girls' childhoods were not concerned with play—they were concerned with homemaking. . . .

"The American principles of freedom and independence were taught in the public elementary grade schools to which the little Chinese girl was sent. And later in school, she gradually learned that such qualities as individuality, self-expression, and analytical thought were the rights of all Americans and were the basic principles of American education. . . .

"If a growing woman thinks at all, the conflicts of these two worlds must be resolved. It is always simple to choose between right and wrong, when white is right and black is wrong. Mind and heart are strained if black in the old world is considered white in the new.

"This discovery becomes a turning point in the life of any member of the second generation as he asks, 'Am I of my father's race or am I an American?' Since the old pattern has been made part of his emotional fiber, his heart may ache with the decision. Everyone is liable to make mistakes before he finds his own right answer. America is a country of opportunities to choose your own way, but freedom of choice can be bewildering if one's decisions have no basis in precedence.

"I think the balance between old ways and new comes only after an understanding of the old ways. Not only the Chinese, but many other groups of foreign ancestry have brought their cultures intact to America. These first generations have tried to enforce their standards upon those of my generation to protect what was familiar to them when they were surrounded with the unfamiliar ways and people of America. For their convenience the Chinese have clung together in their community, but they worked hardship on their children who must eventually go out to make a living in the American community. I used to ask myself why, but now I have come to understand that my parents were only human beings!

"If a group of Americans were in a country as foreign to them as America was to my parents, the Americans would just as carefully protect American traditions, and if their children were born in a foreign country, they would think of their children as Americans, raise them in American ideals, and turn them toward America as their homeland.

"I have found my own adjustment in acting as a Chinese when I am among the old Chinese. I can go to my father, act as his fifth daughter, and pass him a cup of tea with both hands. But in the new American world I have learned to act like an American, and my most important assistance came from teachers in American schools. We forget most of our many teachers, but fortunately I remember four or five who took special interest in a struggling, undistinguished girl and gave me a little extra attention, the only encouragement in a lonely search to find a pattern of living and working which would balance the old world with the new. The hope of a more understanding *one* world lies not only in the quality of the home, but in the perception of those in education, both in other countries and in America.

"At Mills College in Oakland, California, I lost my bewilderment with two worlds. I learned that my Chinese background was my point of distinction. I learned never to count on racial discrimination to excuse personal failure. How easy it would be to say, 'I was discriminated against' instead of 'I did not work hard enough.' But the intellectual honesty I learned through my American education would not permit this shifting of blame.

"The book I wrote not only emphasizes differences. I tried to say that the greatest values are the same in both worlds. Honor, courage, honesty, uncompromise in the face of personal conviction, service to fellow men—these are no different in the old world or the new world. . . ."

The last gathering to hear those words gave her the liveliest question period. They wanted to know about her tools and equipment, how long it took to make a piece of pottery, how she priced her pottery, what kind of Pakistani handicrafts she found admirable. One question was the climax: "What do you like better, Miss Wong? China, America, writing, or pottery?"

The audience was delighted and roared with good humor.

Jade Snow thought and finally replied, "I like making pottery in America."

She had talked to about two hundred groups. It had been so hectic a journey that she couldn't appraise the value of the program on which she had embarked with high expectations. The representatives of the United States program abroad had varied greatly in character and competence. Too many had been neither leaders nor specialists! She had tried her best, and so had Woody, who had truly husbanded her. An old Chinese saying came to mind: "An inch of time is an inch of gold. It is difficult for an inch of gold to buy an inch of time." Both had given their inch of gold and their inch of time for the United States.

According to plan, Jade Snow stopped for four days in Washington, D.C., to make the rounds of various foreign desk officers. She had a great deal to say at the Malayan desk, which was located next to the Indo-China desk. When that officer overheard her report on Malaya, he asked her disappointedly, "Why didn't you go to Saigon too? We needed someone like you there!"

Jade Snow thought: And this is the man we are trusting to handle Indo-China affairs? Aloud she said, "I went to all the posts which put in a request; I could have easily included Saigon, but you're nine months too late!"

Jade Snow finished dictating her findings and recommendations. In due time, Washington sent a long transcript to her, but she never heard any reaction to her report.

CHAPTER 12
THEIR FIRST SON

Throughout that first trip around the world, Jade Snow and Woody sought gifts for their mothers. Independently and unknown to each other, each had requested the same object. When Jade Snow had asked her mother what she wanted most of all she hadn't hesitated. "A doll."

"A doll?" Jade Snow was startled.

Her mother explained, "When I was a child, my father left for

San Francisco, where he was a partner in a fish and poultry business. It was hard for me to say goodbye to him, but he comforted me by saying that he would bring me a 'foreign doll' upon his return. He never brought me a doll, and I have longed for one ever since!"

Jade Snow was perplexed. In all these years in San Francisco, she certainly could have bought herself a doll! Did Mama want to re-create that expectation of someone going far, far away, and returning to her with a promised gift?

When Woody asked his mother, she also wanted a doll. It seemed incredible, and her son asked, "Why?"

His mother answered, "I have had eight sons but no daughter. For years, I wanted a doll to dress and call her mine."

They had looked throughout Asia without finding appealing or important enough little girl dolls. After finishing their State Department duties, they began the search in earnest in Rome. One shop after another quoted outrageously high prices—thirty, forty dollars for the largest, most beautiful models. Woody had been sharpened by bargaining in Hong Kong and India. Although he wasn't sure of European practice, he proposed, "I am from Hong Kong and you are my Chinese wife who knows no English. We will converse in Chinese, and I will use broken English to bargain with the shopkeepers."

At the next shop, Woody pointed and asked, "How much?"
The Italian saleslady quoted a U.S. dollar price.

Woody tried to remember how broken English should sound. "No understanding you-ah. How muchee Hong Kong dollars, please-ah," he said haltingly. It was convincing, for he was having trouble finding words.

"Oh, you're from Hong Kong! How very nice! Excuse me; I got the idea you were from America. There was something about your shoes and spectacles . . . I usually can tell if they are American made."

"Then these dolls are not for you." She took them to a stockroom, where an array of superb dolls was reasonably priced. For Jade Snow's mother they chose a blonde. Chinese children found blonde dolls exotic, just as Scandinavian girls liked black dolls. They decided that the two dolls could not be alike, and one was as much as they could carry during the weeks until they got home. In New York City, at F. A. O. Schwarz, they found a curly-haired brunette walking doll for Woody's mother.

Each mother cherished her gift differently. Jade Snow's mother adorned hers with strands of solid gold and bright jade beads and placed it permanently on top of her dresser. Woody's mother regularly undressed her doll, washed, starched, and ironed her pink organdy dress and white lace cap, redressed her, and returned her to the head of her double bed. No visiting grandchild was allowed to play with that "daughter."

It was joy to reach San Francisco and settle into their upstairs studio flat, for they had given up the Tiburon lease and had stored their possessions in the roomy loft above their studio. Once again, they would be economizing to repay debts and conserve time, the craftsman's precious asset. They thought in three years of marriage that they had learned to minimize tension-building traps.

With the help of Youngest Brother during his summer school vacation, Woody painstakingly made sliding screens of Chinese lattice design. Natural mahogany strips were nailed into frames; parchment was used for backing. Jade Snow varnished the lattice and painted the framework white. They worked nights, after regular business duties. Like her art, the inspiration was Chinese, but the final product was their own innovation. The series of panels partitioned the loft into a living arrangement of sitting-dining area, a kitchen, and two bedrooms. Electricity and plumbing were installed for a washer, dryer, and a shower. In studying the landlord's blueprints, Woody had found that a brick chimney hid a flue. They bought a black iron portable fireplace, and Woody spent several days on a ladder knocking a hole into the foot-thick chimney, connecting to it the fireplace flue elbow. It supplied cozy warmth in their bedroom on winter nights—sometimes the whole iron fireplace would glow red. The former waterfront warehouse was converted into a high-ceilinged spacious apartment.

There was a purpose behind this feverish activity. They were expecting their first child. The happiness of a longed-for baby was combined with the mystery of a first pregnancy, for though no race adored babies more than the Chinese, they considered it uncouth to discuss pregnancy. Jade Snow remembered taking her mother and father to see an American attorney who handled legal affairs for San Franciscans from her father's Young Wo Benevolent Organization. Her father was legal guardian for a Chinese widow confined to a mental institution in Santa Barbara. (The 1906 fire had caught her unable to escape because of bound feet, and she had gone berserk.) There were papers to sign, and Jade Snow, fresh out of college, had come along to interpret. Kind Mr. Ralston was also a family friend. As they rose to leave, he said to Jade Snow, "Tell your parents that my daughter is expecting her first baby, and I will soon be a grandfather."

Jade Snow translated this simple message. Her father turned to her mother and said, "Any subject will be mentioned by Americans, who are not afraid of shame. We do not even see his daughter, and he speaks of her big stomach!"

His wife agreed. "But this is not surprising; Americans are perplexingly different from us Chinese."

Mr. Ralston asked smilingly, "What are your parents saying?"

Poetic license was necessary. "Oh, naturally they are happy for you and hope that everything will go well. Do let us know when the big event happens." She wondered to herself at the double standard which disapproved of discussing pregnancy but celebrated with extravagance the birth of a son. Barrels of red-dyed eggs and sections of roast pig, classical birth announcements, would be delivered to friends and relatives. When the baby was one month old, invitations would be issued to come for open house when chicken-gin soup and pigs' feet cooked in black rice vinegar would be served.

Although Jade Snow did not talk about her expected event, when her parents noticed her swelling body her father advised, "Once a month you take 'Twelve Grand Precious Things,' a combination of herbs from an ancient formula to aid fetal health and facilitate childbirth. In the last two months before baby is expected, you take 'Thirteen Grand Precious Things.' After the baby is born, the brew from 'Birth-Growth Soup' should be drunk."

Mama added, "Eat more of bean cakes and other soy products, for that will make your baby's skin smooth."

Jade Snow continued her ceramic work, trimming the last pieces of pottery and finishing firings ten long days after the baby was due. Her doctor was not worried, and four days later, it was time to get to the hospital. An hour and a half later, their first son was born.

A rooming-in accommodation permitted Jade Snow to nurse her baby, who was wheeled in in a transparent crib. He slept on the crook of his right arm, exactly like Woody. That week of her life was to glow always like a sweet miracle. The miracle was the healthy new son. She saw his inch-long growth of black, downy hair, each tiny nail, each little hair on his knuckles, felt his silky skin, and smelled the fragrance of a new human being. She marveled at the perfectly functioning body which had formed out of their union. Never had she been surer about an Almighty purpose. She felt that He had made them a gift of a son, and they were custodians for his care.

The kind nurses observed her joy, but said knowingly, "With the first child, you want rooming-in. With your second child, you will not want to bother. With the third child, you won't even want to go home!"

Many working women of Chinatown considered it economical to board a newborn infant at a nursery and to return to their jobs, to earn more money than it cost for the infant's care. Her experienced sisters-in-law urged Jade Snow to do likewise. "Think of your husband who must run the business alone for a while; he needs his sleep at night."

But she could not bear to relinquish to a stranger a moment of the baby's development. Dollars could never be equated with a child's worth. This philosophy strengthened through the years, and she was not to change even after the child towered in physical height over his father. She didn't foresee that the following weeks at home would be the most disorganized and physically exhausting of any she would experience. Bottles supplementary to nursing were disagreeable. The infant had diarrhea and hiccups; he screamed and did not distinguish between night and day. Life was a constant stretch of work and sleeplessness. In her exhaustion, Jade Snow felt little tenderness, but Woody was transformed into gentle patience. He helped with the laundry, prepared formula, and took over at baby's bath. At the Red Cross class they both attended he learned that a "football hold" was the proper grip, and Woody, once a football quarterback, applied the technique to his wiggling son.

Father and Mother Wong were first visitors. They inspected the baby's features carefully. His eyes were bright, and he had no blemishes; his ears were close to his head, which was roundly shaped. They felt a right to be critical of their grandson's care. The studio flat with its high ceiling wasn't warm enough; the crib didn't have enough covers. The baby should be carried on Jade Snow's back by the Chinese method, which would give him security and warmth. He should wear a jade amulet to keep him from being startled. He should not be allowed to sleep on his back, which would flatten his head unbecomingly.

Woody's mother came separately. He was her eighth grandchild, so she was very matter of fact. "When I was your age at thirty-one, I was through having my eight sons." She added her own criticisms. The child needed sedating herbs. The whites of his eyes were bluish, proving that he suffered from gas. Therefore his tummy should be rubbed with camphorated oil.

After this miscellaneous advice, the older generation left Jade Snow alone to cope with her irritable infant. Yet underneath their remarks, she sensed that unspoken rare Chinese approval—for the baby was a son.

After that first trying month, the baby began to smile and notice lights. After three months, the mother felt that this new child and she were getting together on the same team. Jade Snow accepted their first dinner invitation from close friends, a surgeon and his wife who insisted that they bring along their new baby. He obliged with his best behavior, taking his bottle of broth in his hostess's arms. Later, they were to become his godparents.

It took six months for a combination baby-caring, working and housekeeping rhythm to be established, for this addition to their family required four hours of her day. She remembered her mother's care of Youngest Brother. Fresh vegetables were briefly cooked and then blender-puréed, as were fresh fruits. Chinese soups were strained and fed by bottle. Fresh chicken liver would be steamed and chopped, then mixed into soft rice. As soon as his front teeth appeared, he munched on tiny drumsticks. Sugars were never added to his formula, and his diet didn't include cookies or crackers. Never acquiring a taste for sweets, he grew up without a single cavity.

His playpen was set up in the basement, where his father operated the humming metal lathe or crunched the jaws of the foot shear. Since his interest span was brief, he would be brought to Jade Snow, who could hold him as she sat dictating. Once a visitor said, "When I came in, I thought you kept birds because I heard such musical sounds, but it turns out to be a baby!"

The first serious illness came, and the first temper tantrum. When influenza persisted for two weeks, he cried constantly. For the first time, Woody's mother came to help. She asked for salad oil, which she poured into her palms, rubbing them together briskly until the oil was warmed. Then she placed her palms firmly on her grandson's stomach and rubbed gently. The process was repeated on his hands and the soles of his feet. She had brought with her a tiny glass bulb, no more than half an inch in diameter, sealed in red wax. The vial contained a brown powder.

"I have raised my boys with these 'Seven Powders.' Half the dosage cannot hurt him," she explained as she mixed that amount with warm water and forced the screaming baby to take the potion. Immediately afterward, he fell asleep, a blessing for him as well as for his parents.

Grandmother was not around to counsel on the first tantrum. Late one afternoon, Jade Snow brought the baby upstairs. She had hand laundry to finish before preparing dinner, so she placed him in his propped-up seat. His suppertime was 6:30 p.m., and he was dry. But he began to cry, and he cried and cried. Perplexed, Jade Snow recalled two opposite Chinese approaches to child rearing. Her mother had carried her babies on her back, wrapped in a double-thickness square cloth, with four wide straps attached to the corners which were brought around front to cross and tie into a secure knot. Her hands were free for work, and the child was carried thus until he walked. Mrs. Wong had been terrified lest her baby crawl under the pulleys and swiftly moving leather belts of factory machines. (Forty years later, when her children got together on a holiday, they discussed their childhood and traced their common inability to swim to their mother's terror and her warnings against physical activity.)

Woody's mother never used a carrying cloth. Her worst problem was a new son a year or, as she would put it, "Three years —two sons." She declared proudly, "I never cuddled a baby. I wouldn't nurse one either. If he had been fed, was clean and dry, I would place him in his crib. If he cried, I would shut the door. If he cried more loudly, I would go to a farther room and shut another door."

Neither situation applied here. Jade Snow wished she could shut a door, but shoji dividers were no barrier against sound or light. She had tried the carrying cloth from her mother, but the baby protested against its confinement.

So now she decided uncomfortably to let him cry, which he did for one hour and fifteen minutes, until Woody came up. By then the baby had thrown up all over himself. Tight-lipped and overwrought, Jade Snow could have wept too. Woody surveyed the scene and, without a word, picked up his son, cleaned him, changed him, and held him, singing silly words. Afterward, the baby ate a hearty supper and was in quite good humor all the next day.

After nine months, he was adjusting happily to life, and Jade Snow again felt outpouring love for him. They cast around for Sunday recreation adaptable to a baby and a dog. Any venture of a few hours involved bottles, thermoses of hot water for warming, containers of food, blankets, stroller, diapers, extra clothes, toys, and other odds and ends they thought necessary to keep a baby amused and comfortable. A leisurely barbecue became the best way to enjoy a sunny day, and that fall, for ten Sundays in a row, they visited a secluded dell in Berkeley's Tilden Park, a half-hour drive from San Francisco. Equipped with the baby's gear, a playpen, a box full of charcoal and kindling, the Sunday paper, a portable radio, the makings for long drinks, and food for a meal, they could throw their heads skyward and forget work.

The three became inseparable. After the baby was a year old, the Ongs tried a buffet party at home for sixteen people. Their son was standing and crawling, and helped to entertain. It became their pattern from then on; if friends were close, they would open their home and kitchen to them, and include the presence of their children.

Acquaintances who would not enjoy a child were entertained at a restaurant, and their son would be entrusted to Woody's mother or Jade Snow's parents. He did not enjoy these infrequent excursions. Once, when they returned to pick him up, Father Wong was standing at his doorway, exhausted and bewildered, holding out the screaming year-old infant. "He has cried since you left, and I have not sat down at all," he complained. If only the baby knew that he was bossing the most exacting disciplinarian Jade Snow had ever known!

As much as she loved this son, her husband, and being mistress of her home, these could not remain her only satisfactions. She was continuing to expand her lines of ceramics. Molded sculptural clay forms were added. Earrings and cufflinks, cigarette and jewelry boxes were designed, and they made new investments in machinery. When Tea Garden Preserves moved from across the street, Woody bought their bronze mincemeat machine, which made a perfect clay mixer. There was that exciting day when their 8-foot-long giant Pyribil lathe with 32-inch swing (meaning it could spin metal up to 32 inches in diameter) arrived from the East and was lowered by crane into their basement opening. The lathe revolved maple forms or "chucks," against which copper circles or "blanks" were shaped, or "spun."

Woody had longed to be free from subcontracting to outside spinners, who sometimes ruined a chuck or mishaped a blank. Sometimes promised deliveries did not materialize, leaving Woody and Jade Snow nervous about their enameling commitments. By temperament and in principle, they found it unacceptable to be at the mercy of a third party. Although Woody had not trained in spinning, an art introduced to America by Germans fabricating parts for the beermaking industry, he had studied a number of books and watched spinners at work, and decided that their own lathe would protect their product from beginning to end.

More and more, Woody took over the reins of their diversifying, growing business. Daddy's statement to the Wong Association describing their affairs "as many as the quills of a porcupine" seemed appropriate.

Soon after their return from abroad, fifty huge wooden crates arrived, containing their import orders. It became necessary to find a sales representative, someone in the huge Chicago Merchandise

Mart, which was a national central location visited by buyers. Jade Snow told Woody, "I cannot go with you because our son cries so when we are both gone. You must choose the right man by yourself."

Alone with the baby, Jade Snow felt perfectly safe trundling him to Chinatown at night, visiting Woody's mother or her parents. It was about ten years after the war, and enterprising young men had started new ventures or joined their parents' businesses, remodeling old interiors and façades into brightly lit installations with modern glass and tile fronts. For instance, Mr. Fong had retired, and his G.I. son, who had claimed a Hong Kong bride, expanded his father's business into several branch stores. Others with promotional ideas seized upon the lunar Chinese New Year theme to bring tourists to Chinatown at a usually dead time of the year—February. Although by custom a home celebration, Chinese New Year became a schedule of public events sponsored by the Chinese Chamber of Commerce and the San Francisco Visitors' and Convention Bureau (carefully planned to occur, somewhat belatedly, after private family observance), including the Chinatown Beauty Queen Contest, street carnivals, and the famous parade climaxed by the huge silken dragon silhouetted in blazing lights, curling down Grant Avenue over the numerous legs of the dancers who carried him. While Woody was gone, Jade Snow took their infant son to watch his first night parade.

Woody left reluctantly and kept in touch by phone. "It's ten degrees below zero here. What can I do at the end of a day? If I go for a walk, I am frozen. I hate being alone in a hotel room, and I don't like nightclubs."

Another day, his call was more cheerful. He had looked up their old acquaintance, the corporate chairman. Far from being annoyed when they turned down his contract, he had become one of their good friends, who respected them for saying no to him. He gladly included Woody in social evenings with his friends and business associates.

But that trip to Chicago proved to Woody that he was loath to travel alone. The fact that countless numbers of successful American businessmen traveled as part of their work made no difference. He didn't care for the negotiating and empty talk of the

American sales arena. He preferred action with few words, within the realm of his own authority. So except for occasional un-avoidable absences, their son and his younger siblings were to grow up with around-the-clock company of both their father and their mother, who did not expand their business beyond its existing scale.

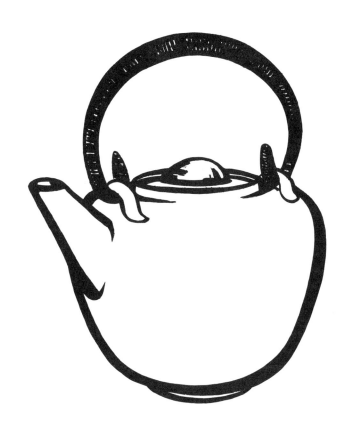

CHAPTER 13
FOUR POTTERS AND A PRIEST

One night after dinner, a Japanese-American travel agent telephoned, wanting to show them a film on Japanese potterymaking. Woody replied, "You can't come now."

"Why not? Nighttime is best to show a movie."

"Because," Woody declared, "my wife is washing her hair and my baby is asleep."

But the stranger was persistent, and they made a later date.

Young Kimura had inherited his father's travel agency. The

film showing was an opening wedge for his real purpose: he wanted the Ongs to lead a tour to Japan and Hong Kong, where most Americans weren't ready to explore alone. If the couple could find an adventuresome group to escort, Kimura would make the reservations and write up the tickets. They were unsure. Leave their business again? What about their son? Yet they longed to see the Orient once more, and it would be a chance to revisit import resources, their relatives, and friends. An agreement was reached.

Invitations went to their private studio mailing list to attract people of congenial interests, whose quick and overwhelming response surprised them. Kimura was ecstatic at the success of "his" idea. Thirty-three men and women from diversified walks of life and various American cities were eager and confident that they would see a different Orient in the company of the Ongs.

The average visit to Japan lasted a week, but their itinerary included three weeks, one of them in Kyoto. Leisure and luxury were featured, and all costs, even tipping, were included. Mr. Kimura paid for the travel costs of the baby, engaging a registered nurse throughout Japan and an amah in Hong Kong. Their two-year-old became the darling of the tour. He adjusted to daily travel and to their group even though he couldn't speak Japanese or English, for his early vocabulary was Chinese.

When they reached Hong Kong, however, he came down with a fever, vomiting, and diarrhea. The hotel doctor advised, "Don't trust the milk here. It comes from clean cows, but it is watered down. Boil it for your son—he has no immunity to local germs." So instead of calling on their relatives, the relatives came to inquire after the child. Seventh Auntie hobbled in on her little feet, escorted by her maid. She carried a pot of soothing broth brewed with fresh watercress. (The Chinese cuisine supplements medical treatment. A progression of soups is traditionally recommended according to ailment. Just as chicken gin is right for after birth, so watercress cools fevers. Recovery from surgery is benefited by birds' nest soup, which supplies quickly digested protein. Anemic blood is improved by steamed beef broth laced with ginger root. Ginseng tea is a tonic which aids digestion.)

How Seventh Auntie admired the coloring and sturdiness of

this great-nephew's body, for local babies lacked exercise and sunshine, which were inadvisable in the tropics. At an early age, milk was dropped from their diet, partly because of expense or unavailability and partly because it was not traditional in their menu. The Asiatic Chinese child was often pale, thin, wiry, and small.

When the Ong son had been checked in San Francisco by his first pediatrician, his weight, length, and general development were the U.S. average for a one-year-old. Since both Jade Snow's and Woody's mother had been under 5 feet tall and less than 100 pounds at maturity (Woody's mother used to say, "I was a mother several times over and remained ninety pounds"), Jade Snow had rejoiced: "Isn't it marvelous that after centuries of being small, Chinese children with adequate prenatal care and correct diet in this generation can become as large and healthy as Americans? Innately our genes aren't of a small race."

The doctor had stopped her conjecturing: "I would have to see the case histories of a thousand Chinese babies to confirm your theory."

Seventh Auntie did not need a thousand case histories. She was delighted to see this first child of a second generation born abroad. Even though the child was sick, she declared in soft wonder, "I used to think that pictures of foreign babies in American magazines must have been artificially contrived, for they looked too robust and beautifully colored to believe. Now that I see a two-year-old Chinese can be this size, I think there must be some magic in your air and food." Gently she stroked his arms. "His flesh is solid." She nodded approvingly.

Upon leaving, she whispered, "Come back to see me again, and I hope next time you will bring a little sister."

In Hong Kong, they enjoyed private reunions with relatives; in Japan, Jade Snow and Woody shared with their travelers the privilege of visiting local potters who became their friends after that State Department mission first brought them together. The Japanese potter, unlike many American potters, worked only when he was in the mood; nor did he maintain a stock of price-tagged wares. He didn't even feel that he had to make a piece of pottery from beginning to end. He excelled in related fields of artisanship and scholarship—training bonsai, painting, calligraphy—

and in such hobbies as keeping rare animals or birds. Being a relaxed person with humane values, his ability to make pottery was only one phase of the cultivated total man (for all the potters were men).

Potters received deep respect, from the Imperial family down to the working man. It was common practice to reach a wide public through exhibitions in department store galleries, where pottery commanded impressive prices. Exhibitions normally sold out; then a collector would approach a potter and say, "Here are so many yen. When you have a piece of pottery you think I am worthy to own, send it to me." The patient buyer did not mind waiting a year for the potter's choice.

It was on the State Department tour that Jade Snow met Kitaoji Rosanjin, born in 1881 and considered the greatest of the older modern potters. He borrowed freely from the styles of old Chinese porcelains and Japanese pottery, but maintained a vigorous personal touch. When they approached the Rosanjin property in Kamakura, a young American saw them. "Woody," he hailed, "what are you doing here?"

"J.B.," Woody exclaimed, "what are *you* doing here?"

They had been students together in summer studies three years before. J.B. explained that he was learning Japanese potterymaking. "This Rosanjin is a real character," he said, "and very temperamental. He has been in a foul, black mood for several days and has not spoken to anybody."

In bitter January cold the little group huddled by the rustic house in its setting of rolling hills and placid fields. "But we had an appointment!" protested the State Department officer escorting the Ongs.

J.B. stared unsympathetically at her. "What difference is that supposed to make to him?"

Finally Rosanjin appeared at the door. He was much larger than the average Japanese, had unruly gray hair, wore heavy, thick-lensed glasses, and was dressed in a Western suit. The group was invited to inspect finished pottery in the showroom. Jade Snow picked up pieces which interested her most and turned them upside down to look at the finish of the foot—for the underside reveals the craftsman's care. Rosanjin watched her in silence. After a while, he ushered them to his inner study. It held a pleasant clutter of books, papers, brushes, and surprisingly, a Western table with chairs around it. They did not have to remove their shoes to enter tatami-matted rooms and sit on zabutons (cushions) placed on the floors.

The unfriendly mood of Rosanjin had evaporated, and he waved his guests to chairs. Ignoring the others, he focused on Jade Snow. Someone brought the customary tea, which they were about to sip politely when their host pulled out from under the table several quarts of excellent Japanese beer. The tea was quickly removed, and glasses of beer were passed. J.B. whispered, "He drinks beer the whole day," and added further information. Rosanjin turned potter when he became dissatisfied with serving dishes for food. Delicious food was his most important reason for living, but he couldn't enjoy eating unless the dishes were artistically perfect. He learned to make pottery to satisfy his aesthetic requirements; and the products of his kiln were dedicated to the serving of food! Now his wares were in great demand by exclusive restaurants.

(An exclusive Japanese restaurant, like a Japanese inn, is managed as a private residence. Guests are accepted only after introduction and by appointment. They are given the private use of elegant rooms with personal attendants, sometimes one to each guest. Each course served is a gorgeous presentation to "feed the eye" before the mouth, and represents the finest culinary achievement.)

After J.B.'s introductory remarks, Rosanjin said he enjoyed Chinese food most of all. He directed his first question to Jade Snow: "What part of the fish do the Chinese like most?"

Mustering her poise, she answered, "The head and collar."

This pleased him enormously, and he began writing a poem about succulent fish. The writing was in Kanji, literary Chinese familiar to educated Japanese. Echoes of those lessons in Tang poetry stirred in Jade Snow's memory, and she finished his poem with the proper words.

The impact on Rosanjin was instant. He waved aside the interpreter and proceeded to wander with Jade Snow in written Chinese, on such matters as food, poetry, and after a while, pottery. What kind of pottery shapes were most suitable for certain delectable Chinese creations?

He asked her, "By the way, what did you say you did in the United States?"

Jade Snow replied, "I am a potter."

Rosanjin threw back his head and roared with good-humored laughter. Everyone looked at him perplexedly. He waved his arms in protest. "Nonsense! No *woman* can be a potter!" The opinion of womanhood in Japan is low, and regard for a potter is high; the two together were incompatible. Unbelieving Rosanjin changed the subject.

"Some day, I would like to see America, but it worries me that I speak no English. So I must go quickly by airplane with a large sign hung around my neck." With red ink and brush, he quickly wrote the words of the sign in Kanji:

THIS IS ROSANJIN, EMINENT ARTIST OF JAPAN. HAVE MERCY UPON HIM, BECAUSE HE KNOWS NO ENGLISH, BUT HE LOVES TO EAT.

"And as soon as I get off the airplane, I'll come to your studio, and the first thing you must do is to take me to a Chinese restaurant and feed me," he pursued.

(Before he died in 1960, Rosanjin returned Jade Snow's visit by coming to her studio, accompanied by a contingent of welcoming committee, interpreter, and friends, on a tour sponsored by the State Department. The moment he saw her, he whipped out a pad and pencil and began writing the names of the Chinese foods he wanted to taste in San Francisco, including sharks' fin soup. His schedule did not allow a dinner with her, but she advised him which restaurant would best prepare what he wished.)

Rosanjin became expansive: "Come outside and visit my studio." Here workers had made bowls and compotes. In the wan January sunshine the newly trimmed ware was drying outdoors on rows of wooden planks. The master picked up a piece which was "leather-hard" (dry enough to handle but damp enough for impressions) and with a sharpened bamboo tool quickly carved a pattern of holes. Jade Snow was shocked. A sturdy pottery bowl was a lifetime asset in the kitchen—for baking, steaming, salad, beating eggs. But not a bowl with holes!

She turned to the interpreter: "I don't understand."

Rosanjin caught her bewilderment, which pleased him. He drove his point home triumphantly. "A moment ago this bowl was an ordinary worker's bowl. Now, because of my holes, it has the valuable Rosanjin touch. I do not need bowls useful for all things; this bowl is good only for one purpose—the serving of beautiful fruits. You will see their enticing colors and textures through the holes."

As they were leaving Kamakura that day, J.B. trailed after them with further information. "See that little farmhouse down the hill? Isamu Noguchi came back to Japan and wanted to stay close to the soil, and he lived there for a while."

The next potter they met on the State Department tour came through an unexpected encounter. Bedlam had broken loose in the town hall of Seto (near Nagoya), a pottery manufacturing center, when the audience roared its protest against the high protective tariffs of the United States (45 percent). As the Cultural Affairs officer moderator looked horrified and helpless, a man arose from the audience.

Unlike Rosanjin, he was dressed in traditional kimono and getas (wooden clogs). His face was unlined, and his wavy hair was rather long. With one Japanese sentence, he quelled his fellow men and disbanded them.

Astonished, Jade Snow asked the interpreter, "What did he say?"

"He said that they were talking foolishness because you are a Chinese artist and not an American economics expert."

The peacemaker was Toyozo Arakawa, who was celebrated for his research into reproducing ancient "shino" white wares, characterized by a milky, thick glaze ground from pebbles, and burned with orange undertones. Subsequently, he was designated a "Living Human Treasure" by the Emperor, and with the title went a subsidy in recognition of extraordinary talent.

Now, moving through Japan three years later with a large group of tourists and a hundred pieces of luggage, it wasn't practical to revisit this friend, but from correspondence Arakawa anticipated their arrival. He came to Tokyo, missed her, pursued her via the night train to Kyoto, and appeared the following morning at their hotel. He did not speak English, and Jade Snow knew little spoken Japanese, but she sensed his urgent wish that they accompany him. With Woody, they got into a taxi and drove through a part of Kyoto new to them. At a narrow side street, they went on foot along a path formed by random stone squares that led into a small temple compound. White walls six feet high and topped by black tiles secluded them from the nearby busy thoroughfare. In narrow garden beds on both sides of the walk grew camellias and other bushes; all was green, all manicured exactly, without a fallen leaf to mar the order. The atmosphere was at once serenity and perfection, and the enveloping silence was not of disuse or neglect, but managed and expectant.

The stone walk ended at a building with sliding front doors of natural wood covered with white paper. Above, Chinese characters carved into an ancient wooden sign meant "Dragon Light Temple." Arakawa struck a bronze gong, creating delicate musical tones. He motioned to them to remove their shoes. Soundlessly, the doors slid open, and before them stood a young priest with a face of peace, clean-shaven head, dressed in a kimona the color of tea leaves. An immaculate white collar framed his neckline. From the time they had entered the gate, the visual impact had been monochromes of greens, browns, and whites, and the temple within retained these quiet colors. But such polished floors, such fragile woods, and such beautiful dull old ink paintings on those paper wall panels! Texture played against texture. Jade Snow felt as if she had entered a mysterious inner soul of Japanese life, a triumph of exquisite architectural balance. Through the doorway of each nearly bare room, they saw a vista marked by something beautiful—one scroll, perhaps, or a single touch of color, a purple clematis in a vase.

Those rooms formed a huge L that sheltered a courtyard; sliding panels had been removed in the mild spring climate, revealing a room-framed sunken garden to be looked at, but not to be entered. The garden-court was dominated by one huge noble pine, leaning slightly with age, and near it, a Korean type of square stone lantern. Smaller shrubs were artfully scattered around the moss-covered grounds. The rest of the world could not be seen; only the garden, its walls, and a canopy of blue sky.

Their temple host told them in English that he had spent his college years studying in Southern California. Thereafter in Japan, he had continued to study English from a private tutoress. He had known Arakawa for many years, since he had studied at a Buddhist temple near his kilns, where the potter always stayed when he visited Kyoto. There was an exchange of words in Japanese, and their host disappeared momentarily, returning with a box which he placed in the center of the group seated on the zabutons. Jade Snow saw its Chinese label, "National Treasure." Within the outer wooden box was a coarse green scarf knotted around another finer box of white wood. When opened, this box revealed a purple silk cloth enveloping a white silk pad. A black lacquered box decorated with gold design and gold label came next, still concealing the contents within. Another thin silky gauze; another box; then little purple pads holding in place another lacquer box shaped exactly like a bowl. Within this box a brocaded drawstring bag contained the National Treasure: a Sung Dynasty tea bowl of generous size, with a "fat" glaze, semimat, semishiny.

Never had Jade Snow seen a bowl like it. She had studied many categories of Sung bowls, but this one was unique, in deep blue-black with iridescent tiny fires, alive like embedded opals. In humility, she accepted with both hands the priest's offer to hold the Treasure. She felt the smooth coolness and turned over the thousand-year-old symbol of the best of a potter's work, indeed symbolic of the best of China's culture, in order to look at its foot. The sturdy stoneware clay had been left exposed, to show the brown bone of its structure. The artist who shaped that foot—how did he feel when he unstacked the kiln and saw this supreme glowing result of one in a million? How many other bowls had he worked on which the kiln fires were not kind enough to deliver in hoped-for results? "How came this Chinese bowl to this temple?" she asked. "What is this temple?"

The garden and temple were an integrated design by Kobori Enshu, famed for his Katsura Detached Palace, now under the protection of the Imperial Household Agency. The paintings on the walls of this Ryoko-in (Dragon Light Temple) had been created by celebrated contemporary artists of the brief Momoyama period.* The Ongs looked around with renewed interest and understanding.

Their host gave them a résumé of Buddhism, which was introduced from China during the Nara period (A.D. 600–794), a religion for the royal elite. By the time of the Kamakura period

---

* 1593–1615, known for vigor and splendor in fine arts achievements. Momoyama, or "Peach Hill," was the site of the ruling shogun Toyotomi Hideoyshi's famous castle.

(twelfth century), civil war, court intrigue, and general turmoil had made death the populace's greatest concern. A new form of Buddhism, again from China—Zen—answered this concern by stressing salvation through meditation, to achieve "divine emptiness," by looking within oneself for the meaning of life and death. The samurai warrior at Kamakura, believing in Zen, developed his own meaning—Japanese chivalry with self-sacrifice, discipline over mind and body, will power and self-control—the qualities of a true samurai.

Simultaneously, the formal tea ceremony (Cha-no-yu), training in flower arrangement, and the planning of gardens, which were interrelated arts, flourished. Zen, the garden, the flower, the tea and its pottery bowl—these are part of one spirit.

The priest referred to the bowl at hand. "Beauty like this is too great for any individual to own, perhaps not even for one country to keep, but it is to be cherished by the appreciative. We have this one perfect bowl. I am only its present custodian between generations. Rarely do I see it myself. But when I do, I see it like new each time."

He carefully rewrapped the Treasure, covering by covering, and his guests felt that it was time to go. Jade Snow asked, "I have not heard your name." The smooth face smiled slightly, showing gold teeth. "I am Kobori Sohaku, descendant of Kobori Enshu." He gestured toward the dominating pine. "And the tree was planted by my ancestor."

This wise, humble, sure, and gentle descendant of a legendary artist and tea master had opened a door for her mind and for her eyes, allowing her to perceive external beauty expressing internal spirituality, a religion unlike Christianity yet in no way conflicting. She was unable to visit China, fountainhead of that philosophy; but because this concept was concurrent and fundamental to the creation of Sung pottery before it was transplanted and nurtured for several hundred years in Kyoto, and because she had been brought into this religious sanctum by an unpredictable series of circumstances, Jade Snow at last found the key to the art which had preoccupied her during a solitary quest of fifteen years.

Not only Buddhism but other transferable Chinese cultural elements flourished in Japan. Kyoto had been saved from bombing during World War II when Langdon Warner personally appealed to Franklin D. Roosevelt to spare the city's unique arts and temples. During this visit, when Peking and Hangchow were not permissible tourist destinations for Americans, Jade Snow found in Kyoto a record of Chinese inspiration and Japanese techniques.

Other artists as well as Rosanjin presented this synthesis; among them Kenkichi Tomimoto, potter, calligrapher, and painter. He painstakingly decorated pure white porcelains with fine Japanese geometric patterns, sometimes taking weeks to complete a piece of important work. But his Chinese brush could finish calligraphy in seconds.

Tomimoto's temperament and personality and therefore his arts differed strikingly from Rosanjin's, for Tomimoto's ego was not coupled with vanity, though he had been famous since 1912. He lived in such a small, quiet house in Kyoto that people visiting him for the first time thought they had come to the wrong place. He never copied designs, but sketched his own directly from nature. One of his books,* which he autographed to Jade Snow, carried this introduction: "When I was young I made many drawings in one day and threw most of them away. Nowadays I make very few but they are all usable. That is the difference between now and thirty years ago.

"To think that I have spent over forty years on foot and on bicycle going over mountains and fields in search of suitable specimens of plants and flowers and these few drawings are the result is disappointing, to say the least."

Tomimoto's humility epitomized the dedicated potter who avoids trick effects; the eternal elements, earth, fire, air, and water, are his supplies and his inspiration. Now he led their group to his simple studio, located near a kiln shared with several potters. His current project was a vase commissioned by the Emperor of Japan to present to the Shah of Iran, and his coloring media were gold and platinum. Since Tomimoto knew English, he talked informally as he worked.

"I grew up in Nara, where my father, an architect, was also an

* A Collection of Designs by Ken Kichi Tomimoto for Decorating Pottery Selected by himself, Chou-Koron Bijitsu Shuppan (1957) 1-2-chome, Kyobashi, Chuo-Ku, Tokyo.

amateur artist of Chinese painting. This beautiful old paper was left by him to me." (Paper and brushes are more than worth their weight in gold to artists.)

In a few graceful brush strokes, he presented his favorite Chinese characters: "Wind," "Flower," "Snow," and "Moon." (In his book, he used the symbols for plate 22, with this remark, "About

風	花	雪	月
Wind	Flower	Snow	Moon

1910 I saw in a mosque letters used in arabesque, and I wondered if I could do the same with Chinese characters. The four characters, Wind, Flower, Snow, and Moon, are often seen on Sung ware, and I have modified them to suit my taste. I still continuously use them in line, circle, or other designs, in blue and white, iron black, or in colors over glaze.")

One did not trouble a great personage without a proper gift. Woody brought him a new handwoven Kashmiri tweed sport coat in a pattern of herringbone squares—off-white and maroon. It would be handsome with his gray hair and mustache. He beamed his pleasure and said, "My son will want this from me," an unusual compliment.

In later years they were to visit Kyoto and Tomimoto again. He was thinner but still vigorous, and building a new, larger home. He had visited Bernard Leach in England. The Emperor of Japan had awarded him a medal for Cultural Achievement upon the occasion of his one-man show commemorating fifty years of pottery, only the second time such a medal had been awarded. Leach had laughed at Tomimoto when he heard about this award. But when, in turn, Leach was decorated by the Queen with the C.B.E., it was Tomimoto's turn to laugh.

This story delighted Jade Snow because she knew Leach as a student, when his worst criticism of a student's piece of pottery consisted of one word: "Indeterminate!" In their modesty, neither artist ever told her what she read later: both had studied under Old Kenzan the Sixth, and the Master had bestowed on both "Certificates of Proficiency."

"Seeing that Old Kenzan died without any heir," wrote folk-art leader Soetsu Yanagi, "Leach and Tomimoto should rightly receive the title of the Seventh Kenzan, for they are the only pupils who legitimately mastered the art of Raku ware. This is a fact which might be of interest to students of Japanese ceramic history. . . ."

The greats among contemporary Japanese potters may be counted on one hand. While both Rosanjin and Tomimoto have died, Shoji Hamada works today in northern Japan in the mountains of Mashiko. Over seventy years of age, he has shared in the vigorous growth of the folk-art movement and remains one of the few survivors. He too has been designated a "Living Human Treasure." Single-handedly, he elevated the standard for pottery-making and the economic base of Mashiko, and unstintingly helped local artists. On reaching him there, Jade Snow and Woody were warmly received by an informal personality, a smiling, sturdy, balding man with glasses, whose worst problems were people and mosquitoes.

The people are some 25,000 fans, interviewers, or collectors who visit Mashiko each month. Yet he feels that those who made a long journey to find him must not be turned away. He toured the Ongs around his extensive grounds. Buildings were handsome, thatched, hand-hewn farmhouses, harmonizing with the earth. Casually, he led them into one dark building, where he knew his way around intimately. He brought out a large Chinese ceramic urn, one piece in his collection, and they discussed it. When he discovered kindred souls, he brought out more and more, and they spent fascinating hours together.

When Jade Snow envied Hamada his inspiring natural setting, he shook his head and explained his second problem: "After the people leave me by end of day, at last I have time to work in the evenings, especially pleasant in the summers. But then the mosquitoes plague me. How can I hit them with clay-covered hands?"

"Oh," Jade Snow cried, "but do you not have any insect repellent?" Apparently not. (When she returned to Tokyo, she got out the rest of her supply and sent it to him.)

She teased this Human Treasure about that famous saying attributed to Hamada: that he never signed his work, because if it was bad, no one could say it was his, but if it was good he might be credited with more good pieces than he actually made. Hamada laughed knowingly, because it is the privilege of an artist to confuse the novice. The artist who doesn't identify his work is securely independent of the need for publicity. He can always recognize his work, but his intimate concern is over as soon as it is completed, for the process of creation is the end in itself.

In no country other than Japan did Jade Snow find so many artists who could communicate with her on the common ground of their working philosophy. Her soul had been nourished as never before.

CHAPTER 14

THE DEPARTMENT OF THE HEART

A year after returning from leading that tour, their second child was born. Though her name in English satisfied the birth registration, the process of identifying the baby girl was not complete. A Chinese descendant must have a Chinese name—a serious symbolic choice, since names indicate character. As common and numerous as English Johns and Marys are Chinese names meaning Perception, Truth, or Love for girls, and for boys: Handsome, Glorious, Prosperous. There are other names less common but no less meaningful. Jade Snow recalled her father's saying seriously when he heard that the adult only son of a good friend had drowned, "He should not have named him 'Lively River.' "

In old China, a man acquired several names in his lifetime: first a "milk" name, followed by a "school" name, a formal marriage name (the form entered in the family tree), and a business name. A name may even be given in death to mark a final important event.

Established families usually picked a series of formal marriage middle names for successive generations of boys, to be shared by all cousins of that generation. The Wong family tree manual listed twenty-four generations of such middle names, of which Daddy's "Hung" was the twenty-first. Even a branch of the family which had moved to Shanghai was tallied in this order. Informally, "Tin" or "Heaven" had been the middle name given at birth to Jade Snow's brothers, as well as to the two Macau sons of Ninth Uncle. When a family got together, they could instantly distinguish seniority.

Their son's middle Chinese name had been thus determined years ago by his paternal grandfather, who had picked the word meaning "Bright" (pronounced "Ming" and the same ideograph as for the Ming Dynasty). When the baby was born, Jade Snow had asked her father to find a name to pair with "Bright." On a piece of red paper he brushed in black a dozen possibilities. They chose the word "Tao" (meaning "way"), which implied correct action based on understanding the principle of things. It is also the word for the Taoist philosophy.

"Hung"　　"Heaven"　　"Bright"　　"Tao"

Girls, who are secondary to boys in the Chinese scheme, did not merit a formal marriage middle name chosen by dead ancestors. Jade Snow's mother-in-law had chosen the word "Beautiful" for an informal childhood middle name for granddaughters born to her other sons, and it was proper that this new granddaughter should follow suit.

Jade Snow fretted. "Beautiful," an inoffensive word, was a cliché. "Beautiful Gold," "Beautiful Shadow," and "Beautiful Flower" were common. She was gloomy about finding a combination for her daughter as likable as "Ming Tao." Woody suggested, "Ignore my mother and decide on something else you would like. Make it simple and call her 'Little Jade Snow.'"

But it was not simple to take issue with one's mother-in-law. So Jade Snow consulted with her Chinese authorities. Her mother's comments were direct: "What is significant about the name 'Beautiful'? What can you do with it? Your father chose his sons' names and I chose our daughters' names. You know how to use a Chinese dictionary."

Daddy suggested constructively, "You decide in which 'department' you prefer to locate your daughter's name and let me know."

The written Chinese language has changed little during thousands of years. Since words were created by meaning, they are listed in the dictionary by their root or radical meanings, or "departments." Within the "department," a word is placed in order of successively increasing strokes. For instance, the name of a plant usually falls in the department of "Grass." One would look for the "Grass" category in the dictionary, wherein all ideographs with "grass" as a component part are organized by number of strokes. Names of metals are found in the department of "Gold;" trees are named in the "Wood" department. Other departments include "Bird," "Fish," "Fire," "Water," "Bamboo," "Insect," "Ship," "Sound," "Meat," "Vehicle"—in all, some two hundred departments exist for the entire Chinese language. Oddly enough, the word "Beautiful" is located in the department of "Deer."

Jade Snow felt that a woman's most essential quality should be in the department of "Heart." At an agreed date Daddy slowly climbed the steps to their upstairs studio-home and sat down with her by her desk, a piece of antique rosewood furniture with open shelves at both sides of its base. Here she kept an out-of-print Chinese dictionary in two seven-pound volumes, printed in Shanghai in 1914, which Woody had inherited from his father. Her father appraised the beauty of the desk and slowly rubbed its satiny surface, but said nothing.

Jade Snow wondered what he was thinking. It was now five

艸 Grass	金 Gold	木 Wood	鳥 Bird
魚 Fish	火 Fire	水 Water	竹 Bamboo
虫 Insect	舟 Ship	音 Sound	肉 Meat
車 vehicle	麗 Beautiful	鹿 Deer	

years since they had worked on the Chinese text of *Fifth Chinese Daughter*. Was he reminded of old times, thirty years ago, when she sat on tabletops in his factory, keeping him company and learning to memorize Chinese? What would he now conjure from the mysterious depths of a mind which could produce verses, parables, proverbs, legends, religious or philosophical pearls of wisdom applicable to any occasion?

Her father reached into his pocket for notes written in red ink on the back of an old envelope. He had prepared five possible girls' names chosen from the "Heart" department with these meanings:

1. Quiet happiness.
2. Kind affection.
3. Gentle love.
4. Thoughtfulness, especially of elders.
5. Saintly virtue, with beauty and moderation (popularly used to compliment superior feminine character).

The last one seemed appropriate. But her father said, "Do not be hasty. Let us keep these in mind and go through the 'Heart' department thoroughly." Then he traced the ideograph for "heart" with his index finger on the desk, and counted the number of strokes softly, automatically, "One, two, three, four," as she had seen him do hundreds of times. Upon reviewing that "department," she was surprised to find words unfit for any name: "Forgetful," "Anger," "Sorrow," "Impatient," "Regret," "Pity," "Evil," "Worry," "Shame," had also been classified by ancient Chinese as matters of the heart. And her father's own name was there, meaning "Constant, dependable, lasting."

After studying each of his suggested five words, they decided that number five would definitely pair best with "Beautiful." Thorough Daddy commanded, "Now write it." Indeed, it was a most complicated ideograph, formed with twenty different strokes and dots. Someday, it was going to be a vexing task for the little girl to write "Beautiful Virtue" (phonetically "Lai Yee") at Chinese school.

心 恒
Heart (Father's name)

小 懿
"tree" form Yee

紹 雪
Introduced Snow

Jade Snow repeated Woody's half-jest, "Why couldn't we have called her 'Little Jade Snow'?"

Her father admonished, "It is never possible for one of a younger generation to take the name of an older person, for that would confuse orderly relationships. A name indisputably belongs to one person only. You cannot call a daughter 'Jade Snow,' but her school name can mean 'Continuation Snow.' I shall write it down for you."

So the Chinese name was settled. Brother and Sister were christened Western style in a double ceremony at which the Mills chaplain who had married the Ongs officiated. It was held at the home of the San Francisco surgeon and his wife who hosted a gala champagne party for their godson's family and friends. "I practically never cook," said their hostess, "but I personally made the blintzes with caviar for this occasion."

The business "angel" who had helped them through the years and his wife became godparents to the baby girl. A third couple, their attorney, was Second Godfather to Ming Tao, and his wife Second Godmother to Lai Yee.

Jade Snow's and Woody's family found this religious ceremony a warmly memorable family event. Mama proudly held her new granddaughter to pose for pictures. Not since their wedding had their families mingled socially with their Western friends. As at their wedding, the figures on this occasion were more significant than the guests realized. Their hostess was a descendant of early missionaries to Hawaii, where Cyrus and Susan Mills had once headed Punahou, their mission school, before establishing in California the college which would bear their name.

That old-fashioned hymn, "Blest be the tie that binds our hearts in Christian love," straddled oceans and embraced races. And no one on that pleasant occasion realized that it would be the last such embrace for Daddy.

Perhaps as second child, she was handled in a more experienced way, perhaps it was true that female infants had less sensitive digestive tracts than boys, or perhaps it was just her temperament. Whatever the reason, fitting Lai Yee into Jade Snow's and Woody's life was not perplexing. Three-year-old Big Brother spent mornings at the Golden Gate Kindergarten Association Nursery School, just around the corner from Grandfather and Grandmother Wong, who sometimes peeked at him through the front yard fence. Within the protection of the premises, Ming Tao could do as he pleased: play alone, or with others his own age. He could climb, crawl, or swing outdoors, or sit quietly inside drawing, painting, constructing—and now he learned English.

Jade Snow was slow to recover her energy after Lai Yee's birth. One day when Daddy dropped by and found her pacing the floor to placate the baby, he said forthrightly, "You need household help. This will not lessen your attentiveness to your children, but another pair of hands can run the washer and dryer, or fold clothes."

"You mean, hire someone to do housework?" Jade Snow thought this was an extravagant measure.

Her father was realistic. "When you children were small, there was always someone around who could lend a helping hand, either Grandmother, an uncle, or some friend who would take you to the park, or meet the family needs enough to lessen the load on your mother's shoulders. But in today's kind of American living, as much as we all wish to help, each is busy at his occupation or lives beyond the Chinatown area."

"I wouldn't know how to find a trustworthy person." His daughter was dubious.

"How about an ad in the Chinese newspaper? Get a Chinese-speaking person for a few hours a day, so that you can still have your private home life in the evening."

An advertisement in the *Chinese Times* found them Mrs. Yip, a youthful grandmother whose husband was a retired waiter. She was cheerful and clean, and she adored children. She and Jade Snow liked each other. Jade Snow knew that no two women performed housework alike, so she explained the explicit routine to Mrs. Yip and left it to her to work things out her way.

What a difference her help made! When the baby was through nursing, Jade Snow could leave her upstairs with Mrs. Yip while she hastened down to work on back orders. Six firings were completed in succession. The boxes went off with Christmas orders to Houston, North Dakota, and Toronto.

Ming Tao, who had been taught Cantonese because Jade Snow and Woody wanted him to be able to converse with his grandparents, got along very well with Mrs. Yip, who was from another Cantonese district and knew a different repertoire of folk rhymes which were taught to children to occupy their interests, train their memories, and indoctrinate them subtly. One which Ming Tao thought was funny described the dismay of a new bride living in her mother- and father-in-law's home:

> Earlier, earlier [I] arise
> But it is said to be too late
>
> Kneeling, kneeling, three embroidered skirts were worn out
> Father-in-law bought a small winter squash
> Steam, steam—simmer, simmer
> It would not cook
> At once, scolded until tears confused

Repeating the words, Ming Tao identified himself with the bride and the effect was so ludicrous he always laughed.

Another unexpected bonus was that both parents could be absent at the same time during business hours. She hadn't realized that for nearly four years, one of them had always been with Ming Tao during the day, or else they had included him in their errands. That fall of 1957 was the tenth anniversary of UNESCO. A national conference for better relations between Asia and the United States was organized in San Francisco, and they were able to act as delegates to lectures and round-table discussions. Political leaders, art experts, and literary representatives assembled, including their friend, U Thant, who was now ambassador from Burma to the United States.

Political overtones did not enter the conference until a final luncheon address at the St. Francis Hotel by U Thant, who pleaded for American recognition of the People's Republic of China. He was pleasantly surprised by the long ovation, in which the Ongs joined wholeheartedly. Afterwards, he invited them to his room for a "smoke."

He offered Woody one of those little black Burmese cheroots which even their beautiful women smoked, and the three of them reminisced about life's remarkable surprises, that they should see each other again so unexpectedly after four years and halfway around the world!

That evening, the conference delegates were feted at a gala reception given by a civic-minded hostess who supported diversified cultures and arts, and whose spacious home was a handsome example of modern architecture. Jade Snow and Woody were the only Chinese who stayed near U Thant, for at the time, Chinatown's population was nearly all pro-Taiwan, and the Nationalist Chinese consular representatives coldly bypassed him with eyes averted and noses in the air.

As stimulating and rewarding as these intellectual and social experiences proved, they couldn't detract from the satisfaction of climbing up the bare oak steps to their studio home, where the noisy welcome of three-and-a-half-year-old Ming Tao and the quietly grave regard of Lai Yee were reserved for them. Public life was never going to matter as much as the tranquil gratification of home and family.

CHAPTER 15

TRAVELING: PROBLEMS AND PRIVILEGES

Few pleasures are greater for an American traveler than recalling his adventures abroad, and in the days when tourism to Asia had just begun, those 1956 tour members spread word-of-mouth advertising in their home communities until the Ongs' regular studio affairs were interrupted incessantly by visitors and mail inquiries on travel advice. San Francisco was the West Coast Gateway to the Orient. When Woody found himself giving away so much of his time, he investigated the requirements for becoming a travel agent.

Working hard, he succeeded in being licensed by the International Air Transportation Association. Certificates of appointment by airlines followed, enabling him to sell their tickets.

They planned an ambitious three-month group tour for the spring of 1958, as far away as Mandalay and Bali. Their children were to accompany them, but Lai Yee's godmother, their attorney's wife, asked, "How are you going to manage a tour if the baby gets sick and can't travel? Why don't we take both children at our home when you leave?" Jade Snow knew the person who extended this generous offer meant it. With relief, they moved the children and their everyday necessities to her Palo Alto home, where a nurse helped in their care.

They flew off with twenty-five followers via Vancouver, on a Canadian Pacific plane which made an unscheduled refueling stop in forlorn, dark, and icy Shemya, Alaska. They disembarked to enjoy coffee in a quonset hut while the aircraft was being serviced. When they were airborne again, a tour member rushed to Woody, crying in dismay, "Mr. Ong, I have left my passport and air tickets in Shemya!"

Woody, who was about to doze off, jumped up asking, "How did that happen?" She was one of the younger women, and had not seemed flighty.

"One of the group asked if anyone had a U.S. airmail stamp, since it was the last chance to use one. I offered her one from my travel wallet, and after coffee, I forgot the wallet."

Swallowing a tranquilizer, Woody went to consult the plane's captain. Since Shemya was an unscheduled stop, they were sure that the documents could not yet have been picked up by anyone. Radio contact located them and a plane lift was arranged. In Tokyo, Woody guaranteed her entry into Japan without passport or visa. This was only the first of numerous problems he handled for tour members over the years. The errors, apprehensions, carelessness, unreasonableness, and forgetfulness of American travelers away from home, sometimes funny, sometimes exasperating, usually inconvenient, could fill an unreadable book.

They organized successive tours biennially for another ten years, during which they became acquainted with additional out-of-the-way places and updated themselves on new tourist facilities. Between tours they advised special-interest travelers who liked these remote places and traveled to those areas via custom-planned itineraries. While on tour, Woody assigned rooms, claimed baggage, and worked with local operations personnel; Jade Snow checked restaurants and menus, and lectured interpretatively to the group. At home at the front desk between tours, Woody met the public and travel trade representatives while Jade Snow in the background kept up with her art and handled correspondence. This change in career emphasis began with the 1958 tour.

When they arrived in hot and humid Taipei, they expected the privilege of meeting Mme. Chiang Kai Shek, who would welcome them as the first large American tourist group. Rushing to the plush Grand Hotel, reportedly built by Mme. Chiang for foreign guests, they changed to dressy tropical clothes before transferring down the hill to a large high-ceilinged government reception hall. Mr. Lee, her secretary, greeted them in friendly fashion, telling them that his daughter had gone to Mills. Through a military-guarded doorway came Mme. Chiang. A hush fell as they regarded this legend of beauty and greatness.

She was not tall, but her handsomely erect stance gave an impression of height. That slim figure would have been the envy of any woman her age or younger. Her dress, the traditional Chinese cheongsam, was made of navy blue satin-back crepe, ankle length and slit. The collar was high; the sleeves were short. No trim appeared except for three sparkling matched diamond clasps half an inch in diameter, two fastening the yoke below each shoulder and one between at her throat. Huge sparkling sapphires, which Jade Snow guessed were larger than a thumbnail, and bordered with tiny diamonds, decorated her earlobes. Encircling one wrist was a translucent apple-green jade bracelet. On her hands were white mesh gloves. Her feet were small, shod in dainty black lizard pumps with little spike heels.

The heart-shaped face was fair; the skin smoothly unwrinkled; the black hair simply coiffed. The eyes were friendly, flashing with alertness. The lips were smiling. She projected that magnetism which is a special gift and combined it with the poise of someone used to the public eye.

Mr. Lee had instructed them to rise before she entered, and to give her a standing ovation. Then Mme. Chiang, in faultless English, asked them to be seated in a semicircular arrangement of chairs. She faced them against a background framework of her delicate brush paintings, hung in traditional scrolls.

After the Ongs were introduced by Mr. Lee, Jade Snow acted as spokesman, presenting each person in the group and giving his city of residence.

Easily, pleasantly, Mme. Chiang asked how they were enjoying their trip. Jade Snow summarized it briefly. Mme. Chiang turned to the group. "Do you have any questions?" One member asked politely how the children of refugees were educated. The majority seemed too tongue-tied to speak. But there is often someone in a group of Americans who feels he is obligated to break a silence with an echo from his brain; in this case it was an older woman from Illinois, who ruffled the smooth atmosphere with an odd question, "Do you think there is more Communism in Japan or in Formosa?" There was an awkward pause; the Ongs were aghast. Mme. Chiang's smile remained just as composed. Swiftly, she countered, "Well, you have just spent three weeks in Japan. Suppose you tell me!"

Lamely, the questioner replied, "I wish I knew."

Mme. Chiang remarked in ringing tones, "You are now in Free China, where we believe it is important not only to hold your own beliefs but to allow for the reasonableness of the other man's belief." She added, "I personally do not think that the masses of Chinese people in Mainland China are Communists, only the administrators."

Another lady from Pittsburgh tactfully changed the direction of the interview. "Do you find your paintings a source of relaxation?" Mme. Chiang replied, "My paintings are not a pastime; they are hard work."

The secretary whispered to Woody that the time was up. Mme. Chiang could not know that she had also granted Jade Snow a symbolic reward. To immigrant Chinese who had worked in vain in the United States for dignified recognition, Mme. Chiang's 1943 visit to the United States (when her picture addressing Congress was on the front page of every newspaper) had at last given them a taste of that longed-for "face." Jade Snow, fresh out of college, had written a request to see her at her San Francisco stop, but her secretary had politely refused. It had taken fifteen years to realize her wish.

Taiwan was not the only country which Jade Snow and Woody were exploring for the first time with this 1958 group tour; for ever since she had heard the Indo-China Desk officer's remark, Jade Snow had been curious about that unvisited land. But in planning to include Vietnam and Cambodia, she had no premonition that the group would be led into areas they would never be able to see again.

If the Ryoko-in may be considered representative of the spirituality in Japanese culture, the Bien Hao Temple may be considered indicative of the decadence of Saigon. Its buildings were badly in need of repair. Bright idols substituted for Buddhas, and children clambered over them in play. In dim recesses, war gods and peace gods stood amid air heavy with incense. Piles of dead leaves drifted about, and in seemingly as meaningless a pattern, thin monks wandered around. Never had she seen religious personnel so lacking in dignity. One tour member declared, "They sure look like bums!"

Beds and water crocks were scattered around the open courtyards and corridors. In a larger compound, small huts had been constructed to house monks in training between the ages of eight and twenty-five. The monks were sacrifices to the gods, sent by rich Vietnamese families who believed that the gift of a son would ensure personal wealth. The pathetic novices were allowed outside of the temple only once a year. They could not have any outside visitors. Jade Snow was told that "Bien Hao" meant "demented ones" because the novices often went mad and committed suicide. (Years afterward, she was not surprised at headlines reporting the South Vietnamese monks' self-immolation in protest at the Vietnam war.) Jade Snow wondered about the character of the Saigon population itself. How many were actively Catholic and how many indifferent Buddhists?

There was little time to delve for answers, for the next morning they had to depart at 4:30 A.M. for Phnom Penh. In working with Air Vietnam to arrange that unscheduled, special flight, Woody made friends with its Chinese manager, who arranged for their tour to be admitted into the Cambodian Royal Palace the next morning. They passed into a world unlike anything in Western life. This was the natural setting for Prince Sihanouk and his Queen Mother.

The private museum of the royal family was packed with memorabilia. Gold-embroidered ceremonial robes and heavy golden swords, talismans made of rhino horns, small and large jeweled hats for royal horses and elephants—these would not be seen by most tourists.

International gifts included a contemporary jade urn and ivory screen from the People's Republic of China, and an entire gold dinner service with silver flatware from Napoleon III, engraved with his crest *N*. Into a large glass case had been tossed hundreds of exquisitely handwrought and heavy gold bracelets, anklets, necklaces, next to open enameled boxes glowing with gems—emeralds, diamonds, and rubies. In corners of the cases, piles of gold coins and diamonds defied an attempt to count them. A number of golden combs were included, each set with half a dozen enormous diamonds.

The palace guide explained, "It is Cambodian custom for each queen to have her personal jewelry. Here are the precious jewels of many queens."

Photographs included a large, erect silver frame around the friendly countenance of Chou-En-Lai, but other pictures were piled up like the jewelry without order or identification.

They left the museum for the Silver Temple, built in 1880, when the French were lavishly wooing Cambodian rulers. As at any holy place in the Orient, they removed their shoes before entering a dim chamber, about 40 to 50 feet high, 80 feet wide, and 160 feet long, decorated with the best from Europe and of Asia. The incandescent lighting from French crystal chandeliers fashioned with delicate porcelain inserts supplemented daylight subdued by tones of stained glass windows. Walls were richly decorated by frescoes depicting details of royal life and Buddhist themes. The center of the room was completely dominated by Buddhist sculpture.

A gold superstructure had been built nearly to ceiling height. At the pinnacle was a large Buddha carved of pure green jade, while at the base was a huge, 200-pound solid gold Buddha, protected by a glass case. The gold Buddha had diamond eyes. His open palms were crusted with smaller diamonds, and his body dazzled with clothes of diamonds. Both sides of this Buddha were flanked by attendants: smaller Buddhas, all solid gold, all dressed in diamonds. The altar was accented with a pair of enameled gold urns from China filled with huge bouquets of starlike jasmine blossoms; their heavy sweet fragrance permeated the temple.

While their eyes feasted on the glittering sanctuary, their bare feet were delighting to a once-in-a-lifetime sensuous thrill. The Silver Temple derived its name from its floor, which was entirely paved with 8-inch squares of coin silver, melted, cast, chased with line designs, and buffed by French artisans. Eighty years of rubbing by royal bare feet had bestowed upon its cool surface a mellow satin smoothness. That morning in Phnom Penh, the group was aware that they were enjoying a very special privilege arranged by the Air Vietnam manager who, like other Chinese they had met, thought of what he could do for them rather than what they could do for him—and was no Chinese stranger.

CHAPTER 16
TO GOD HE WENT

After nearly three months of travel away from the American world, the tour had disbanded and the Ongs were homeward bound with mixed emotions. Anxiety about Daddy was uppermost, for he had suffered a stroke a year and a half ago and Youngest Brother's letters told them he was now bedridden, though he did not want Jade Snow to shorten her itinerary. She had shepherded him through a variety of medical appointments, not only for his hypertension, but for treatment of a malignant tumor in his right shoulder. After retiring, as part of his household responsibility he had continued to walk long distances carrying his corduroy bag loaded with grocery purchases from Chinatown. He had refused to stop when he felt pain.

As anxious as she was to gaze once more at her father's dignified face, she dreaded finding the spirit of a great man hopelessly depressed. Returning to creative ceramics would be relief from problems of handling tourists, but her work also included the tiresome details of quarterly tax reports, paying large bills, and coping with unexpected visitors. She yearned to see, hold, and hear her children; yet she knew they meant the end of quiet.

Honolulu broke up the long flights and offered a chance for brief respite. Both of them were exhausted by close and constant work. When at noon the next day Woody was still asleep, Jade Snow wandered alone to the beach snack bar, where a mahi-mahi burger, avocado salad, and buttermilk were American tastes savored anew. At rest, she found it strangely moving to watch a normal American scene: the active enjoyment of leisure. On Waikiki Beach were all ages and sorts of people. A pregnant mother in her maternity bathing suit was wheeling a year-old child. Balding, paunchy older men with their fat wives were swimming slowly and with effort. Young beach beauties were methodically tanning their lithe bodies. Fathers snorkeled with young fry. Whole families, all ages, both sexes, were laughing exuberantly.

In the Orient, the rich who had leisure would spend it sitting, savoring expensive food in public; but few men and even fewer women hurled themselves into physical activities. Jade Snow could not single out any individual American as remarkably attractive, but by reason of their healthy, straight bodies, clear, clean skins, and general *joie de vivre*, they were all handsome and beautiful, and they seemed supremely unaware of their unique blessings and freedom.

Jade Snow felt compelled to examine her own standards. Before her were hundreds of beneficiaries of this peculiarly American gift. Would this vigorous pleasure and freedom ever be hers too? She had sprung from the same soil as those San Franciscans who labored bravely in Chinatown, barely making ends meet. This was the theme of her father's and mother's life of accumulated sacrifice: today's work, forgoing pleasure, for tomorrow's security. At that, Daddy felt obligated only to ensure his sons' education. What would she count essential for herself?

Her Chinese training had hammered her to do her duties well. Such discipline, after satisfying her parents, had been useful in realizing personal ambitions in the Western framework beyond Chinatown. But home was where her heart was held, and she was more ambitious than her father, for she believed in providing equally for her daughter and her son.

Loving her, her husband supported her in her career and did not disagree with her goals. Respecting her self-determination, he helped her at home. But as a Chinese male, he also had the option of not doing what he didn't feel like doing; the proper functioning of domestic details was within his wife's province. He paid the bills, but it was Jade Snow who suggested activities, shaped values, and introduced taste. His wife found being a home executive more arduous than being a business executive, although both roles had to be balanced. Children's needs were unpredictable and never-ending; yet no worksheet report would be made at the end of a housework week. And without the happiness of her husband and children, she could have none herself.

Full comfort was not yet in sight. While they were economizing to clear debts and accumulate enough for a down payment on a home, how about the present price in weary nerves? The Chinese said, "In fair weather, chop wood for rainy days." Or, "Don't wait until thirst before digging your well." How much wood is enough? How many wells? Or should one live as if there will be no tomorrow? Fortunately or unfortunately, tomorrow will come. Between the plodding hopelessness of many Asians' every-day existence and this casual panorama of Americans at play, who lived the happy medium?

The Ongs enjoyed four days of rest and the hospitality of good Chinese friends, the Hus, who loaded them with local gifts of field-ripened pineapples, red anthurium, and great branches of lichees freshly harvested from fifty trees which Mrs. Hu's mother had transplanted to Honolulu when she immigrated from Canton. Nothing Jade Snow could have found in the whole wide world could have delighted her father more than the lichees, for they carried the flavor of Canton to his jaded appetite, and reminded him of early summer in China.

She chided him in good humor, "You have told me all my life that in China the squabs are fatter, the fruit is sweeter, and the flowers are more fragrant. But I haven't found the Macau squabs fatter; in fact, most things grow smaller."

Her father, never at a loss to explain, replied easily, "When people are starving, do you expect the squabs to be fat?"

They had been gone so many months that Daddy had news for her too. After years of a childless marriage, Oldest Brother (who lived a block away in a pair of flats he owned) had fathered his first baby, a boy not yet a month old. At last, God had blessed him with his life's desire, his first son of a son, to carry on the Wong name.

"I have named him 'Moon Tong' [meaning "Full House"]." Her father tried to smile. His deepest wish had become reality, though he would not mention that he could never see this baby grown. Daddy never had a chance to enter the name of this son in the nineteenth generation of the Wong family tree manual.

His physical condition wrung her heart. He was marking time, for the cancer had spread throughout his body. There were moments of complete lucidity when he quoted old poetry. At other times he sat with closed eyes, seemingly in a coma. Forgetful of a recent meal, he would have a sudden desire to eat again.

Her mother, faced with the bills of a long illness and the support of her youngest son, would not give up her seamstress job. Each afternoon upon returning home, she cooked for the three of them and nursed the invalid through many long nights. Fatigue made her impatient and irritable.

Youngest Brother, now sixteen, seemed to accept the inevitable fate enveloping a man he felt old enough to be his grandfather. Daddy had never been the companion to him in the way he had observed the fathers of his American schoolmates being friends to their sons.

Ming Tao and Lai Yee, at ages four and one, returned home suntanned and healthy. They regarded their grandfather with some awe. Ming Tao knew him with deep affection as well, for during those weekly doctor's visits, he had accompanied them. When it pleased him, he became general in command of his mother and grandfather. In downtown traffic, he would march ahead, swing around, and command, "Halt!" Even though Jade Snow was impatient with the game, his grandfather always complied in mock seriousness, standing with a slight, admiring, indulgent smile until the boy gave the signal, "March!" Besides, Grandfather had already given him his first calligraphy lessons. Holding the white little hand in his wrinkled brown one, he had shown the child the correct brush position: again, a ball of newspaper had shaped the curve of his fingers.

Each person in this intimate family life had entirely different relations with the same Father Wong.

In a few more days it was July 4, and they observed his last birthday in the Wong kitchen. When he had passed his U.S. citizenship test, her father had changed the celebration from his Chinese birthdate of the tenth day in the fifth lunar month to the fourth of July. Once he gave up the possibility of returning to China, he adopted America in full.

Woody helped his father-in-law to shave and put on the coat to the new Hong Kong suit they had had tailored for him. The deep blue British wool with random flecks of bronze and peacock was the finest fabric he had worn. He fingered the material silently and appreciatively, as if he regretted that he would never have full use of it. Jade Snow was rewarded to see his shrunken frame so well clothed. How does one ever know which gift will give full pleasure or utility in time? One moves, works, lives, and acts on faith and assumption that tomorrow will come. One satisfaction today makes a memory for tomorrow. There was once a time when she never saw Daddy open gifts, for it is rude to open packages before the donor. Besides, Daddy, the saver, found it uncomfortable to enjoy too many gifts at once. He would stow them away and open one at a time when he felt like a gift.

In their own studio-home, they found increasing happiness in their children. Household routine could be approached with a new patience. Ming Tao seemed deliriously joyful to be in his old haunts again. Walking or climbing stairs together, by habit he would take his mother's right hand. He noticed the tiny new ring on her little finger, shaped like a small crown, a Thailand gift from Woody. He looked solemnly at the colored stones and asked, "What's that?"

"It's a princess ring," his mother answered.

"Princess! Princess! That's what you are, my princess!" And

for many years afterwards, "Princess" was his nickname for her. When, at unexpected moments, they heard him burst out with loud cries of delight, Woody remarked, "I suspect that his devotion is ours forever."

No matter how equally Lai Yee was to share in what they could provide, her brother had had three and a half years of them to himself. Little Sister was sweetly delicate and clinging to Ming Tao as well as to her parents. To them, she spoke in Chinese, but at her godmother's she also mastered two American terms, "Hi" and "Thank you." She seemed less secure than her brother, and would not let her mother out of her sight. At night, she awoke crying, and Jade Snow wondered how the third child on the way would affect the alliance between these two older ones.

She had resolved that for the next six years, she would cut down drastically on civic and creative activities. Not only a growing number of children but aging parents on both sides were dependent on her. After this third child was in school, she could expand her life again. There would always be an audience interested in another book, another exhibition, new experiments in clay or enamels.

Two weeks after Daddy's birthday party, Youngest Brother called her to go over their father's accumulation of Chinese books, as he was clearing their basement during summer vacation. Their mother complained that she would have to pay the garbage man to take away what Youngest Son wanted to dispose of, some of them valuable volumes of pre-Communist Chinese publications. Though Jade Snow agreed to help, she wondered why she should care about saving them. She had little time to pore over references; she doubted if her children would ever hold Chinese academic interests.

The stacks of books looked like an arduous job for her to handle at this stage of pregnancy, so Youngest Brother filled and transported foot lockers to her studio front door. What to do? To bring them to her basement meant certain mildew, as the building was on old land fill below San Francisco Bay's high-tide water line. To bring all the unsorted books upstairs was both backbreaking and indiscriminate. So together with Youngest Brother she sat down on the hardwood stairs, sorting for hours.

Youngest Brother remarked, "I knew you would know what was

worth saving, but personally, I wouldn't care if they were all tossed out." She thought his reaction strange. Of all the children, he had been most outstanding in Chinese.

Many volumes were translations of the Bible, which she saved for the church. Novels were put aside to return to her mother, who enjoyed fiction. No qualms were felt as they tossed out the major part of their father's lifetime accumulation, larger in books than in dollars: philosophical reflections on World War II, medical guides, religious essays, religious posters, yearbooks or annual reports of the YMCA and the Wong Association, outdated hymnals. She saved art books and calligraphy examples, collections of chop marks, for herself.

Some of the volumes appeared to represent dollars foolishly spent, yet Jade Snow saw in them the need of a man to know more than what the Chinese newspaper carried, knowledge beyond the Bible and church meetings. Without access to a Chinese library (which was established many years later) it had been the only way of improving his mind in the restricted Chinatown environment.

The last suitcase surprised them both. Bundles of books had been tied with cord, their thick marginal edges carefully labeled in black calligraphy and further identified with ties of white cloth tape bearing more calligraphy. The tapes identified each of the eight children's Chinese study books, commencing with "Wong the Oldest," "Wong the Second," and so on. Within a bundle, each book had been meticulously covered with paper covers, some browned from forty years of storage. Work papers in each child's tiny, careful hand were also bound together.

What should they do about these? The man who had preserved each child's Chinese progress would soon have no use for them, nor did his children want them. The books were mute and poignant testimony of how much their father cared and how little his children cared. Pages out of the past on geography, letterwriting, science, were quaintly outdated. She turned to Youngest Brother. "How do you feel? Here are yours too!"

He shook his head vigorously. "No, don't remind me. Those were tough days of learning which I hated."

Saving her pile, Jade Snow discarded the others. But for weeks afterward, she was haunted by those bundles. They spoke of a father's pride in his children's education, his often repeated conviction that education would be the key to their freedom and status, prizes that he had never received in good measure. They were silent souvenirs of hours spent disciplining each child's mind and habits, albeit the child recalled only the discipline with emotions ranging from distaste to resentment. In a taciturn tradition, in a life dominated by the pressing necessity of work, that tutoring might have been the only mental exchange and sustained companionship between father and child during their lifetimes. Jade Snow had never seen these bundles before. What did they mean to a father who didn't even keep pictures of his children, only of his parents? Was he sentimental about them or did he save them as he did thread, buttons, and old boards? She would never know because it would never be proper to ask him.

As they sorted, sister reflected to brother, "I'm saddened by Daddy's going, more than the fact that I will miss him. It seems that his whole life has been spent pinching pennies for his children."

Youngest Brother replied, "Don't you think he did it because he wanted to?"

"Yes, of course, he acted on conviction. But though his children all respect him as a father, do they love him as a person? Is what we see around us in America better, children who love their parents without respecting them? If they do not respect them, can that be real love?"

"Well, maybe it's more important to be respected," said her brother. "He never asked to be understood, and I don't know how well he understood us."

"That's true," Jade Snow recalled. "He never talked about his problems—or his disappointments—or accomplishments. Maybe it was the way he was brought up. I think that our father never had fun: it was mandatory to work and save, not to enjoy life. You know, it must have been hard for mother to live with him, even though she had a similar background."

Her brother was thoughtful. "I know if he had his way, I'd still be going to Chinese school every night. You remember that I won the American Legion Award for all-around achievement when I graduated from Grant's eighth grade, at the same time that I was studying to get the top percentages at Hip Wo School. But last year, when I began Lick High School, it was rough. I was literally pounding my own head one night when Mom told Daddy I had to stop Chinese school. A real explosive uproar followed. Daddy told Mom that he was trying to help me keep my heritage, and she was trying to pull the cat's tail when he was trying to train the cat!

"Mom said she wasn't against my learning Chinese, but she wanted a sane son. And you know when Mom makes up her mind, she wins. Daddy went to his room and moaned for his mother. But ever since I stopped Chinese school, I can enjoy American school."

Jade Snow reminded him, "But don't forget your Chinese studies formed disciplined learning habits. Why else do you think you did so well in Grant? At sixteen, you know more about some subjects than Daddy. We must admire him for rearing us with success when he didn't even known how to write an English letter."

"Well," admitted Youngest Brother, "I never thought of it that way!"

Jade Snow thought: Here is the baby son adored by all, yet he has not perceived that Daddy too has had a right to be himself. Our father sacrificed for the family he cherished—but he stifled their affection.

Small wonder that so many of their Chinatown contemporaries did not understand their parents either. It had taken years to adjust her vision from fear to compassion for a man who had lived by his principles, and to realize that it was his duty to train his children his way.

Yet what had those of her generation to boast, they who had become more educated than their parents, who were able to dress well and drive freely beyond Chinatown? Though they could acquire the property denied their forebears, had they eliminated their problems? For some, overcoming the pangs of that poverty which had aggravated the torment of adolescence while mired in an alien culture became their life's primary purpose. They left Chinatown slums, emigrating in their own way for better housing, to merge in low profile into white American neighborhoods, to forget their parents' problems and personal anguish, and to provide a better life for their children, the third generation.

Some of those who did achieve financial success and integration became deeply concerned about their children's lack of psychological and cultural identity in an American environment. If parents could afford the expense of sending them to study in Taiwan or Hong Kong, as some did, their consciences were assuaged. Or if they could give their young those material luxuries which had never been theirs or their parents'—then they felt that they too had harvested the American fruit of success. But working-class Chinese had no easy way to buy culture for their children, and the burden of their ambition could be relieved only by giving of themselves as Daddy had done if they had some education and the same conviction; otherwise, they could only watch powerlessly as their children turned to rebellious ways when they grew too large for corporal punishment, and there was not enough money to satisfy growing demands stimulated by the American environment. This was to be the curse of Chinatown, and it was just beginning.

Soon after disposing of the books, she received a telephone call from her father. He asked for an ambulance to take him to the Chinese hospital, "to make life easier for your mother," he explained, "where I can rest in peace."

Jade Snow hurried to him. There was no need to discuss what both knew. As they waited, she asked if he had any special request. "No." He shook his head. "Take these from me."

He put into her hand his old gold wristwatch and a rectangular black lacquer box. When she opened its hinged lid, she discovered within its imperial yellow velvet and satin lining a heavy silver medal, shining through its tarnish, attached to a red and white ribbon. On one side of the medal had been struck the Chinese words, "Guardian Prince of the Second Rank—With many arrangements Supporter of the Revolution." On the reverse it was dated: "The Great Ching Dynasty Second Year of the Emperor Sun Tung." * Thus her hand held the last material remembrances

from him to her: one a reminder of the minutes passing today, and the other, a reminder of his country, 6,000 miles and half a century away. This was an award given him by Dr. Sun Yat Sen for having sold bonds to raise funds for training rebel military corps of the Tung Meng Hui.

* Last child emperor, who ruled from 1908 to 1911. Hence the medal was dated 1909, the crucial year leading to the collapse of Imperial rule.

"Supporter of the Revolution"—that was cause for wonder. What motivated Daddy to work that hard for Dr. Sun's revolution? It was more than sympathy for someone he knew; they shared a common religious belief in human worth and social improvement, the new faith which had moved Daddy to write home to China that he was staying here. She was convinced that Daddy worked to support the Revolution so that those millions in China, women as well as men, would someday have the opportunity for work and education. Theoretical idealism was adapted to practical reality: speedy emancipation required the technique of revolution. Daddy strangely combined deep caring with individual nonconformity, the fuse of a potential revolutionary.

Jade Snow could spend little time with her father at the hospital because of her young children at home. At six o'clock one morning Woody answered the phone. He turned to her. "He's gone," he said tersely. Daddy had died alone, symbolic of a lifetime of aloneness.

It was August 17, 1958. He had gone to his God, wanting to, believing in Him. Dry-eyed and prepared as she was for this termination, Jade Snow's loneliness engulfed her though she was surrounded by her own loved ones. "Dear God," she prayed, "if he be with You, reward him at last. All he was and all he had, he gave away."

She knew that henceforth, every time she read Chinese or looked at other human beings, at life, at the world, she would be reminded of his views, and would ache for that unstated companionship which existed in the Chinese world between her father and herself. At thirty-six, she could no longer turn to him as head of their clan, a source of wise counsel, philosophical strength, a handy Chinese reference. No more was there a reason to shop for a delicacy, or dip aside a pot of home-brewed soup. No more would she ever write to him another letter in Chinese, referring impersonally to herself in the third person, commencing in correct form with reference to the addressee placed graphically on a higher level than the body of the text, "To the Great Person of Father, as looking from below your knees, respectfully regarding you . . . ," then in half-size idiographs: ". . . little daughter jade snow. . . ."

No more would she receive a letter from him, written economically on part of a sheet of paper, beginning without title space in correct form for one older addressing one younger, "jade snow beloved daughter, know and understand. . . ." *

Now she must be the fountainhead to her own family, transmitting what she knew of the Chinese culture, establishing her own kind of strong ties with and among them, guided by the speculation of what her father would have done or said. His physical shadow would tower no more. Instead, her children, her mother, her brother would be turning to her, and she to the second male to follow.

* There are no upper-case characters in Chinese.

PART II

FIRST PERSON
SINGULAR

After Daddy's death the habit of referring to myself in the third person could gradually be changed to the use of the first person.

CHAPTER 17
NOW WE WERE FIVE—THEN SIX

Six days after Daddy's funeral service in his church came our eighth wedding anniversary, also the day our second daughter was born. It was too soon for feelings of joy to rise above grief. Life became a confusion of emergencies. The baby looked jaundiced, and there was a possibility of a total blood transfusion. I came home from the hospital to find Lai Yee's nurse waiting to bid us farewell, for her husband was hopelessly ill. Woody rushed between airport and pier to receive the Hong Kong editor of the Chinese edition of *Fifth Chinese Daughter*, who had flown in as an airline inaugural guest and required hospitality, and to meet his daughter, who arrived by ship and wished to be our houseguest until her college term began in the East.

Mother needed help to settle Daddy's tiny estate, to dispose of his belongings, and to order his gravestone. On that Sunday, the hot water tank burst, and there we were, with a four-year-old, two babies in diapers, a houseguest with an accumulation of cruise laundry, and an editor using our studio home for press conferences. Lai Yee came down with a temperature of 106 degrees. Whatever sense of humor I used to have about the rich variety of life disappeared.

Still, in time some routine was found, with fresh help from Chinatown. Fortunately, the new baby was cuddly, smiling, and did not require a transfusion after all. Counting Woody, at least one member of the family always needed comfort, and all slept and ate at different times. To relieve me, Woody took our oldest two on business errands or studio work. He was one of the few bank clients who regularly brought in deposits accompanied by a boy dressed in an Indian costume and a daughter in a stroller.

One morning when the baby was six months old, a quiet hour allowed me to sit down at the Chinese dictionary once again. Again, I turned the pages to the department of the "heart." My work was simplified. I found that Daddy had used Woody's business cards to mark the volume at each page of possible name choices. I found also the red-inked memoranda on the back of the old envelope, and the black brushed ideographs on red paper which dated back to the occasion when he was choosing Ming Tao's name. I could compare the declining strength of his brush strokes within the four years, caused by the shoulder tumor.

In choosing a Chinese name for our new baby I was guided by her characteristics. She was affectionate, sensitive, dependent, and extremely feminine. In the sort of world developing around us, I thought she would need steadfast and cautious qualities. Acutely aware of Daddy, I studied the department of the heart, to choose a name which would pair with "Beautiful." Seriously I considered "Perception" but decided on "Wisdom," for to me "Wisdom," pronounced "Wai," would require "Perception."

Wai

Even more frustrating and exhausting than the lonely fight to succeed in the ceramics business (for I could organize my time toward that one goal) were the two years that now followed. "Bones and sinew are tried and trained," according to an old Chinese saying. Not unlike other mothers of small children, I awakened one to six times a night. Studio work was catch as catch can, because the Christmas rush was on. I did not have time to read the morning paper, and fed the two youngest at the table along with myself. They required bottles alternately, and Lai Wai soon learned to yell just as loudly as her older siblings. On December 1, one child after another became seriously ill. Only during Lai Yee's hospitalization was it diagnosed as salmonella. It was six months before all the children regained sound health.

The battle had been physically tiring and psychologically trying. Subtle hints from both sides of the family insinuated that we were not healthfully housed. Most of the married members of our families had long ago bought homes in outlying suburbs, and some had already traded them upward, while we were still economizing at our studio. Woody and I have a saying, "Together through thick and thin." That winter we looked at each other, and said, "It's awfully thin."

When Ming Tao was five and started kindergarten, he seemed to understand he should help. One day after the conclusion of his "Mickey Mouse" TV hour, I asked him, "Will you help me set the table tonight?" When he did a creditable job, I asked, "How about giving me a hand wiping off these fingerprints?" This was also performed so well that I impressed on him, "You have a job from now on." At our next family party, Ming Tao was overheard saying gravely to his cousins, "I must do housework from now on."

Beds to make, heads of hair to comb, white shoes to clean and to tie, noses to be wiped—hands that had shaped pottery bowls were soothing small fry instead. Once a week, sixty nails had to be cut, six ears swabbed clean, and together with baths, these physcial jobs were taken over by Woody. "I used to bathe my brothers," he said, to prove his qualifications.

The three children were developing personalities which would indicate their natures when grown: Ming Tao, who had been taken to church by Grandmother and Grandfather Wong from childhood, said "grace" nearly every night, invariably requesting God to help him "grow big and strong and full of energy." When he was not talking to God, exuberant Ming Tao admitted that he was also full of ideas, an enthusiast "do-er." Only when it came to picking up toys or clothes did that enthusiasm evaporate.

Lai Yee was a quiet fighter, loyal and now emphatically independent. She did not want her bath yet, nor her hair combed now. Or she did not want to leave her bath yet, or be dressed. She also used her vocal cords to drive her points home effectively. On the other hand, after quietly amusing herself, she neatly gathered up after her brother.

Little sister was clinging and tractable, but she was also restless, often crying for reassurance at night, unsettled by day, wanting to go out. When thwarted, she would angrily shake the fragile shoji doors, as Woody said, "like a tank!"

It was time to try to find a house. The growing travel business could use upstairs office space. It would have been less of a financial problem to buy a tract house at lower land values away from Chinatown, and start the commuting which seemed the American way of life. To move to the suburbs would assure the children's needs for sunshine and wholesome physical activity. But if we wished them to be confident that their Chinese roots were a source of strength, not a burden of conflict, we felt that they needed to grow up near Chinatown, not far from the loving wisdom of their Chinese grandmothers, to appreciate their unique dual heritage. Ming Tao was six, and ready not only for American school but for his first Chinese grade.

We began looking for a house within walking distance of Chinese school and studio, so that we could continue to be psychologically and physically close to each other. For months we searched. Our list of "musts" included a sufficient number of rooms to enable each of us to enjoy privacy, yet not so big that we could not maintain it without help.

It was nine months before we came across a want ad that offered a four-bedroom Victorian house west of Chinatown, a single-family dwelling in a district surrounded by flats and apartments, and just around the corner from Sherman Elementary School. Woody and I drove there, liked the white house with green shutters and a mahogany front door, picked up our children and Woody's mother, who was babysitting them, and toured the house once more. At once we decided to make an offer. A house, like a person, is never without flaws, but communicates instantly the character it represents. We were positively naïve in not checking out wiring, plumbing, termite inspection, and all the possible defects on a list with which experts arm the prospective buyer. But the old building which survived San Francisco's 1906 earthquake had a serene appeal, and after we hurriedly moved in ten days prior to leaving for another tour to the Orient, we were content to wait until our return to bring the house up to date.

It made a great difference in our peace of mind as we traveled with our group that spring to know that Woody's mother was also enjoying for the first time windows open to fresh air and sunshine in every room. Wild birds fed regularly in our blooming garden where our children played safely in their sandbox or at their swings. Hiromi, a gentle maid from Okinawa, cared for children and home, respectful of the firm Chinese grandmother.

Our son was taught how to walk twelve blocks to the same Chinese school that I once attended at our church. My mother was horrified. "If I had an only son, I would never permit him to walk to and from school through that Broadway traffic."

It was not usual to disagree with Mother, but I explained, "I cannot let fear of an accident prevent him from a Chinese education. If he doesn't start this year, later he will not like to be with boys younger than himself."

The next two years could be said to be years of realization. After our tour, we shopped in Hong Kong for furniture. Now the two girls would have their hand-me-down cribs replaced by custom-designed rosewood beds, with matching dressers and desks. All of our beds were placed with the heads pointed east, for Daddy had taught me that we should sleep in the direction of the earth's rotation.

Woody agreed that our home should be our refuge. It would

hold young and old family members when we grouped for family reunions. We began to bring the house up to our standards, adding a bath and redecorating. Woody changed the steep grade of the garden by bringing in carloads of spent mushroom soil. Into this area went a new species of double white camellia, developed by Dr. and Mrs. John Lawson of Antioch, California, a gift from them in exchange for permission to name it "Jade Snow." That this hybrid in the tea plant family, whose ancestry springs from Chinese origins in Yunnan, should find a place in my corner of earth has been another of life's unexpected rewards.

Major remodeling was required for the center of our family life: the kitchen. We spent months studying appliances, working with designers, laying down scale models on paper, and finally evolved a room large enough for eating, studying, cooking, barbecuing, laundry and storage, with a balcony overlooking the garden. In travels to the Orient, we had marveled at the functional and pleasurable dimension that balconies added to rooms.

Woody and I have little disagreement over money, in-laws, religion, children, or business. But cooking is a different matter. Our first quarrel on our honeymoon occurred when we were preparing Chinese food for our hostess on a Montana ranch. Woody was cutting an onion for sweet and sour pork. "Don't cut it in slices; it should be in squares to go with the shape of the pork cubes," I told him. This kind of mistake couldn't wait overnight for correction. Woody had stared at me. "There's only one way to cut an onion," he said.

"No, there are many ways—slicing, dicing, mincing. . . ."

"You're crazy. What differences does it make how you cut an onion anyway!"

Never having heard such a bigoted and dead-wrong remark, I retired to my room in tears.

Now, in this kitchen, Woody had his set of knives and cutting board; I had mine. He had his barbecue pit with its terra-cotta flue; I had my wok. He had his sink with garbage disposal; I had mine. Never should we have a fight again.

With the wok installed next to four burners set in a gas-fueled island cooking center, the children were to grow up watching me cook. Their study tables were only a few feet away, so that homework could be supervised each evening as I stood at the stove.

Upon returning home, all feet rushed to the kitchen. Only closest friends and gathered families have been included in kitchen dinners, when the study tables are pushed together with our dining table to form one large eating area. Warm teak tones of the wood cabinets, oranges and yellows for the painted surfaces, and the butterscotch browns of the Mexican mosaic counters have made a practical and cheerful family room.

This extravagance was deliberate, since I spent more time here than in the living room. Knowing that we would not leave much of a financial legacy, I wanted to teach our children the self-sufficiency to stand up anywhere. I considered cooking one of those necessary skills. Good taste includes food choices as well as environmental aesthetics, and delicious but sound nutrition is a basis for their good health. The kitchen was our demonstration lab.

Hiromi married and moved, and was replaced by efficient Misako five days a week. I returned at noon each day to cook lunch and keep tab on house affairs, bringing from Chinatown the dinner groceries which she would wash and cut. At 5:45 P.M., we picked up Ming Tao from Chinese school, and as we arrived at the front door, Misako was ready to go to her waiting husband. For many years, this would be the pattern of our daily routine.

Our cherished Christmases began, something new. One of my classmates sent us annually from her home in Oregon a freshly cut tree with the fragrance of the forest, exciting for all ages to trim. A hundred boxes came from grateful tour members who remembered our children, and it was a trial to their patience to wait for Christmas morning. We could now reciprocate with home parties for lovely Christmases enjoyed with different godparents who for years had shown us the true graciousness of that American tradition.

In the spring, we dyed Easter eggs and hid them in the garden, or, if it rained, in the house. The children would get in line, and we would give the youngest a few seconds' head start. As they grew older, the hunts continued, but instead of hard-boiled eggs which we couldn't finish eating, we substituted hollow plastic eggs into which we tucked small coins.

Party time or every day, we worked and cooked and played and studied together. We also traveled together, sometimes on short motor trips within California, occasionally beyond. In a long trip to Hawaii we included Woody's mother. (Because of that earliest training in filial obligation, neither Woody nor I could enjoy excursions without inviting our parents—when he was alive, my father with my mother, and later Woody's mother, had Sunday dinner with us every week.) The best plans do not always turn out well, for in Honolulu Lai Yee broke out with chicken pox and had to be quarantined; then Lai Wai's turn came when we were sailing home on the *President Wilson!*

I also introduced the children to museums and libraries, pleasures which became familiar to all of them. Ming Tao would save his weekly allowance to buy art books. One birthday when I asked Lai Yee what she would most like to do, she said, "Drive to the Legion of Honor and paint," and we did. Our children were not to experience my childhood fears of the world beyond Chinatown.

When Ming Tao was eight, he said, "I would like a baby brother." His two sisters were five and four; both adored babies and seconded the motion. "I have to think about it," I said. Everything seemed to be going so well. We loved our children very deeply, and I felt in my Chinese bones that in them was whatever immortality one could be sure of. Who knows, though I believed in God, what would come after death? Pottery, writing, speaking, our arts, our work had their place, but the living gift is the most creative of all, for in the young is the hope of a better world.

Besides, the three children had arrived at a new plateau of self-sufficiency. After returning from our tour, we noticed their changed habits. They no longer ate in front of the television, and after a meal each brought his dishes to the sink. They helped each other to bathe and buttoned one another's clothes. They patiently made their own beds, which Lai Wai did by climbing right in to pull blankets even. Our work load was physically reduced, even though they weren't angels.

When Grandmother Ong turned them over to us, she said with relief, "I enjoyed being here, but it was a great responsibility. I am glad to say that there were no serious illnesses. Now do not spoil them, for I have had all the time to train them which maids cannot do. If they do not do as I tell them, I just sit there until they do. I might have spoiled my sons, but I have not spoiled my grandchildren."

Later, I had to find out from Ming Tao what "Po-po's" (as Grandmother Ong was called in Chinese) secret was. "Did she scold you; did she spank you?"

"No . . ." He thought. "I can't remember what she did. She just acted as if she expected it and we had to do it. I guess she hypnotized us."

Our daughters reported that Po-po gave them delightful treats. It might be tiny, tasty, Oriental peanuts, or soft, moist buns filled with spicy meat. Sometimes, there were shreds of sharp, red ginger, and even chewy American candy bars, which Daddy and Mommy seldom provided. They had also learned nonsensical Chinese nursery rhymes,

> The little sparrow stole some oil to apply
> She made her feathers shiny and went home to visit her mother.
> But she fell down and became covered with sand.

Or:

> Walk, walk, walk.
> Walking along the street, you might pick up an orange.
> If the orange tastes good, then the street was right to walk.

They recounted with groans Grandmother's memorable medical rubs. "When we bumped our heads she would boil an egg and rub our foreheads with it, *hot*. If we had a cold she took Vicks and rubbed our chests. How it smelled!"

Eventually I said to Ming Tao, "When you are nine, sister will be in first grade and youngest sister in kindergarten. If you can be more independent, Daddy and I would also like one more baby. But we cannot know if it will be a sister or a brother."

It was a brother, born in June 1963. The moment his head was delivered, he was screaming in the delivery room, and to this day, he hasn't stopped protesting. If he had been my first child, I would have been so perplexed that he would also have been my last. When Ming Tao's godmother, who would also be his, came to see the newborn, she exclaimed, "This is no baby; it's a person." He was rearing his head, impatient with his crib, wanting out. When one listens to the tape of his christening, one cannot hear George Hedley's soft voice over the three-month-old's comments.

For his Chinese name, using the same middle name "Ming," we chose "Choy," (meaning "Talent"). Its nuances were confirmed by the dictionary, but it had lodged in my mind for more than twenty years. At the Hedley's campus home, a gift to his missionary father, a huge handsome horizontal red silk banner, hung above their fireplace, on it the Chinese words, "Talented Soldier of Christ."

Choy

This child presented a first problem dealing with allergies. We threw out all feather pillows and replaced the jute rug pads. Being the youngest made him competitive and impatient to add his voice to the general din. When the three older children were playing a game he couldn't understand, he could find the one necessary element, rush off, and throw it down the heat vent, effectively ending their fun. Partly because of his exuberant personality, partly because of his sensitivity, and partly because of his many problems, life in the Ong family would never be the same again.

At the age of two, while the head of the Allergy Clinic at the Kaiser Medical Center was testing him, he ran off with his stethoscope. It was ridiculous to see the eminent doctor chasing Ming Choy down the corridor, and when caught, this patient anticipated descending wrath. He looked up and asked innocently, "What time is it?" At this, the doctor helplessly checked his watch and told him the time, forgetting his stethoscope. For years afterward, Ming Choy found that this question disarmed nearly anybody formidable. No one refused to tell him the time, though there was no reason why he needed to know.

Every day he was cause for fresh laughter, but he was also too impatient, too stubborn, challenging our backs and our patience. Woody called him "a monkey with the hands of an octopus, and like lightning, he never strikes twice." Every night, he cried one or more times in his crib, giving indication of his own stresses, and I would rise to comfort him. For almost four years, I did not enjoy one night of unbroken sleep. But as I staggered up in darkness, agonizing, I scolded myself, "Aren't you glad you have a son to awaken you? Soon enough, you will never awake again."

The girls' worst problems were their double loads of homework, for they had also commenced Chinese school. Yet they still had hours to see favorite TV programs, to bicycle or play ball. Lai Yee's nature now seemed shy, but she was easy on the nerves. Lai Wai, competing with a new brother, was moody, explosive, and temperamental, yet marvelously eager to help others. One minute she was sunshine and the next minute she acted as if her last friend had disappeared.

When life again settled into routine, Woody instituted a new custom; on Sundays we held a "show and tell" hour. At about 5:00 P.M. each child would talk on his feet in front of our fireplace for fifteen minutes about any project of real interest—art, pictures, or compositions. The family listened, criticized delivery style and asked questions, and as the children vied with each other to find unusual subjects, from drawings depicting the habits of bats to original music played on the guitar, these hours gave us another dimension of family pleasure.

Woody found that children were more interesting to him after they "could talk back," and gradually he taught them how to fish and, as he had taught my youngest brother long ago, he also taught Ming Tao how to re-create a great Chinese art and sport: kite making and flying.

CHAPTER 18

OF CHINESE KITES AND ASSOCIATIONS

Toward the end of February when winter rains temporarily halted, we took the children for a Sunday drive. Near San Francisco's long Marina Green, Ming Tao noticed a number of flying kites—the commercial kind made of two crossed sticks covered with printed plastic. "Daddy, will you buy me a kite like those?" he asked.

Woody was scornful. "They are so elementary, and the cheap plastic stretches. See how they flap? See how some keep diving

164

for lack of balance? So they fly, but are they beautiful or graceful?"

To help Ming Tao understand that kites could be more than toys, I explained, "Kites have been a great Chinese pastime. By the old lunar calendar, shuttlecock-kicking season ended with the seventh month,* when kite flying began. On the ninth day of the ninth month, after a great feast, the season's kites were released to the skies to chase off evil spirits. Keeping a kite after that date would bring bad luck to the house. Each season, a family created another new kite."

Ming Tao was fascinated. "I didn't know all that."

Woody picked up the subject. "You know, those old kites ranged in shape from a dragon to a centipede. There was even a design which released firecrackers! They might carry decorations like mirrors, feathers, or tassels. I've heard of some small enough to fit into your palm, and others large enough to lift a man!"

"But, Daddy, you were born in San Francisco. Did Grandfather tell you about them?" Ming Tao sensed that his father might have a personal tale of Chinese kites.

"As you know, I was born at Brenham Place and Clay Street, facing Portsmouth Square," Woody began. "There I noticed flying kites with fantastic shapes, maneuvered by a white-haired, white-mustached old man. This lone aristocrat was employed as caretaker of the Sam Yup Association Building, where he utilized the conference meeting room to make kites. When the park became too dark for me to shine shoes, I pestered him into teaching me his tricks."

Ming Tao wondered if the Sam Yup Association had been one of those "Tongs" he had heard about.

"No, Tongs use force, but *Sam Yup* means *three dialects*, and they call it a 'Friendly Society.' Their members are from three neighboring Cantonese villages with similar dialects." Then Woody added, "It is only recently that newcomers who speak Mandarin or Shanghainese have arrived."

We were driving to narrow Grant Avenue, jammed with motor and foot traffic from weekend Chinese suburban visitors, who

---

* About September 1.

wished to replenish refrigerators and pantries with Chinese vegetables and groceries. No food store could afford to be closed on weekends. Woody's mother, who had moved to an apartment off Grant Avenue, was always home. On an impulse, we left the younger children with her and brought Ming Tao to the Sam Yup Association. After we rang the bell, a buzzer released the door lock, and Woody warned, "Be prepared to climb."

Three flights up, the president of the Association, Mr. Lee, greeted Woody warmly, for he had been principal of the Chinese school that Woody attended. Woody explained that he wanted to show us around. "Do you remember that old man who used to make kites?" he asked.

Mr. Lee suggested, "Mr. Choy, who used to teach you at Chinese school, was our former president for many years. He may be able to help you."

Woody remarked, "My, how this place has been changed!"

"Yes," Mr. Lee agreed, "we spent a great deal of our reserve funds to enlarge and modernize these headquarters."

Gorgeously hand-carved Mongolian ebony square Chinese chairs, the Association's first property, had been placed against the walls. Interspersed among them were tiny matching tables. Such furniture was an art of the past generation, as were the majestic yellow porcelain vases with multicolored overglaze decorations. On one wall between the two flags of the United States and Taiwan was mounted the pictorial story of the Sam Yup Association's history. These relics dated from kitemaking days. But the setting was updated by an acoustical tile ceiling with indirect lighting, hardwood floors, and a huge black plastic laminated conference table which could accommodate dozens around it. A sanitary drinking fountain had replaced the old teapot in its basket, formerly used with community tea cups immersed in an enameled pan filled with cold rinse water.

Mr. Lee was proud of their improvements. "Over a hundred years ago, we started at the San Francisco waterfront, at Pine and Kearny streets. Now we total five thousand voting, financially contributing members throughout the United States. On the West Coast, we have branches in Stockton, Fresno, Los Angeles, and Mexico."

We glimpsed a spacious, spotless, white-tiled kitchen, and as we left, we noticed some open cartons of decorated red candles and incense punk. To curious Ming Tao, Mr. Lee explained, "It is nearly time for 'Ching Ming,' and these offerings are ready to go to our cemeteries. We will add whole roasted pigs and boiled chickens. If a particular spirit once liked cigars, cigarettes, or liquor, his relatives will supply them too. On the nearest Sunday morning to 'Ching Ming,' Chinatown will be crowded with buses chartered by each association. The spring ritual is observed by Chinese all over the world, from here to Burma."

As we left, Ming Tao remarked, "Think of the tourists and other Chinese who walk by this locked door without realizing what is upstairs!"

Back at Grandmother's, she asked casually, "Did you find what you wanted at the Sam Yup Association?"

When Woody explained our new interest, Grandmother exclaimed with surprising excitement, "Don't tell me that he is going to take up kites! I have not forgotten the terrible shock I experienced at Brenham Place. A friend called at our flat. 'I think that is one of your sons out there on the rooftop.'

"I ran outdoors, and saw you running along the ledge overhang, four stories above the street, without any rail between you and certain death below. You were flying your kite and not looking at where you were heading. I dared not call to distract you. I have shivers yet when I think about it.

"Yet in those days, who had a car? The trees in the park were in your way. Ming Tao is lucky that you can take him to open space to fly his kite."

Woody was astonished. "I was only telling him *about* kites. Who said anything about flying them?"

Grandmother alone could give an order to his Daddy, so his son seized the opportunity. "Please, Daddy, you know so much about kites. I want to learn how to make and fly one too."

Woody countered, "It isn't that easy. Chinese kites can be made only from select bamboo and a special tissue. It's been so many years since I made a kite, I don't know where I can get those materials."

Our son was unconvinced. "I see bamboo all over Chinatown."

"Any bamboo won't do. Kite bamboo should be large in diameter and straight, with its joints or nodes some inches apart."

"But if you made a kite, can't I try too? Please help me," Ming Tao begged.

Woody could not resist adding, "In fact, I made quite a few kites, for the Park and Recreation Department used to sponsor annual kite tournaments. Participants included children up to high school seniors. Those were exciting days! I won a few prizes myself."

Ming Tao mused, "Nowadays, we make things with our hands, such as model ships and airplanes. I wonder why more boys and girls don't make kites?"

Woody said, "There are books on Western kites, but none on Chinese kites. I think that with the old-timers disappearing, it will be a lost art. Soon, there won't even be memories."

Again Ming Tao requested, "Daddy, I want you to show me."

"I'll think about it," Woody promised.

So, one Saturday, after Ming Tao had learned his lessons, Woody offered to search for kite materials. Parking at the south end of narrow Grant Avenue, known as Dupont Street in my father's time, we climbed the little rise toward Pine Street.

On the three blocks up to Sacramento Street (which is still called "Street of the Tang People" by the Chinese) dozens of shops, large and small, filled with "art goods and curios," catered to tourists. Then we reached tearooms, restaurants, and the Chinese press. We were elbow to elbow with tourist visitors: servicemen in foreign uniforms, Indian women in saris, Pakistanis in pantaloons, Australian boys in shorts and knee-high socks, and Americans who, by their dress and faces, came from cities other than San Francisco. Eager cameramen dashed before moving traffic to snap exposures of unique architectural profiles.

Against brick walls were the hodgepodge colors of painted iron grille balconies: bright green, somber yellow, or reds. Roof and storefront overhangs jutted out. Some were handsome colored tile with upcurved pagoda corners, and others were corrugated iron with canvas drop sides. Customers underneath could dispense with umbrellas during rainy days. Even the street lamps were different. Green spiraled posts were topped by hexagonal amber glass shades which subdued night lighting. (In earlier days they were globular paper lanterns.) Intricate fretwork and entwining dragons were silhouetted against the frosted glass. No wonder this area of San Francisco stimulated the curiosity of the outside world! The exotic flavor of another culture prevailed.

But to us, the Chinatown where we grew up meant familiar home ground. Among new faces, we saw old friends and, occasionally, relatives. It was pleasurable nostalgia and anticipation for our generation to browse here. Toward Clay and Washington streets, grocery stores began. Chinese men held little children by the hand; perhaps they were fathers or uncles who loved small fry. Taking them out would relieve hard-working mothers in crowded rooms. Housewives were about, choosing dinner groceries. Open packing boxes displayed whole salted dried fish, and crocks were filled with preserved duck eggs encased in damp black clay.

The last block of Grant Avenue, before it crossed into Columbus Avenue and North Beach, was almost entirely devoted to food stores. Live squabs, turkeys, and chickens huddled in cages, swimming fish in window tanks delighted watching children, and in season, frogs or crabs crawled in open crates. In markets of Southern Asia, where it is hot most of the year and refrigeration nonexistent, shoppers buy poultry and fish alive in order to know that they are fresh. When Cantonese first settled in San Francisco, they established the live poultry-fish markets with special Board of Health permits. These nontransferable licenses were granted for certain addresses, and later they were not granted at all, so fewer and fewer such markets exist.

I often shop on this Grant Avenue block. Gourmet foods at reasonable prices, such as fresh salmon and asparagus, show up when they are first in season. The busy merchants seldom converse, even after years of patronage. But once after I had given new travel calendars to owners of the vegetable and poultry-fish stores, they unexpectedly relaxed their tongues. Both had known my father, who shared their village origins. Thereafter, the vegetable merchant always knocked off a few cents from the adding machine total. Mr. Chong, the poultry-fish store proprietor, told me more: "Your father taught school to my father in China, and he taught me when I attended the Young Wo Association School here; later, he taught my daughters. For three generations we are indebted to him." It was pleasant to do business with Daddy's friends.

As Ming Tao noted about the Sam Yup Association's hidden functions, so the problems of Chinatown merchants may not be realized by tourists. White power has been squeezing them in more subtle forms than the mob violence of the last century. Unions picketed, claiming the right to slaughter ducks at their farm source. Instead of caged quacking birds, the carcasses would thereafter arrive in packing boxes. Taking a cue from that success, another union sent pickets to prevent shipments until Mr. Chong signed up for membership on behalf of all his employees. Union dues were not part of the Chinese workingman's budget; their boss had to pay for them. Increased fish and poultry prices had to be passed on to Chinatown residents.

Another harassment was added. The wholesomeness of fresh-killed live chickens suddenly was declared the responsibility of the U.S. Department of Agriculture inspectors, and proprietors like Mr. Chong had to pay for a full-time inspector, with overtime rates on weekends. If the inspector went off for coffee and the staff continued working, he would, on returning, pour kerosene on chickens he hadn't "inspected."

"What does he know about a sick chicken?" Mr. Wong was incensed. "*I* know what is a sick chicken. For fifty years, I did not need an inspector and none of my customers had ill effects. It cost me over fifty thousand dollars to put in the equipment they required. It is so hard to do business, I think I will soon retire to Hong Kong."

Chinatown residents not only paid hidden costs; the economic opportunities of many were limited by racial discrimination. As Younger Brother had discovered, other more lucrative trade unions do just the opposite—continue to exclude membership by race. These are just two examples of methods which box in the poverty of the Chinese. Woody and I have known of these limitations. Ming Tao was merely beginning to be conscious of race hurdles.

Having walked Grant Avenue without finding the bamboo, we retraced our steps—at this end, through a predominantly Chinese crowd. Recently arrived mothers from Hong Kong wrapped babies on their backs, while teenage American-born girls wore shorts. Some people conjured up another era by their dress and features. A stooped, old lady in her black Chinese coat, side fastened to the waist with brilliant green jade buttons, and baggy black trousers was slowly threading her way, supported on the arm of a young girl. She was slow not only because of age, but because of her six-inch-long feet.

As Ming Tao stared, Woody explained the cruel practice of binding feet. "They were a status symbol of being well born, for a woman who tottered on her feet couldn't work for a living. The process was painful as bones were broken and wrapped under the foot; long-term binding prevented growth, and a little girl's ankles were permanently swollen. Even when the binding was discontinued, victims were left with deformed, undersized feet."

We had reached an importing shop where a saleslady friend could find bamboo sticks only for drapery rods, small in diameter, with close-together joints four inches apart, and not quite straight at that. These wouldn't do. On an inspiration, Woody turned into Sacramento Street to find a small shop which specialized in bamboo accessories and furniture. He greeted the store's proprietor, Mr. Kong, a man about our age, and explained our quest. Mr. Kong added to our knowledge. He disappeared into his basement and returned with several lengths of bamboo, from half an inch to two inches in diameter.

"This piece of bamboo is from Japan; it is slightly crooked at its nodes. This brownish bamboo from India has whiplash flexibility, fine for fishing. You may have heard them called 'Calcuttas.' And this greenish bamboo from Brazil is also in the fishing rod class.

"But here"—he picked up a straight, refined-looking length—"this is what you want, Tonkin bamboo from China. I have a limited supply imported prior to 1950."

He held up the end. "See that golden cast of its external patina, almost like an enameled coating penetrating about one-eighth inch into the bark? This is characteristic of Tonkin; wood cannot equal it. Your frame will be rigid as well as resilient."

Woody examined it and marveled, "The nodes are as widely spaced as any I have seen—over a foot apart."

Mr. Kong's answer surprised us. "This is female bamboo. Nodes in the male bamboo run closer, perhaps only six inches apart." Woody counted three dollar bills, but Mr. Kong refused. "I don't want you to pay me. Take these samples with my good wishes for fun ahead."

With this partial success, we were encouraged to continue our search for kite paper. At the doorway of a stationery store stood the owner, gray-haired Mr. Chow, in animated conversation with a friend. Woody greeted them with the conventional phrase, "Is everything well with you?" Then he added, "Do you remember that upstairs custodian who used to make kites?" The store proprietor and former Association president recalled him but couldn't remember his name. And he didn't carry kite paper either. "Try the next block on Grant Avenue near Washington Street. They display ready-made kites from Hong Kong, so they may have kite paper," Mr. Chow suggested. "Besides, one of the clerks has been with that store more than thirty years, and knew that man."

At the recommended store, the elderly, slightly built salesman indeed had known the old kitemaker. "His name was Chan, and we were very friendly; we even attended Chinese Kung-fu classes together." Behind his old-fashioned metal-rimmed oval glasses, his eyes held a faraway look. "That Mr. Chan was surely independent! He wore glasses too, smoked a pipe, and had a nervous twitch in one eye."

Woody exclaimed excitedly, "That twitch! That was he, all right! I had forgotten about that twitch!" Then he asked about kite paper.

"It is this kind of paper," replied the clerk. "I use small squares to wrap the slippers which I sell."

He produced a square of light buff paper with a visible vertical grain. "You can tear off many strips of this paper along its grain, but you cannot tear horizontally. Its lightness, softness, and strength come from its unique fiber content," he explained.

A young man in his late teens who had been listening to us volunteered that he had flown kites in China. "You use damp strips of this same tissue to bind the joints of the kite. Afterward, it dries tight."

Woody agreed. "I remember spraying water on the finished kite surface before I colored it, to make it taut."

When they discussed kites with noisemaking devices, Woody recalled, "That old kitemaker once constructed a kite with a humming device. In those old days, its noise so distracted the work horses that the police asked us to cease flying hummers."

Ming Tao asked about fighting kites, and though Woody had no experience with them, the onlooker had. "In China, we used what we called 'elephant glue,' stiff, strong glue. We took the thinnest glass, like that in discarded light bulbs, pounded it into dust, and mixed it with the glue. We dipped the kite line into this mixture and let it dry. The glass-covered line was reeled onto a spool held by double handles, for we wouldn't want to cut our hands.

"In a kite-fighting contest, two opponents have prepared abrasive cords. The trick is to fly your kite higher than your opponent's, by getting yours up with greater speed and skill. Then you manipulate your kite to dive and descend to saw off the opponent's line. But then, he might outmaneuver you!"

Other customers gathered to listen and nod with comments or their fond recollections. (Informal crowds gather quickly in Chinatown, drawn by a curiosity on the street or an interesting subject at a lunch counter. Let there be a murder or a robbery; then the throng vanishes. Afraid of trouble, no one wishes to witness.) It was astonishing how many older Chinese remembered vividly the pleasures of their childhood pastime, and were willing to discuss them, for the moment no longer strangers to one another.

At home, our family assembled to design our kite, and I wondered, "I have never seen a dragonfly kite. Will that work?"

"Why not?" asked Woody. "Strange, neither have I. Ming Tao, go get your book on insects."

In the illustrated section on the dragonfly family, there was a "May Fly." I liked its wider wing formation and long, graceful tail. "Let's try the May Fly."

Woody sketched a construction plan. He studied the component elements and got our ax and a sharp, stout boning knife, and put on a pair of working gloves. Then he threw on the kitchen floor a pile of newspapers for a cushion and tried to split the bamboo with the ax. After several resounding whacks, the sturdy material resisted him. "I hate to dent this vinyl flooring," he muttered. "Let's go downstairs to the garden room and use the concrete floor."

The family watched as he achieved the first split. With the second split, he obtained a straight piece about three-eighths of an inch wide. At the third split, the ax went off at an angle and the pieces broke.

"Never mind," he reassured them. "That can be used for a minor part. I am working on the three most important structural members: the two front ribs for the wings which must face the wind force, and the body, which must be rigid. These lengths must be sound and straight."

Seated on a stool, Woody whittled until the sticks were free of splinters. His left hand pulled each bamboo length—inner node side up—along his braced thigh, while the boning knife in his right hand stripped it smooth. Control was necessary, for one clumsy slip of the knife would destroy the evenness of the stick.

I exclaimed, "This is hardly a pastime for a child. That knife has to be handled carefully."

Woody answered, "Naturally. But kites have long been a Chinese family project. An adult starts teaching the children."

He continued to show our son. "You can whittle and work as much as you want. Someone with lots of time will make the bamboo as smooth as possible with fine sandpaper. But for now this is good enough. Let's go back to the kitchen and shape these sticks."

Woody held the bamboo length of the May Fly body so that its midpoint was over an open pot of boiling water. After the steam softened the bamboo, he gradually bent it until both ends met, and he fastened this loop with an elastic.

"Eventually, I will use those short pieces as ribs to reinforce this body section," he explained.

"But it looks awfully short. Only half of the wing span."

"I can lengthen it by piecing. You go by what looks right. The finished product improves on the sketch."

I agreed. "Like any other work of art; accidents of creation even in a kite may be unexpected dividends."

Woody was searching. "Where is the paste I asked you to make?"

It is possible to use store-bought white glue, but as a part of our home product, I had made the paste.* Woody tore off half-inch-wide strips of the tissue paper; after moistening them with the paste, he lashed and overlapped them around each kite joint. Then his son took over, following his father's example.

Slowly, over a series of hours, the skeleton of the kite evolved. The wing stretch of four feet was tautly bowed by cord attached to the center hollow body frame, which measured about two feet long and eight inches wide. Woody instructed Ming Tao to attach cross bracing at various points of the body frame. Then using two quarter-inch-deep, two-inch-diameter bamboo rounds for eyes, Woody drilled holes straight through so that they would rotate around a ten-inch bamboo skewer. Our son became excited as he saw the kite taking shape. Carefully, he lashed the skewer across the head. (Sections of plastic conduit kept the eyes in place.)

Woody surveyed its looks. "It's too complicated to fasten the May Fly's second pair of lower wings. This would look better and handle more easily if we added a tail section." So he redesigned and constructed the tail which was hinged to the body with two twine loops. The frame was finished.

"O.K.," Woody said. "It's all yours."

Ming Tao was dismayed. "I haven't covered a kite before."

"You have the paper. All you do is lay the frame on it and draw the outline, cut, and glue to the bamboo. You've been cutting and gluing ever since I can remember."

"But the paper isn't as big as the wings!" Ming Tao objected.

"Piece it!" Woody left him.

When his son occasionally had trouble, Woody relented to give him a hand. But typical of Woody's way of teaching was his "sink or swim" attitude, having literally nearly drowned himself before he learned to swim. When the tissue wrinkled, a fine spray of water tightened the slack. At the lower edges of the wings, Ming Tao pasted double thicknesses of tissue for reinforcement. What started to be May Fly looked more like a gigantic bird, too big to handle at home, so it was transported to the studio.

---

* Recipe for kite paste: take 1 heaping tablespoon flour, mix to a smooth paste with cold water, and add water to make 1 cup. Add 1 teaspoon sugar. Place in saucepan. Add 1 cup boiling water and cook, stirring constantly and boiling until color is opalescent. Stir in ½ teaspoon of ground cloves or cinnamon. Strain into jar. Keep refrigerated.

The fun part for Ming Tao was to paint the bird. He used poster colors in swirls of magenta, yellow, orange for the wings and made the body blue. One side of the tissue-covered eyes was red and the other side green. Painting was Ming Tao's forte. The kite was named "Phoenix," queen of Chinese birds.

The job of searching and working, on and off, had taken months, during which Ming Tao doubted and Woody remained confident. At last they would fly it, Ming Tao still doubting, and Woody still confident. From his tackle box, Woody took a salt-water fishing reel. He said to me, "Bring some strips of rags for the tail. I am not sure how many I need, depending on the air currents and how this goes up."

"I'm not going to bring any old rags. Let me find something which would look nice in the air," I replied. Black, natural, white, and red raw silk left over from pajamas made artistic partnership. We piled into the station wagon with the kite, the children, the fabric, and the reel.

1—Revolving eye spaced by hollow tubes pivots on bamboo skewer. 2—Hand-split and sanded bamboo strut joints are bound with paste-soaked paper strips. 3—String is used for three-point bridle system attached to bamboo edges of wings and end of body section. 4—String loops are used to hinge the mobile tail.

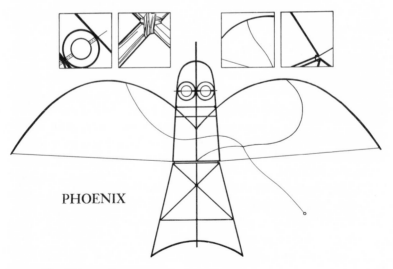

PHOENIX

At the Marina Green, Woody pierced two tiny holes in the tissue about midpoint on each of the forward wing frames and another hole at the end of the body. He cut off enough twine from his fishing reel to form an equidistant triangular bridle, about 21 inches long on each side. Then he fastened his reel line to the bridle. Some strips of raw silk were tied to the tail.

The moment Phoenix was lifted from the tail gate, she was eager and restless, catching the slightest wind movement and reaching for heights. Woody remarked, "Wind currents are tricky; although not apparent at ground level, higher up they may be strong. Nor should it be necessary to make a panting run to get a kite up."

The kite was having trouble. It went up, but soon it swooped and darted. Woody looked at it critically. "More tail," he muttered, and reeled it in.

We attached more tail, but she would not gain height; again, she was pulled in. The younger children wandered off, but Ming Tao became anxious as I attached more cloth. Finally, I gave up and tied a whole yard of red silk at the end—not very artistic, but it gave weight. "Stabilizing, like a ship's stabilizer," Woody explained. "It's not scientific; got to play it by ear."

Thank goodness, that did it! She rose like the proverbial phoenix from the ashes, up and up. Her powerful wing span in brilliant waves of color soared against the pale blue sky. Her revolving red and blue eyes gazed downward at the world from a 200-foot height. We understood why the tissue edges of her wings had to be reinforced: they flapped continuously in lively fashion, at a 40-degree angle to her body.

Ming Tao was enchanted. "Let me hold the reel now."

Then each daughter returned, wanting to hold the reel. Even tiny Ming Choy was successful with his turn. The bird seemed to hypnotize casual onlookers into a captive audience. Drivers stopped their cars for a better look.

After we had had our fun, the kite was brought to the studio and hung by its beak, waiting to be flown again, the only one of its kind in all the world. Sometimes we ask if walls could speak, if that statue could talk, what would it tell us? If Phoenix could talk, she would have told of a father and a son re-creating a Chinese art more than two thousand years old.

CHAPTER 19

"WHEN THE BOAT IS ROCKING, DON'T LOOK FOR TROUBLE UNDER THE BED"

One happy summer, Woody and I evened the score on having treated his mother to the Honolulu trip: we took my mother with our children to Kauai, where we feasted on abundant mangoes, papaya, bananas, eggplant, and avocados; local natives netted us fish, and we picked our own pineapples from the fields which surrounded Papaa Ranch. It was possible to cope with the youngest's bottles and diapers, and my mother didn't worry about the right clothes or inability to speak English. Ming Tao built sand castles and watched in fascination as rising tides carried them away; the girls gathered sea urchins at low tide; Ming Choy dabbled in a brook, catching frogs; Woody took my mother sightseeing; and I had a chance to write.

When we flew home to San Francisco, we were met by Woody's Oldest Brother instead of Misako and her husband, Fred. "Fred died of a heart attack!" was the tragic news.

So we returned to confusion not unlike the confusion after my father's death. Comfort to Misako and Fred's funeral were our immediate concerns; then we picked up the reins of business when it was the staff's turn for vacations, and cared for children while unpacking fifteen suitcases. Woody lost his voice, and Lai Yee fainted in class, cracking off part of her front tooth.

The frantic atmosphere affected our baby. He would not accept any substitute for Misako, whom he had known since birth, and attacked any new applicant, literally kicking her out. He attacked me if I did not pay instant attention, and finally, he attacked himself by hurtling down the stairs with a toy peg in his mouth. He tore a bleeding hole in his upper front gum, but we could not find the missing tooth. Fourteen days later, it descended halfway, crookedly—he had driven it into the roof of his mouth!

I was afraid that he would destroy himself. The child psychiatrist told me, "The boat is rocking, don't look for more trouble under the bed," and advised us to hold Ming Choy in physical restraint when he rebelled, to protect him and those he attacked.

That Thanksgiving, after having entertained our families, and finishing the last dishes at 2:00 A.M., I awoke the next morning and found that I could not walk. Physically constraining our supercharged cub had wrecked the delicate balance of my back.

We devised a new plan. Instead of depending on one maid, we used a combination of three: a day worker who left at 4:00 P.M., Misako in to help with dinner, and a schoolgirl on weekends. If one of the three didn't show up, we weren't going it alone for long. I never dreamed that I would be so dependent on domestic help. Our fourth child was so hyperactive that no grandmother could come to our house again to take charge while we traveled; so we postponed tours.

The rocking boat was subsiding. After an awkward beginning, Ming Tao was adjusting to junior high. He made a detailed report for anatomy, drawing all the human bones and muscles, and was building a model of Shakespeare's Globe Playhouse for which I made curtains. At home, he helped with mowing the lawn or watering. At the store, he ran errands and began working with copper. After watching his father during playpen days, he was manning the machinery on his own.

Ming Choy turned four. He had some idea of danger, so that he did not dash madly out into the street or lean out of a window. But we could never leave him near an open ladder because we would find him calmly sitting on top. One day, he threw his arms around me and declared me to be the best mother in the whole, wide world. I was so touched, I asked him tenderly if he were the best boy in the whole, wide world. He replied modestly, "No, just in California!"

Since birth Lai Wai and Lai Yee, nine and ten, had worn uncut braids, now long enough to sit on, causing turmoil every morning to comb, and every week to shampoo. With their reluctant consent, Woody washed their hair, I braided it anew for the last time, and then—snip, off came each. When I held up the 20-inch long shiny twists, they acted as if I grasped living appendages amputated from their bodies. Each screamed and wept and ran to her room. Later, Woody hugged them in consolation, while I wrapped their queues and locked them with precious documents. I doubted if Chinese males had been so personally reluctant when the Empire fell and they were freed from the queues which had been the sign of their subjugation to Manchu tyranny. Our braid cutting was a symbol of our girls' passing from carefree childhood to a new life of responsibilities.

They became conscientious babysitters, entertaining their small brother at home or taking him to the park. It was no longer necessary for an adult to watch him. But every morning when he appeared in the kitchen, it was a signal for me to stop cooking, sit down on the stool, and hold him on my lap—all 45 pounds—to "love-love" for a minute.

I remember a Mother's Day prayer when my sisters and nephew had also gathered in our home. (Oldest Brother had died of a heart attack.) Mama, who kept silent when Daddy was alive, made her own kind of grace: "We are mothers and children together at this table laden with food and drink. Give the mothers the wisdom and outgoing love which they must transmit to their children, so that they in turn will develop their wisdom and outgoing love to work in the ways of our Lord."

Family love extended beyond my home. Youngest Brother won a handsome Regent's scholarship that covered part of the tremendous cost of a medical education in Los Angeles at the University of California. An exchange of letters was prompted by my sending him a news article describing the establishment of a Chinatown clinic for mental problems, a breakthrough in the traditional Chinese wall of contained and ignored emotional difficulties.

He was excited by the article, for he was aware that young Chinese had suffered from many of the conditions mentioned in the article: anxiety, learning disabilities, as well as stammering; the barriers to free talk within the family, and the same "dead ends" that existed in our family! Ever since graduating from Lick High School, he wrote, he had wanted to thank me (but there was that family barrier to free talk) for arranging his two years at Grant Junior High, a deeply traumatic experience because he was removed for the first time from familiar Chinatown and thrown among white Americans. It proved to be a major turning point in his life.

The news article I sent was an early expression of community concern over maladjustments which might produce destructive young misfits in Chinatown, nearly all new arrivals from Hong Kong. By the mid-1960s, after the Kennedy Refugee Act, nearly 15,000 newcomers had been admitted, of whom 9,000 gained permanent status. No longer was Chinatown the homogeneous culture it represented originally. The numbers of new arrivals were too great for comfortable absorption either in Chinatown or in the larger white community. White-staffed public schools were not prepared for an overnight expansion of language instruction for teenagers who didn't know enough English. News reports of social unrest appeared short years after that first story of cultural limitations:

Royal Hong Kong police have been in close contact with the San Francisco police intelligence unit and homicide detectives. Hong Kong police have helped identify certain suspects here.

Some arrivals had existed in an educational vacuum in Hong Kong. At twelve years of age all were required to take examinations to qualify for further education; and if they didn't pass, they were barred from school but could not obtain work permits until they were fourteen. Invariably, teenage children of working poor parents drifted into street habits during that two-year no man's land between twelve and fourteen. Those who came to San Francisco continued the same lawless habits, moving away to relieve family crowding and living in isolated rooms where they seized on "easy" ways to support themselves.

Besides the murders, there have been numerous armed robberies and plenty of acid throwing and window smashing, the tactics reserved for shopkeepers and restaurant owners who dislike paying for protection.

This new generation was the tragic by-product of postwar China, young people whose parents were less daring, less intellectually ambitious than the refugees who knocked on my Hong Kong hotel door for help in 1953. Relocated in crowded urban settings, these refugees were straining for necessities and status; someday, some of their children would steal to obtain them.

Chinatown's unemployment rate is nearly thirteen percent, while it is six percent for San Francisco as a whole and under five percent for the country.

The language barrier was one cause for unemployment; unfulfilled physical and psychological yearnings were its results; and such temperaments as refused to be cemented into the misery of poverty tried criminal rebellion. The high school with the largest number of Chinese students—whom most white teachers normally prefer to teach ("San Francisco's elementary school teachers believe that Chinese children are the most intelligent students and the highest achievers in the integrated classroom") —also had the city's highest number of suspensions. Alienated young Chinese have altered the kind of social services required in Chinatown.

There is nothing exotic about the fact that 41 percent of its population lives below the poverty level, nor is it exciting that Chinatown has the highest TB and suicide rates in the United States. Marginal workers live marginal lives. Overcrowded in the 1880s, it remains that way today.

San Francisco's Chinatown is probably the worst ghetto in the country. More than 60,000 people are packed into forty-two square blocks: 885 persons per acre, ten times the city's average.

The churches, the Y's, government-subsidized programs, have rallied to assist the elderly, to grapple with housing problems, and to organize constructive activities for the young, such as child care centers and day camps during idle summers. Few of these young have any idea of the pains which my father and others like him had suffered to foster the Chinese institutions which have survived more than half a century for them to use today. Missionary work now takes another form. But a doubled population of 60,000 on a poverty base cannot be self-sufficient; and those who commit sensational crimes are less than a quarter of 1 percent (of Chinese population).

However, police believe the actual criminal element in Chinatown is small. They say no more than 150 persons, mostly teen-agers, are responsible for all the crime, and these are the gang members.

Since 1969, there have been seventeen murders associated with Chinatown youth gangs.

Elders hurry home before dark, condemning lawless "bad boys." "You read too much about Chinese crimes along with black crimes," my mother regrets. A shocked community wonders why this new breed of offenders has no cultural pride, and will not melt into the stereotyped pattern of long working hours for the substandard wages of previous generations. Yet is the temper or code of these "bad boys" much different from that old code of the Tongs? Some Chinese murderers have a self-image of courage; they justify the act as "righting a wrong," and if caught, they accept their punishment passively.

Banks at every corner exist where none were before, a temptation to daring robberies which sometimes succeed.

YOUTHS ON TRIAL FOR MANDARIN TOWERS JOB

Two 19 year old youths charged with involvement in the May 14 armed robbery of the Mandarin Towers branch of the Bank of America are being tried before a jury in U.S. District court.

The robbers had worn women's stockings as masks and had tried unsuccessfully to shoot out bank cameras which took pictures of them in the holdup.

Human greed and blind rage are expressed according to today's changed styles.

The present turmoil in Chinatown is, some observers believe, an open revolt against intolerable social conditions. And the youth gangs are the knife point of the revolt.

Banks can afford expensive, modern fronts. Glittering new restaurants can pay for kitchens installed according to the building code. But other façades hide overcrowded quarters; for war brides and newcomers settle in the same rooms where single men used to cluster.

Many of the working people live in dormitory-like buildings and keep their possessions in suitcases because there is no closet space.

Three federal housing projects have been completed, but housing is still insufficient. Landlords do not bother to modernize living facilities for uncomplaining tenants, who are glad to find any place at all in Chinatown. Only six out of a hundred homes have adequate plumbing. Yet there are some residents of Chinatown who cannot merge into white communities even if they wanted to: recent working-class immigrants and older Chinese who don't speak English.

SELF-HELP PRESSURED BY SEE-SAW FUNDING

Nestled inconspicuously on Old Chinatown Lane, Self-Help for the Elderly is an administrator's nightmare. Living from hand to mouth in a literal sense, spending half of its time scrambling for money, the agency and its director don't know when the bottom might fall out.

The independent elderly remain here rather than move to live with grown children in outlying neighborhoods, and do not complain if their successful progeny have become too busy to look after them. That retired elders, low-paid workers, and unhappy youth should begin to demonstrate like other minority groups arouses surprised comments in the white community.

My mother is one of the older Chinese who enjoys living alone in the home Daddy and she bought. She has never longed to return to China. Her interests are with her children here. Youngest Brother has graduated, completed his residency and training, and is now a psychiatrist. "His name is on a door," she says modestly to relatives. My other younger brother, who now has four daughters, asked her to live with him in Los Angeles, where he continues working in industrial management, despite the resentment he encountered from Caucasian workers. "As long as I can use my feet," my emancipated mother asks, "who wants to move where one has to depend on driving?"

Woody and I were also thankful that we had our feet, and that we had found our home just before that population surge. For soon after our boat stopped rocking from child care problems, it began to shake from financial ones, and remarkably, the children who had done the rocking before now helped to steady the ship.

By 1968, Ming Choy was in kindergarten and one full-time live-in worker could cope with family needs; so we organized another tour to the Orient. After months of work arranging reservations and mailing brochures, followed by inquiries and correspondence, our investment of time and dollars was sabotaged by President Lyndon B. Johnson's recommendation of a prohibitive tax on foreign travel. The tax did not pass Congress, but the possibility frightened prospective travelers. Each day Woody would scan the mail apprehensively. We shuddered at successive requests for deposit refunds, until we were down to only six members. We could not cancel our obligation to these nice people who were anxious to go and willing to pay a break-even surcharge, but it was not a profitable exercise.

Upon our return home, our Bolivian housekeeper produced a cable saying that her mother was ill, and off she went. We had a financial family conference with our children, who were four-teen, eleven, ten, and five. Every round of shoes for dress and play cost us $100 for eight pairs. The cost of domestic help was more than mortgage payments on the house. Ming Tao was the spokesman. "We love our house. Don't give up our house!"

I faced them with the alternatives. I couldn't do another full-time household job, but we could all divide that work; and they agreed on a cooperative schedule. Additionally, Ming Tao went to help at the studio each day after school, and we paid him as we had paid schoolboys for twenty years. He would save toward his college education, relieving us of part of that burden. Each child was paid for housework hours. They would buy their "extras" with this money, and later, they also bought their own clothes. Ming Tao became leader at home; when we had to accept an unavoidable dinner invitation, or to extend one, he supervised dinner and the younger children.

In our division of labor, each took pride in helping to pull the load. I told them of Eric Hoffer's saying in reference to the University of California that campus maintenance was more important than the gift of buildings: to make a gift is only a one-time affair, but to work and keep it beautiful while in use is a lasting challenge. The children would say in a discouraged way, "Mom, after hours of hard work, everything looks just the same." And I would try to convince them: "We may not remark about a clean room, but we would certainly notice a messy one."

There had never been a summer that I could talk the children into going to camp. "Be close to nature" was one of the reasons I gave. "We love nature already," they retorted. "Make new friends" was another reason. "We have enough friends already," they countered. "Get away from home chores"—I thought that would prove irresistible. "We'll only get other chores," they said firmly. This summer Woody suggested that it was time they learned how to cook. So each child took a turn once a week to plan the menu and cook dinner. I would take him or her marketing. "How do we pick?" each asked. Fresh mushrooms with closed caps, firm cantaloupes with heavy netting, fish with shiny scales and red gills, the tiniest eggplant and zucchini, heavy heads of lettuce, thumping watermelons for deep resonance—all this they learned. Ming Choy felt sorry for any child without the fun of shopping in Chinatown, for he was fascinated with the marine specimens which were displayed—even including frozen species from Hong Kong.

Our meals included non-Chinese dishes. Ming Tao enjoyed seafoods and learned to cook a wide variety. I remember one marvelous dish of fillet of sole Veronica, for which we peeled grapes, and another of fresh abalone which he pounded before frying. His taste was expensive, but his results were usually excellent. His sweet and sour pork combination was so good that my mother asked him to cook it for her Chinese New Year's party! The only failure I recall was our first attempt at crêpes Suzette, which didn't flame, though their flavor was divine. (After all, Woody was asked to come home with Grand Marnier at $12 a bottle!)

No meal included more than one new dish to learn. With his complicated sole recipe, Ming Tao chose canned minestrone, hot French bread, and buttered noodles. When he was attempting the crêpes, he had broiled lamb chops and frozen string beans.

For Lai Yee, squab is a treat. There are as many ways to cook squab as chicken, but a simple way for a young learner is simply this: Split the squab down the back. Then salt it *double*. (In other words increase the amount of salt to twice as much as you think it should have. It will taste wonderful.) Put in a heatproof dish on a rack in a large pot, with boiling water up to the level of the rack. Steam about half an hour, until cooked. We can stretch a jumbo pound-and-a-quarter squab by adding half a pound of fresh pork butt or two pork chops, also salted twice over (which increases steaming time to one hour). The juices are spooned over rice, while the squab and pork, which share flavors, are cut into small pieces to share. As with any Chinese dinner, we would enjoy two other dishes—soup, vegetables—each cooked with some meat, to round out the menu. (Half a chicken may substitute for squab.)

Lai Wai's favorite is tomato-beef, great for emergencies, requiring only a pound of flank steak in the freezer and a 16-ounce can of tomatoes in the pantry. Slice the flank steak thinly across the grain. Marinate with 2 tablespoons soy sauce, 1 tablespoon sugar,* 2 tablespoons oil. In a wok or heavy iron pan, such as a Dutch oven, put in 3 tablespoons oil, heat until pan is very hot, put in a crushed clove of garlic, add the meat, and toss quickly a few seconds, until partially brown and still red inside. Remove to a bowl. Heat the tomatoes, breaking them up, and adding 1 tablespoon soy, 2 tablespoons sugar. Thicken with 1½ tablespoons cornstarch dissolved in water. Turn off flame. Add beef and serve at once with rice. (Onions and green peppers, separately sautéed, may be included.)

A rice expert in Houston told me that Americans have thrown out in potatoes what would support the rice industry. Long-grain Texas Patna rice is a daily staple for us. Our children were taught the importance of washing rice thoroughly, by scrubbing and rinsing, each process repeated three times, followed by three more rinses until the water runs clear, to eliminate talc and dust. The Japanese electric rice cooker is automatic and foolproof. In Hong Kong, restaurants use the gigantic size to keep contents warm.

Ming Choy votes for chicken. At six, when it was his turn at dinner, he managed this: a fresh-killed and cleaned 4½-pound roasting chicken was salted as usual. Our oval electric roaster with its rack was preheated for 15 minutes at 325 degrees. He put in the chicken breast side down, fat from the cavity on top to keep it basted, and covered it. After half an hour the chicken was turned over and roasted another half hour. He calls this "chicken with the yellow skin" since it doesn't brown. Its juiciness is delicious over rice. For this meal, the giblets were diced (we helped him), boiled in chicken stock, and frozen peas added at the end. After the broth was turned off, a beaten egg was stirred vigorously into it, making "egg flower soup."

Ming Tao once said, "Why is cooking so hard? It is only a matter of good taste."

"Ah," I replied, "but how many people have 'good taste'?

---

* We use raw brown sugar.

We are heirs to a great cuisine, and you have been exposed to it since birth."

Ming Choy had now begun Chinese school. Brave on top of a ladder, he was "scared" of this unknown, so I accompanied him to register, and waited in line with other parents or grandparents who were also anxious to have their newest generation remember the old. When the strangeness wore off, he liked making new friends and developed a phenomenal ability to concentrate and to reproduce the ideographs. As a matter of fact, he spoke and understood little Chinese. While his older brother had spoken only Chinese until that first 1956 tour, Ming Choy had spoken only English because it was used by his older siblings and household helpers (even though Woody and I spoke Chinese). His earliest environment was American: nursery school, toys, baby books; later, magazines, newspapers, and television were also apart from the Chinese world. In an accelerated culture even half-generation environments differ. When occasionally we expected to be detained at work and he walked to Grandmother Ong's after Chinese school, she would be forced to communicate with him in broken English and would be as relieved to see us as my father had been when we had gone to pick up crying Ming Tao.

"I can't sit still with your son. His temperament is like yours as a child, but he's as restless as a flea and jumps around just as much!" Grandmother addressed her complaint to Woody. "In a flash, he was on my kitchen step-stool trying to unlock my door. If there's a bed in the room, he jumps on it. If there's more than one, he tries them all."

Ming Choy has kept that charming childhood naïveté of absolute shining trust in what we say and do, and we, who feel the pang of a less entertaining childhood gone forever, are guilty of fueling his excitement, stimulating his readiness for new adventures, so that we can enjoy life with the double perspective of his reactions as well as our own. At nine, the age when Ming Tao was ready for a brother, that brother still believed in Santa Claus, and we joined in the game to hang up our stockings and keep him young one more year.

His sisters were improving in housework and learned to organize their time. Inevitably, they sometimes criticized each other over fancied or real insults, but though I had despaired of caring for two in diapers when Lai Wai was born, now they were companionable, consulting with each other, laughing together, window or real shopping as a pair, sharing secrets, hopes, and fears.

Thus, we could be glad that these years of growth and learning, living and loving, went well enough. Ming Tao took up photography, and the guest room became his dark room. He bought his guitar with personal savings. The girls learned how to bake, sew, and iron. All four children were interested in pottery and enamels.

To keep them nourished was a serious concern. Milk was consumed by the gallon. No matter how tight our budget, we never limited the children's food, as ours had been in childhood. I was in the kitchen as much as I was at the office. Each morning I arose at five thirty to find the breakfast menu written down, and the lunch sandwich fillings requested. I remember one day telling an American friend what the family had had for breakfast:

> Ming Tao: Mushroom, turkey, and bacon omelet.
> Lai Yee: Spanish omelet with fresh tomatoes.
> Lai Wai: Bacon and onion omelet.
> Ming Choy: 3 strips of bacon with 2 fried eggs.
> Woody: Veal cutlet with 1 fried egg.

(Omelet varieties, like egg foo young, economically use bits of leftovers.)

My friend cried out, "That's permissive eating."

I thought a minute. "Maybe I am overreacting to my youth when I had to eat all of what was served, including what I disliked. Besides, when I forced Ming Tao to eat a cheese omelet, he threw up."

That night, I told my daughters as I tucked them in bed, "I think I am spoiling you." I recounted a Chinese story told by my father to justify being strict: In China, a mother spoiled an only son by nursing him with breast milk even after he entered school. Every day he would come home and have a pull at her breast. Not having been denied anything, her son grew up without character until he became a criminal to support his spendthrift ways. He was arrested, served a jail sentence, and returned home to his mother, who promptly offered her breast to him again! Biting off her nipple, he said, "This is to teach you a lesson for spoiling me."

My two girls, now twelve and thirteen, screamed with horror at this story. Moral or not, it was obnoxious. In his room at his desk, Older Brother heard the outcry and asked what was the matter. I repeated the story and he remarked dryly, "Well, it shows that he did grow up."

The girls demanded to know what Brother had said. When I told them, they shouted down the hall, "Oh, oh, it was a boy who bit the nipple. A girl wouldn't!"

I relayed the message to Ming Tao, who refused to comment and made a face.

I left to go downstairs. The girls yelled out again, "Where are you going?"

"To get myself some hot milk so I can go to sleep."

Ming Tao called out, "Get me some too."

"What, and spoil you?" I asked.

"No, mine will be from a cup."

We could laugh together even in the times of stress which continued for the next two years. The boat would rock again, and we were fortunate that we had a crew to help.

CHAPTER 20
BLACK AND RED DAYS

The 1970 business recession lingered, stagnating our business. I sustained a fall from a neglected street depression adjacent to the excavation for Chinatown's Holiday Inn structure, which was to provide one floor for the future Chinese Cultural Foundation. That injury prevented me from making pottery for some time. We let all the staff go and narrowed down the business to Woody, myself, and the three older children, who came every day after school. By then they had completed elementary Chinese school.

I did not press them into Chinese junior high because I heard that some of their schoolmates were associating with those "bad boys" from Hong Kong, and played hooky by leaving their books in school, then disappearing. Both the disrupted school and parents of students became afraid of possible incidents. It was dark in the winter at 8 P.M. dismissal time.

Lessons had expanded their Chinese vocabulary from simple to complex forms and also had emphasized traditional qualities of family cooperation, honesty, hard work, patience. A typical lesson was entitled: "The Foolish Old Man Moving a Mountain." Each sentence was in seven rhythmic words, and there were nineteen sentences.

The foolish old man was past ninety years old.
Although aged, his determination was strong.
Because the high mountain obstructed his doorway,
He found it inconvenient to pass it.
He wanted his family to cooperate
And level the mountain's 700 miles' height.
From East of the River, wise people came to look,
To warn the old man against his folly.
The foolish old man heard them and replied hastily.
Old brother, you see I am weak; but my heart is that of a child.
When I die, I have children; children will continue to work.
Children will have grandchildren and grandchildren will have children.
Children and grandchildren will attack the mountains.
The mountains cannot grow higher but only diminish.
Sons and grandsons will not end.
It is only important that they have firm resolution
How can I be afraid that we will not succeed in moving the mountain?

It was Ming Choy who was learning to memorize this lesson. The rest of us struggled with its practical application. Unable to make pottery, I could do the enameling; the girls took charge of more work at home. Ming Tao undertook the lathe work, freeing Woody's time for travel planning. We gave up leading tours.

Personal grief engulfed us again. Woody's mother was found at home unconscious from a stroke, rushed to the hospital, and mercifully died three days later. I think she was prepared, knowing that her end was coming. A few months before, she had given back to me all the jewelry and furs which Woody and I had bought over the years for her, saying simply, "I cannot give equally to all my daughters-in-law and grandchildren, so I am giving back to those who gave to me."

One of Woody's younger brothers and I had been planning a party for her seventy-second birthday, which would have been in a couple of weeks. When she was seventy, she had said that she didn't wish the customary seven-decade huge banquet celebration, because she ached for her absent son Norman. We planned to surprise her at our home this year by getting all generations of the family together. It was heartbreaking that when we did assemble, it was after her funeral, when we offered a buffet supper for forty-six.

At that dinner, my mother was depressed and hinted that her turn would be next. She reminded me of the saying, "When you are grown do not travel too far from your parents. Be aware of their age. If they are older, be glad and be fearful: glad that you have enjoyed them so many years, and fearful that there are not many years left."

When I asked her about observing mourning for my mother-in-law, she answered, "When your father died, you were not asked to restrict your activities or to wear mourning. Customs change. There are still people here who will not go out for a month. When I was a girl, Chinese observed mourning for three years, during which they sat on mats or low stools and let their hair grow without cutting."

When sixteen-year-old Ming Tao heard this he was tickled. "Boy, the Chinese had the right idea—pads and long hair!"

Believing that our children should face the reality of death, too, we brought them to our private family viewing of their grandmother in her casket. They saw the customary deck of playing cards, the cup of Scotch, the package of cigarettes, and heard the Chinese music tape being played—these had been more important to her than the flowers that now crowded the chapel. And they said, "Po-po looks like plastic."

"Po-po" had been a precious part of our heritage. Losing her was hard on Woody, for a man is disciplined not to cry or to talk about his deepest feelings. While he said openly, "It's a blessing she passed away so quickly, because she could not have endured being an invalid," we heard him sob just once. Man's first shrill infant cry of need for his mother has intensified into his desolate voice of bereavement. No matter how logical death is, the finality is difficult to bear, and the unknown beyond chilling to contemplate. A child from conception is on his way to separation from his mother, and by slow degrees she encourages his independence, so that her physical death will not be his emotional death. But however prepared, the reality is painful.

August is an emotional month for me. Lai Wai was born and we were married that month. But it was also the month of my father's death, and it was oddly coincidental that Woody's mother should be cremated on August 17, the date of his death. Ming Tao and Woody vehemently protest my looking at the Chinese calendar leaves which predict astrologically auspicious days for action in red, and ominous days in black. August 17, 1970, was a "black" day, and I cannot count the many other "black" days on which we have suffered dire events, such as a store robbery or a flood from broken pipes. I know, of course, that it is coincidence. My mother reconciles reality and superstition by saying, "Be glad of the small misfortunes, for they cancel off larger disasters." When our puppy died, she comforted, "The death of a round hair mammal was a substitute sacrifice for a deeper loss."

Astrologically 1971 was the Year of the Pig, which brought us additional difficulties. Moving our business was the first; after our landlord's death the bank for his estate asked a new rental way beyond our means. The horrendous necessity of moving a twenty-year accumulation on three floors boggled our minds and quavered our knees. Yet, what choice did we have? We could not retire, and we couldn't start looking for jobs. Conventional work hours were incompatible with caring for our children.

I began by going through storage files and personal belongings. Woody began by selling equipment no longer essential for a small staff. Eighty percent of my files were destroyed without a second thought; on checking them, I regretted how much energy and time I had devoted to paperwork. After paring down our equipment to essentials we had a better idea of the space we required. We began looking for a new location in a light-manufacturing zone, yet suitable for Woody's travel business. Real estate agents were indifferent; not enough money was involved in a lease to fire their enthusiasm. Needing advice, I made an appointment with the head of the real estate department of our bank, whom I didn't know, but who should have some of the answers I didn't. He was gracious and helpful. "Decide where you wish to locate, walk into a store in that neighborhood, and just ask how much rent they pay," he said. "Then you will know whether you can afford it."

I was incredulous. Surely, I would be kicked out for being rude. But it was the clue I needed, for the ideal location would be near home. So I started by talking to our Chinese shoe repair man; then I poked my head into a rundown German wholesale bakery. The baker's helper was an accountant from Hong Kong who didn't know enough English for his profession here, but by learning to make bread, he earned $800 per month. Few Chinese remain strangers to other Chinese when it comes to discussing a Westerner. I learned that his employer was retiring because of necessary surgery. I was given the landlord's name, and Woody and I negotiated to take over his lease.

We had to build a loft for storage, but the ground floor, with two separate entrances, satisfied our needs: a travel office, an adjacent display area for imports and ceramics, plus a back area for manufacturing. Woody and I worked with a contractor to design a new front, demolish obstructions, install the loft, and bring electrical and plumbing work up to code standards. Naturally, everything cost double what we first estimated.

The old lease was up on September 1, and our timetable was to start moving August 1 to the new location at Polk Street and Broadway. Heavy machinery was transported by skilled professionals with special tools and trucks, who charged $60 per hour. Fortunately, it was school vacation and our junior crew, ages seventeen, fourteen, and thirteen, could help in other loads. The second week in July, just as we were in the thick of preparations, I learned that I had to undergo surgery. The doctor talked to me on a Wednesday. By Sunday I was in the hospital. Having had major surgery, the idea of an operation did not upset me, but its timing seemed nothing short of disaster. When I adjusted to the idea of ten days to two weeks in the hospital, two weeks resting at home, and no driving for a month, I thought: The contractor has to finish up the work anyway. I shall rest and then do the unpacking. (In fact, I had a notion the break might be good for me.)

Woody had to keep the house going, buying groceries and cooking for four appetites increased by physical work. He was also moving, watching workmen, and getting estimates. My mother's reasons for advising me to marry were proved correct. After surgery, with intravenous nourishment taped to my arm, seeing his distracted silent face at my side, I murmured again, "Awful thin."

My being home eliminated one worry. Our children were tenderly solicitous. Each daughter alternately stayed home with me, while the other daughter and Ming Tao worked on moving. Mercurial eight-year-old Ming Choy, no less thoughtful, would shuttle back and forth as his interests dictated. Mostly, he enjoyed getting into our king-size bed to look at books "to keep you company."

Now Woody was faced with the last phase of vacating the old studio. Not trusting construction workers among our many small and beautiful art objects, he decided that home offered the safest temporary storage. When I was well enough to venture downstairs, I found unexpected objects under coffee tables, benches, along hallways, jammed into the basement.

On nights and weekends at home another big job involved the bulk mailing of 4,200 moving notices. Lai Wai and Lai Yee typed each customer's name and address, ascertained zip codes, stuffed and sealed envelopes. In our living room already filled haphazardly with studio inventory, bundles tied according to zip codes were piled high on the rug.

> When there are blessings, we will share together
> When there are calamities, we will bear together,

is a familiar Chinese refrain. I made a rare request of Mama to come and help. This Po-po also loved her grandchildren. Though she believed it unnecessary to compliment them verbally, she showered them with practical gifts. An excited phone call might come from her: "Seconds in pants have been returned to our factory, some nearly their sizes, and I can alter them to fit." She knew more accurately than I did each child's growing measurements.

When I offered to reimburse her, she refused. "Come and pick them up." If for a while the rejects should miss the size of one of our four, she would find in her basement some remnant yardage left over from Daddy's manufacturing days, and make one or more pairs for the neglected child. The sturdiness of corduroy and weight of denim from thirty years ago contrasted noticeably with today's thinner goods.

As we worked for hours on the envelope job, there was a rare chance to talk face to face. She noted how our children were cheerfully helping. "They do not have the same concept of time or money that we did as children," I commented, since it is custom for a mother to demur when her offspring are complimented. When I was little, to my embarrassment, my faults or oversights were emphasized in a seeming debate with visitors.

"Of course—times have changed. I regret that my mother died without having enjoyed the diversions of today. She never saw colored movies or was entertained by television. On the other hand," she shifted her direction, "you know English, so you can easily keep up with the times."

"Oh, my children say I am old-fashioned. I do not acquire the latest styles. If I have something satisfactory, I wear it ten or fifteen years. They tell me that my hobby is saving!"

Mama agreed: "I wear the same everyday clothes, but I try to have new dresses for special occasions. No matter how well dressed you are, someone else will be better dressed, and no matter how modest your appearance, you will be better dressed than another."

"It isn't just clothes—they think my standards are old-fashioned. As much as they like the pants you give them, I ask them to wear skirts to school; pants are for play or work."

Mama agreed and was reminded of an experience with Youngest Brother. "Each generation surely thinks parents are old-fashioned. Wait until they are parents; then they will hear the same refrain. When Youngest Brother came to visit me, he told me I didn't know how to enjoy life. 'Don't rush to do dishes after dinner the way you always do,' he offered. 'I will do the dishes while you enjoy your digestion.'

"I sat. He poured a wasteful amount of detergent into the sink, released a roar of hot water to fill it with a mountain of overflowing suds, and threw in *all* the dishes, including chopsticks, iron pans, and knives! Then he announced, 'Now you leave them alone. In the morning they will be clean.' Off he went. I sat there contemplating. After a while, I couldn't stand it. I did the dishes."

I laughed.

"In little to big things, your children will differ from you," Mama continued. "However, you must stand firm in your beliefs, even when they have learned more about different subjects, acquire different skills, and converse more fluently than you. They cannot know more about people. You are fortunate that your children like you, your business, and your home. When each of my sons was fourteen, it seemed to be a signal for a separation of interests. Ming Tao is still active with our church—I saw him painting the walls not long ago. Your father would have been happy that this grandson continues to work for the Methodist Church. Children of the Wongs do not usually disgrace their name."

Indeed, Ming Tao was devoting most of that summer to the physical labor of packing and moving shop tools, lifting, loading, unloading, and putting things into place. He was taller than his father, and these two generations wordlessly mustered their maximum physical strength to adjust the final positioning of the heavy machines.

Activities were reaching a feverish pitch to meet a self-imposed deadline of August 20. It had been our pattern to travel as a family every two or three years. This year, before I knew about my surgery, we planned to fly to and drive in Canada for three weeks. Travel with children offers rich rewards but requires different planning. Accommodations with swimming pools in which to splash at end of a day's travel delighted them. Confirmed reservations were essential for six beds each night, six spaces in a plane, and an automobile large enough for fishing equipment and luggage. When we observed our children working their hands and hearts out, we could not cancel those reservations.

Mr. Jung, who operated a cleaning establishment next door and who loved flowers (how many cleaners raise orchids on their premises?), would water our garden. The post office would hold our mail. So on August 22, leaving envelopes scattered all over and feeling that it was madness to leave, we flew to Vancouver. If we did not carve out this vacation for ourselves, the time would be gone forever.

Because fishing was poor (Ming Choy was the only one who landed a cut-throat trout), the keeper of the Pine Bungalows at Jasper National Park made a gift of trout sufficient for our dinner, and later in Edmonton we celebrated our twenty-first anniversary together with Lai Wai's thirteenth birthday at our hotel—the Château Lacombe's revolving restaurant. The change of pace lifted our spirits; the children recovered from what Woody called "moving piecemeal."

This was fortunate, because the problems we discovered back home were totally unexpected. Waiting mail included a notice from the Board of Education that Ming Choy, who like his three older siblings had been going to school one block from home, would be bused to third grade more than a mile away. I accompanied him on the first day's ride and found that his new classmates would include six black girls, three Chinese boys, one Chinese girl, and two Caucasian girls; only fifty percent of those assigned to the class had shown up. The "rich cultural mix" vowed by busing proponents wasn't apparent. Furthermore, the school nestled by a freeway, had been an economic opportunity unit for poverty students, and was one block from a venereal disease clinic. Its windows were fixed translucent glass blocks, apparently to keep out freeway noise.

Our eight-year-old could not understand why being Chinese required him to transfer from our neighborhood school so that a child of another race could take his place. While visiting the assigned school, he had begun coughing in the schoolyard under the freeway fumes. His doctor advised reassignment to another location, since Ming Choy had a history of asthma attacks. I wrote to the Board of Education and to the superintendent of schools; neither replied.

In the meantime, the Chinese community, which lacked the organization, finances, or articulateness to protest effectively the busing of their children away from their Chinatown home base, established several "Freedom Schools" close to home. A modest tuition was charged. We enrolled Ming Choy pending action on my letters. The first day I watched him standing with most of his Chinese classmates in rooms not yet equipped with chairs or desks, since the hastily formed classes in the Seventh-Day Adventist Church were unprepared for the enormous response.

Another two months passed. Ming Choy liked his school, but he began to speak English with a Chinese accent. I appeared at the office of the San Francisco public school superintendent. The secretary was nonchalant. "We've misplaced most of the appeals. Start all over again and ask your doctor to write a letter directly to us."

Eventually, Ming Choy was reassigned to a school within walking distance eight blocks away. He had his first experiences in an integrated classroom: his lunches and pens were stolen, and he was mocked and hit by black boys. When he came home, he asked Woody to teach him how to fight.

Our hearts sank when we hurried to our new studio. The contractor who had promised that everything would be ready had taken on another job, and there had been little progress in our absence. Even concrete had not been poured at the doorways. Paint colors I had picked at his request were not even bought. July, August, and September went by without income. A completion date had not been stipulated because remodeling involved too many uncertainties. October found Woody and me unable to be idle; we were sanding and painting. Why are the building trades privileged to work or not to work, a unique code which allows them income from multiple sources while we who pay them delay our schedules helplessly? I do not begrudge their legitimate wages won and earned. I not wish them exploited, but I do not like to be exploited either. As Second Uncle's son-in-law says, "In the United States, income doesn't depend on scholarship. Calligraphy will not earn a person much respect. But if he can weld two pipes together, he will never starve. Brawn, not brains, commands power and money for the average American worker."

November went by. Gas essential for enameling and pottery kilns flowed when the lines were completed on December 29, far too late for Christmas orders. In January, coincidentally with my fiftieth birthday, I received unique gifts: a sink, hot water, and a new toilet. Phone calls, letters, even threats of lawsuits had been ineffective—only time drifted us into our turn to merit the contractors' attention at last.

Shojis salvaged from our old home were finally hung that

January, to screen work areas from public circulation. We had been betrayed not only in delays but in costs, for the lists of "extras" staggered us. I told Ming Tao, who was in his last year of high school, "What we have saved for your college education is now nailed to the walls."

But life did begin to look up. The remodeling was functionally effective and visually attractive, and the move has improved our life. Two blocks from home, it enables each of us to go to and fro independently, economically, and conveniently. Instead of rushing home at 3:00 P.M. to meet our youngest after school, he can come to us for help in homework—and as he grows older, to help us.

We had achieved the separation of home and work counseled to me as a bride, but enjoy the nearness which saves nerves and time. We hope for more red days than black, a few years of calm sailing with ourselves as ballast and our entertaining youth for crew, and no more troubles from under the bed.

PART III

CHINA TODAY

AN EXPLANATION

In pages following, "China" means the People's Republic of China, which finds the phrase "Mainland China" repugnant. Taiwan is designated by that name. When a Chinese speaks to another Chinese about the People's Republic, he often uses the idiom "The Great Continent." Today's national Chinese language is not known as Mandarin, an obsolete adjective, but as Putonghua (meaning "common language"). For Western readers, Putonghua will be referred to in this book as the "Peking dialect." "Hanyu pinyin," or Putonghua, translated by Chinese phonetic alphabet, is sometimes called the "Latin system." *

Thus, some Chinese proper names may appear in a number of English forms because of various phonic systems, and may not be standardized in the use of hyphens, upper case, or several words run into one word. This book uses the form normally familiar to Western readers.

* An excellent reference for Putonghua using the Latin system: C. C. Huang, *A Modern Chinese-English Dictionary for Students* (University of Kansas; published in Hong Kong by Standard Sing Tao Printers, 1968).

CHAPTER 21
THE LONG WAIT

My father had crossed the Pacific as a steerage passenger, one of five hundred bodies crowded into two tiers of berths in holds below the water line on the ship, each hundred men to one water closet. During the thirty-five long days and nights between Hong Kong and San Francisco, he could leave his two-foot-wide berth to promenade on the five feet of deck space allotted each passenger, which he did frequently to escape the dark, tedious, rolling, hot hold, noisy with the endless small gambling games of his fellow

Chinese. He had a great deal of time to think over the pain in his heart from his first disobedience to his beloved mother.

After her curse he had gone to see their village fortuneteller, hoping to find comfort from him. The fortuneteller had studied his features, and then the lines of his hands. He asked for the date and hour of his birth and, combining the data, had made this judgment: "I see that you will cross three bodies of water, each one greater than the one before. But you will never return across these waters."

Indeed, my father had first crossed the Pearl River tributaries as he traveled south from Fragrant Mountains to Macau. Next, he crossed the waters from Macau to Hong Kong. On the iron boat for his third crossing, he traveled across the largest body of water on earth, the Pacific. Whether his mother's curse and the fortuneteller's prediction were indeed clairvoyant or whether he was so intimidated by the memory of their words that he never let himself return to the land of his ancestors, my father never saw China again.

I suppose that in my several journeys by air across the Pacific, from San Francisco to Hong Kong and from there to Macau, I had symbolically retraced my father's sailings over two of the three waters he had crossed. During the 1956 tour for Mr. Kimura, we left our son with his amah in Hong Kong while we boarded the slow boat to Macau. Woody escorted our tourists and I took a taxi to visit Ninth Auntie, remembering her remark of three years ago, "The next time you come, I may be leaning on a cane!" I had deliberately not notified her, for fear a banquet might materialize.

I found Auntie without cane, and presented her with red packets of money from my parents and a shopping bag of Western goodies: biscuits, candies, nuts, and fruits. Ninth Auntie was surprised and yet not that surprised. She went downstairs to borrow a phone to find her oldest son. Her younger son was not in Macau, because he had gone to China. "Why?" I wondered. It had been reported that Chinese were trying to escape from Communist China, and to hear of her son's reverse direction struck me as extremely odd.

In the half shadow of her room, lit by daylight through a small upper window, the unsmiling tiny woman explained with a trace of bitterness, "We have no money for a college education in Hong

Kong. He wishes to be a medical doctor, a long and expensive training. But if he goes into China only as far as a couple of provinces away, he can acquire an excellent medical training without tuition fee."

"And after he completes his training?" I inquired.

In the same expressionless voice, Ninth Auntie replied, "He must practice where the People's Government assigns him."

As my eyes opened wide, I stifled the big question: Will we ever see him again? Instead, I said noncommittally, "He must have thought it over thoroughly before taking this step."

Auntie nodded dejectedly. "He had no future here. What could he do with 'freedom'? There he will learn what he has longed for, and he will be useful and wanted. We are permitted to correspond and to send him food parcels. Sometimes he must share these parcels, but we do have 'comings and goings.'"

On subsequent visits, I would knock on her door and call out "Jade Snow" when I heard her voice asking for identification. She would open the door with a simple remark, "I was thinking this was about the time of the year you would show up, if you were going to show up this year."

One such call had happily coincided with another guest: Second Auntie visiting from Fragrant Mountains, dressed in black cotton coat and pants just like Ninth Auntie. A shy, tiny, pretty widow who had been my widower uncle's second wife and had nursed him the rest of his elderly days, she was quietly happy to meet me, and told me that life in Communist China was no horror. There was no longer fear of bandits, and though rice was rationed, she had enough to eat.

How joyful it was, on another Macau visit in 1968, to find that my cousin, now a doctor, had returned from China to Macau where he had been born, to attend his ailing mother. Since she was an elderly widow, the Communist government had kindly permitted his exit to this city of origin, though he had to leave his wife and infant son in China, which was the land of their birth.

In June of 1971, despite my mother's anxiety and admonitions (since in San Francisco she is exposed to more conjectures than facts about China), it was natural that I should have no fear of applying to Ottawa's Chinese Embassy for permission to enter China. I drafted my letter to them just before the month of studio moving, unaware of impending surgery, for by then the first American visitors and other overseas Chinese from San Francisco had returned with enthusiastic reports about their excursions to China.

That winter, when news broke that Richard Nixon would be visiting Peking, we grew hopeful that our visas would be granted. Early in January when the end of the studio remodeling was in sight, we began to plan another leave from home and business. To bolster our shaky cash position, we took out maximum loans on our life insurance policies, and when these amounts were insufficient, the best of our Japanese art collection and my personal jewelry were offered to collector friends. Some bought from us; others extended loans.

We left the business in charge of a temporary employee, a young woman with excellent credentials. Eighteen-year-old Ming Tao was given power of attorney. He and his two sisters would take care of the shop after school each day. We were glad now that our move had brought our business close to home. Fourteen-year-old Lai Yee was to take charge of the cooking, and Ming Tao would help with the heavy shopping. Housework and nine-year-old Ming Choy were everyone's responsibility; but thirteen-year-old Lai Wai assumed the major share. All of them agreed to work—for the first time I heard their criticisms of past housekeepers' habits and cooking—they decided to be independent.

Visa requests to the People's Republic of China ask applicants to state their expected entry and exit points. Most visitors to China choose the convenient daily train that leaves the Kowloon station in Hong Kong, only a few blocks from the Hong Kong and Peninsula hotels, and arrives in Canton in less than three hours. But as if in an exorcism, I chose the inconvenient combination of bus and boat route out of Macau, which would cross the Pearl River tributaries five times (there are no bridges) and, in the course of an all-day journey, would pass through my father's ancestral village. Physically and symbolically, I should at last complete full circle the pilgrimage across that third water of the Pearl River, to carry my father's spirit back to Fragrant Mountains and break the curse of long ago and far away which had bound his bones to American soil.

Seventy years had intervened between my father's travels and my own quest. How unlike were our expectations and our directions, and how grateful I felt at the commencement of the trip, a feeling normally experienced upon returning home. We flew the Great Circle route, spanning the Pacific in only seventeen hours instead of Daddy's thirty-five rough days. To ease jet lag and be bright upon arrival in Macau, we made an overnight stay in Tokyo. The next day we landed in Hong Kong and went immediately to Macau by hydrofoil, a ride of an hour and fifteen minutes, to see Ninth Auntie, my cousin "brothers," and by now, also a "niece" and "nephew" born to the older of those brothers.

At 6:00 P.M. we alighted from the taxi and looked around to get our bearings. Their new address was down a small alleyway partly obscured by a stall selling knives. As if by appointment, an Italian motor scooter came up and its driver called, "Fifth Older Sister." The voice belonged to my doctor cousin. I rushed up and shook hands, an American mannerism effusive by Chinese standards.

He and I regarded each other. He had gained a little weight and looked confident. Woody yelled, "Get off the street before you're run over." Village passers-by and street vendors gaped at us in wonder. It was going to be the first of many stares before our travels ended. No matter how conservatively we dressed, our carriage, our coloring, our health, even our shoes shouted that we were not Asian-reared. Tin Wai steered his scooter into the alley, and we climbed five flights to the top floor, where his mother was cooking dinner, while the seven-year-old daughter and nine-year-old son of Tin Yow made a pretense at their homework. Auntie brought welcome tea. Tin Yow appeared, but his wife was visiting her family. Their home was now airy, well lit, and spacious. Tin Yow's family lived with Auntie in the flat, and Tin Wai's office-apartment was just below. Auntie, having gained weight, looked well and relaxed. We accepted her dinner invitation for the first time with the polite phrase, "Please do not dress a chicken or kill a duck."

Auntie's reply was equally polite, "There is no time to dress a chicken or kill a duck. I am only going to offer you salted fish and green vegetables with rice."

"But I know that the salt fish of Macau is famous," I accepted graciously. (Even now in San Francisco's Chinatown, fish and poultry dealers come from this area.)

What to drink? It was 82 degrees and over 70 percent humidity, though their high location with cross ventilation was not uncomfortable. Tin Yow offered beer from Tsingtao, a famous agricultural seaport area in China's Shantung Province.

"Salt fish" expanded into a lavish menu. Segments of barbecued goose appeared side by side with slices of barbecued pork, over which delicate plum sauce was poured. Oxtail-potato soup from Chinese cans was something new to me. Huge fried tropical pompano and rice steamed with New Year's pressed, salted duck and cured sausages crowded the table. There were fried pork chops too. When we protested the extravagant array of dishes, Older Brother waved his hands and said that it was no trouble; the barbecued items had come from a delicatessen. They always bought fresh food twice daily. Our reunion was a joyous excuse for permissive eating!

I looked around for old Auntie, for I was unhappy that she did not join us at table. Her sons explained, "Each of us must eat, then return to our work schedule, and the children are on school schedules, so she has gotten used to waiting on us. After we all leave, she enjoys herself at leisure, picking on what she likes."

Our dinner conversation in Macau in early March of 1972 was naturally centered on Nixon's visit to Peking the previous month. In the United States, I had been very moved when I observed the television close-up of Chou-En-Lai waiting, then shaking Nixon's hands upon the President's arrival at the Peking airport. An expectant hush during the waiting and the greeting was broken as the Chinese band played "The Star-Spangled Banner" before presenting the Chinese anthem. Like me, my cousins reacted to the Chinese courtesy in raising the American Stars and Stripes, colors of a nation which had been anything but friendly to them for more than twenty years. Chinese viewers who understood the English remarks (or heard them translated into Chinese) from on-the-spot commentators found American ignorance of Chinese customs and local facts deplorable, for they had indignantly denounced the coldness of the Chinese, apparently confusing restraint and dignity with indifference. They had been displeased that there had been no cheering, and that the Nixon motorcade did not cause any work stoppage on its way into Peking. My cousins asked, "How many American workers would stop for a Chou-En-Lai motorcade into Washington, D.C.?"

Days later, at the end of his China visit, one well-known commentator concluded on television again, "Well, one thing comes out of all this: the Chinese are individuals!" Reality had begun to collapse a hundred-year-old composite stereotype of a "typical Chinese" created by movie roles, fictional clichés, and advertising caricatures.

Of the various gifts we brought, what fascinated the nine-year-old boy most of all was a huge Sunkist orange which had found its way into my flight bag from the airplane. Dried fruits and chocolates were ignored, while he wheedled and nagged his grandmother into peeling the orange. Then, despite Woody's protest, he quickly swallowed the major portion as Ninth Auntie unprotestingly took the tiniest taste.

The hour passed too quickly, and we left when Tin Wai went down to his apartment to see waiting patients.

Since we planned to leave for China via Macau, we went the next day to the China Travel Service, branches of which processed all travel into the People's Republic. Our apprehension about meeting with representatives of the Chinese Communist government evaporated at once. Far from being tough, they were genial, courteous, approachable—even curious about our lives—and without bureaucratic airs. With Cantonese as our shared language we were mutually at ease. We filled out local visa applications in Chinese, produced pictures of our children born of our Chinese union, listing their Chinese names, and also furnished the Chinese names of our brothers and sisters, together with their addresses. In a review of our qualifications, we were interrogated for two and a half hours. I had to remember the years in which I attended every school and my age when I began working while studying. In what Chinese and American organizations was I active? That these included the Golden Gate Kindergarten Association (a natural affiliation, given my three oldest children's attendance) and the San Francisco Hearing and Speech Center (work with the deaf has been neglected in Chinatown, although the percentage of Chinese children suffering from hearing problems is higher than in other San Francisco ethnic groups) seemed to strike an immediate chord of approval; work with the helpless was also China's concern. That I was also on the Advisory Council for the Friends of the San Francisco Library did not strike any chord. Later I learned the reason.

We were asked to state our purposes in visiting China. I desired to explore the origins of her pottery tradition. It had not occurred to me to bring what the official asked for next, pictures of my work in ceramics, but I said that I could demonstrate in the field if given the opportunity. Not wanting to thrust ourselves upon Second Auntie as her guests, I had decided not to ask to visit her in Fragrant Mountains.

Woody was interrogated separately. (We had privately discussed the advisability of mentioning his brother Norman. Fearing rejection of our applications if Norman should prove to be in disfavor with China's government, we had nevertheless decided to mention him, for we had heard that China detested dishonesty.) When asked his reason for wishing to visit Peking, Woody boldly produced Norman's last letter, which listed his return address as the Peking University Physical Education Department. Our interviewer expressed interest but little surprise.

We were also asked what kind of travel arrangements we preferred. We said we wanted to travel independently, not with a group tour, to the usual places—Canton, Peking, Tientsin, Shanghai, Hangchow, Soochow—plus other unusual places of personal interest: the Ching-Te-Chen kilns in Kiangsi, and perhaps Sian to the north, site of recent excavations.

My impression was that China was very careful whom they admitted and that to ask to visit China was to ask to be welcomed as a houseguest. Any host wishes to know whom he is inviting, and where the visitor is going. We were told to wait ten days to two weeks for Peking approval of our applications.

We returned to Hong Kong to complete financial arrangements with the Bank of China. Introductions are invaluable, and the son of Seventh Auntie arranged to have us meet the manager of its small Western branch located in a wholesale produce area. Eleven workers clad in dark blue cotton Mao jackets and trousers were working away silently in a room with simple furnishings from China. The manager and assistant welcomed us with cigarettes and cups of tea, and while the letter of credit was being made up, there was easy talk in Chinese with no mention of politics. I had a feeling that it was their first experience with Chinese from the United States.

"Do not have any fears; do not have any 'guest air' [stand on formality]. You're going home. The people of China work with individual or group purpose, and have the confidence that *no visitor can take anything away from them.* Everyone will be anxious to help you instead, so much so that those who have the direct contact with you will be the envy of others who have not. Whatever you do not understand, ask frankly. The Chinese character hasn't changed—only the economy and social structure have."

I had already sensed this, and their concern began at once. I had a sore throat; immediately the assistant brought forth some blue pills for me to swallow with the tea, and sent a messenger to purchase additional pills for a cold. As we left, the Chinese equivalent words for "Thanks"—"I am not worthy of this service"—came automatically to my lips. They replied indignantly, "What kind of language is that? We do not know it."

Then our waiting began. We spent the first ten days in a prearranged quick swing through Southeast Asia, updating ourselves on the latest tourist facilities and improvements in Bangkok, Penang, and Singapore. Our return to Hong Kong coincided with the local version of Japan's "Golden Week" in May when three national holidays close most businesses. Here, we stayed commencing with Good Friday on March 31, to the holidays through Easter Sunday into the "Ching Ming" pilgrimages the following week. During this week it was impossible to get into restaurants between 12:00 and 2:00 P.M. or 7:00 to 9:00 P.M., but it was wonderful to see as many as four generations enjoying food together. Hong Kong's three million Chinese continued the national custom of including children in their celebrations.

Two weeks passed. There is only so much looking around at Hong Kong shops that one can do without visual indigestion, for a surplus of luxury goods faces one on every hand. We began to take walks instead of taxis, to wander into side streets instead of hurrying from one big store to another. We found we could no longer wander into lonely neighborhoods during the evening, though four years ago we had gone everywhere at any time feeling safe. Their newspapers vied with American ones in presenting horrible tales. Crime had increased 25 percent. Corruption everywhere undermined morale.

After exhausting Hong Kong's interests, we took the train for a round-trip excursion to the border town of Shensui and peered at tantalizing China beyond. Then we made a boat excursion to Lantau Island to visit its splendid Buddhist temple, but our enjoyment of these self-created adventures was marred by anxiety.

Stories of the Peking visit of the Prime Minister of Malta, of Chou-En-Lai's trip with him to Canton, of a group of American students coming out from China, of 20,000 visitors expected at the spring Canton Trade Fair, filled the press. So we said to ourselves, "Wait a few more days. Canton is overwhelmed by the volume of travelers." We decided that because of our request to follow our own timetable, our applications probably entailed special clearances. We were neither V.I.P., experts, nor grandparents visiting a native village.

For two people accustomed to the American tempo of getting things done, it was hard to cling to our courage and wait out our course. All that I knew of Zen, and the Chinese philosophy of seizing the moment and flavor of *now*, challenged my temperament. It might be un-American, but it was Chinese—why *not* wait? I remembered my mother's frequent admonition, "Believe in God, for the most difficult burden in retrospect will prove to have served a purpose for the best."

A few people in the travel trade knew of our waiting, and when Woody told one of them that he was 95 percent sure we would be admitted, he replied, "Ah, but there is always that five percent chance!"

So we concentrated on that Chinese art of waiting: patience. If one did not receive a negative reply, one could hope for a positive one. We had been told to be in our hotel room each day from 5:00 P.M. to 6:00 P.M. to hear from Macau. Each day we rushed back, jumping each time the phone rang, only to be disappointed. Like expecting a delayed airplane, we were poised in unbearable readiness. More days went as we fretted that our children were carrying unaccustomed loads, the business in San Francisco at a standstill.

After four weeks, we decided that our time was up, our hope for visas futile. Our air tickets would expire on May 16. This Saturday we would have a fun night for the first and last time at Gaddi's, and enjoy an elegant evening of dancing and dining until very late into Sunday morning when Hong Kong went into summer daylight saving time at 3:30 A.M. When I finally woke up the next morning, I said to Woody, "I'm not going anywhere; I'm going to write up my notes and start to pack."

It was then that the telephone rang! Our applications had been approved to travel without restriction in China for as long as we pleased. If we could reach Macau tomorrow, we could commence our journey toward Canton. Even as I was galvanized into action, one thought surfaced: "I have been preparing for tomorrow all my life!"

CHAPTER 22

CROSSING THE THIRD WATER

As I attended to practical preparations, sending some baggage home, storing parcels, buying films and cassettes, trying to wrestle with the logistics of what to bring without knowing where we were going or what conditions we would find, these activities persuaded me that it was true, I was going at last to China.

The average temperature was only 41 degrees in Peking, the newspapers informed us, but knowing that Canton, in the sub-tropical zone, would be our next stop after Macau, we needed clothing for warm weather too. On April 17 we arrived at the China Travel Service in Macau, where the girl receptionist knew all about us, asked for our U.S. passports and health inoculation cards, and dismissed us. I was puzzled. There was no paper work, no receipt issued, no travel costs requested. "What about money?" I asked. Woody was equally concerned. Money was always his responsibility when we traveled. The young lady said we could not take any Ren Men Bei (Chinese yuan or RMB) into China, but could convert our Bank of China letter of credit, Hong Kong currency, U.S. traveler's checks, or cash after our entry. We should get our luggage to their office, she said, for it would be traveling separately by truck, and we were to show up by eight o'clock the next morning for departure by bus.

We repacked three heavier bags (one suitcase of clothes for each of us, and one canvas bag stuffed with such extras as dry skim milk, orange juice crystals, instant coffee, and paper products) and kept with us in small manageable bags such necessities as reading matter, medicine, film, and cameras. The one item I had forgotten when I packed at home, and could have done something about in Hong Kong, was my binoculars. Upon calling again at China Travel Service, a tall, good-looking young man I shall call "Comrade A" * presented himself to us. He was dressed in a white shirt and dark trousers. He beamed, was talkative and reassuring, and introduced himself as a native of Macau, who naturally knew my cousin doctor. Therefore it seemed appropriate that he should ask us to a back sitting room for tea. His vocabulary indicated that he was well educated. Without beating around the bush he led our conversation into international politics. Since the China Travel Service was an office of the Chinese government, he spoke with authority. With bewildering and pleasant informality, for about forty minutes we learned some of their official policies.

"France and the United States are the only countries which have

Comrade

* "Comrade" in Chinese literally means "same aspiration."

not occupied Chinese territories, so we should be natural friends," Comrade A began. "But with the U.S. Seventh Fleet occupying waters around Taiwan, anything China may do to 'reclaim' Taiwan as her own land would automatically involve the United States and provoke international consequences. If the United States will withdraw her military intervention, then we can settle Taiwan within our Chinese family. Generalissimo Chiang has been assured by Chou-En-Lai that he can remain as Taiwan's governor without personal threat, but Chiang doesn't want to lose his present power."

I must have looked at him incredulously, for he certainly did not fit any idea I might have had about an official Chinese Communist. He asked me about life in San Francisco, and expressed sympathy that my parents had to emigrate so far from home to seek a better living. "Naturally they had to escape the old landlords' regime which squeezed the people mercilessly, and the bandits who stole what little else they had left," he commented. "Even after the Nationalists fled, the bandits were still active."

We discussed Vietnam. Comrade A said, "That is another question." (To label a matter a "question" is a polite Chinese understatement for a very serious problem.) "But the 'questions' of Taiwan and Vietnam are the responsibility of the U.S. government. China recognizes that the American people are friends."

When we strolled out into the office reception room we were astonished by the feverish activity and the mountain of luggage which had arrived for handling during our brief absence. We were not the only ones leaving the next day for China, and the other Chinese, who for the most part were planning to visit home villages, were loaded with gifts for relatives. Most of their personal belongings were packed into huge blue and white striped duffle bags closed with metal rings, and then placed into locked net bags for security. (Local Chinese residents cannot bring gifts into China—only overseas visitors.) Flat, circular-shaped, sewn burlap sacks contained unassembled bicycles, and other square canvas-wrapped bundles held unassembled sewing machines. There was a surprising number of bright red, blue, or green plastic articles, such as pails and pans for household use. I found later that plastic articles are not plentiful in China.

No wonder that when the receptionist had looked at our three suitcases, she asked if we were planning more purchases. I hadn't understood. "Am I to bring our own bedding and towels?" She smiled sweetly and answered, "No." We realized why the Travel Service had requested early delivery of baggage, for it was now stacked up to the ceiling. Our lonely bags had also been secured within net bags, and were perched precariously on top of the pile. "They're not crushed," I commented. Woody's satisfaction was different: "The better to start us off first."

When we were given receipts to claim our luggage at the truck terminal in Canton, we asked to arrange transportation by private car, so that we could have the driver detour off of the main highway and take us through my parents' village, but no such car was available. Sixty or more persons were expected to leave in the morning on conventional buses; we would share a nearly new Mercedes (called "Benzie") minibus with a few other passengers. A huge red poster above us proclaimed in English, "The United States Is Imperialistic! Down with Aggressors and Running Dogs!" while the staff continued to regard us with smiles.

Only a few details remained after our check-in. We invited the Wong family to lunch at the new, gigantic (for Macau) Lisboa Hotel. It delighted the two children to be excused from school, but "Please," they implored us, "no Western food." Afterward, Woody and I recorded a last cassette to send home to our children, informing them that no mail could be forwarded to China since our itinerary was unknown, but in an emergency a cable to my cousin would reach us through the China Travel Service. "Keep writing once a week and send the letters to the Peninsula Hotel in Hong Kong, where they will be held for our return. That has to be within a month because our air tickets will expire." We promised to return by end of May, in time for Ming Tao's graduation from Lick High School, and Lai Yee's from Marina Junior High, and for Ming Choy's and Woody's birthdays the first part of June. I tried not to worry about home. While I had no doubt that our children would survive physically, I worried about their getting along with one another without an adult in command.

That night in Macau, the Wong family gave us a gala bon-voyage dinner. Remembering our disappointment years ago at the undernourished squabs of Macau, my cousin doctor provided a memorable feast, catered by the famous Smiling Buddha Restaurant, whose cook and owner was one of his grateful patients. Now that Macau's economy had improved because of the huge influx of Japanese gambling tourists, the squabs were well fed.

We had been invited by Comrade A to see a movie that evening, so after dinner we were driven by our cousin to the China Travel Service. We climbed four flights of stairs past floors of simple rooms that housed overseas Chinese leaving for China the next morning. In the fifth-floor auditorium, Comrade A quickly gestured us to rear seats on one side. "You will see better," he explained. The room began filling up with other Chinese, but only we seemed to be Americanized.

Woody whispered, "Look what's on the wall beside us." It was a picture of smiling, benevolent-looking Chairman Mao. "I think it might be the place of honor," he added. Comrade A translated the movie commentary from the Peking dialect.

The first film showed acupuncture techniques perfected by doctors working on themselves, who injected the needles into the outer calf, wrist or ears, and twirled them to induce anesthesia. In rapid succession, we saw a gallstone removed, lung tissue cut out, an appendix operation, a tooth pulled. Clamps were everywhere, but we saw little bleeding. Patients were eating during the operation or immediately afterward. Western observers in the operating room were also filmed.

Comrade A told us, "The Soviets refused to ship us color film, so we Chinese are now producing our own."

The second film began with the command by Mao Tse-tung that the "blood-sucking parasite" be eradicated, for by attacking mammals, it had made ghost farms of hundreds of acres of land in Chekiang Province. There had been no cure for the disease in a land where the value of human life counted for nothing, where practical scientific research had been precluded. The afflicted community conducted a massive campaign to cover with fill the canals contaminated with the giant water snails, host carrier of the schistosomiasis parasite, and to educate farmers to wear rubber boots when tilling the soil and planting rice, because the parasite burrowed through bare feet. Mutual cooperation would have been unthinkable in the old days, when a farmer with a tiny plot would divert his neighbor's water for his own use.

On the following morning as we were boarding the "Benzie"

at eight o'clock, the driver told us to take the two front seats beside him. A big crowd was moving toward the large buses. Many of them looked sickly, and we learned that they were seeking medical aid in China. The Macau-China border guards who begin their activities at 8:00 A.M. obviously were familiar with the vehicles and drivers, for Chinese trucks moved freely in and out. It was hard to believe that as our driver handed over a batch of papers, we could immediately proceed through those forbidden gates, because just eight or ten years ago I had come with a group of tour members and had stopped to stare longingly through these same gates. At that time, a Chinese truck had approached from the "Red Flag" side, loaded with huge baskets of foot-long Chinese stringless green beans, and as it drove past us we had been startled to see the custodian of those beans turn to raise his fist and shake it at us angrily.

This morning we entered Chinese territory uneventfully. Two young Chinese soldier guards checked travel papers and "needle certificates" (yellow international inoculation records). Minutes later, our Benzie and the other buses reached Kung-Pei, the border town where Chinese customs and immigration officers checked incoming and outgoing traffic. Even in this short distance we noticed a different look in the pastoral scenery. Bent figures, working in unusually long rows of twenty-four to thirty, testified to communal effort. Water buffaloes were in evidence. The houses had thatched roofs not so thick as those in Japan. Perhaps in this mild climate a thick roof was unnecessary.

Disembarking at the border town, we entered a very large waiting room with tables around its perimeter, possibly arranged for luggage inspection. Three large red posters with calligraphy decorated the walls. We were seated under the one expressing anti-U.S. slogans (was it so that we wouldn't see it behind us?). As I copied the political messages on the other two, I had to refer to my Chinese-English dictionary. (The present regime has radically simplified old Chinese ideographs, which have remained remarkably unchanged for thousands of years. Those of us educated elsewhere cannot always recognize the new "shorthand" words.) An Army guard came over, dressed like the border sentinels: khaki trousers, coat and cap, with a red star in front of his cap, and two red velvet rectangular patches on his stand-up collar tips.

He spoke Peking dialect, but Woody and I had taken enough private lessons in San Francisco to understand him. When I explained my perplexity, he admitted that he too sometimes had trouble with the abbreviations, but this form would be easier for a new generation to learn. When tea was brought in, we noticed another change in tradition. The blue design on white porcelain with the translucent white rice pattern was classical, but now the tiny delicate cups had handles.

Our buses returned to Macau for a second load of passengers. Woody and I were requested to follow a young girl, dressed in a similar Army khaki uniform, with two pigtails peeping below her cap. While the rest of our party remained in the big room to listen to a woman lecturing over a loudspeaker, we entered a small parlor, sparingly furnished with a comfortable davenport and a goldleaf-covered bust of Mao Tse-tung flanked by two gorgeous carved ebony stands supporting pots of flowers. We were asked politely if we wished the floor fan to be turned on in this open pavilion, for it was about 75 degrees. We were given forms in Chinese that asked us for lists of the currencies, precious metals, cameras, and watches that we carried. Since I had left all my jewelry in Hong Kong, I had only my watch and wedding ring to report. The customs inspector, another young Army man, paid no attention to pens or paperbacks, but my cassette recorder fascinated him, as did magazines and hardbound books, which were examined carefully and released. He returned to the recorder. Was it a radio receiver too? No, I told him. Switch it on and show him, I was asked. As it happened, my commentary was on the varieties of fish I had seen that morning when our minibus had passed the market at the wharf, for Ming Choy is an avid fish buff. I showed the inspector pictures of my children, for whom I was recording my impressions of China. He counted the number of tapes I had brought, and asked us to add them onto our declaration.

The Army girl returned with our travel papers. She seemed surprised that the inspector was not through, and when he talked to her in Peking dialect about the problem of the cassette recorder, she fastened him down with a stare of steel. "What is your decision?"

"Well," he capitulated, "It's all right, but like the films for their two cameras, they must bring out with them the same number they are bringing in. The films will have to be developed for review before departure."

Our baggage was then taken away, and Woody was told to change his Hong Kong dollars into Chinese currency: RMB (yuan) 2.25 to U.S. $1.00.

The Army girl processed immigration formalities. Extra passport photos had been attached to our travel permits, which she pointed out were good for six months extendible to a year, but limited to one entry. (This news was excruciating. How hard we had tried to get into China, how much we wished to see, and now we couldn't fully use the generous time allowance!) At each hotel stop, we were to obtain validating arrival and exit stamps on our permits, which included the destination "Peking." There the China Travel Service would authorize subsequent cities which we could visit. Later, I learned how valuable the two words "Bei-Jing" * were, for most visitors to Canton—for instance, those attending the Trade Fair—were not permitted to travel there.

These procedures had taken us two hours, but the other travelers were not yet finished. Uncertain about the day's provisions, we had left the Lisboa Hotel with sandwiches and two bottles filled with clean water, for who could have eaten a breakfast at 6:45 A.M. on the way to China? It was only nine o'clock by China's standard time when we were escorted to a large airy dining hall facing a courtyard. The hall was empty, but a group of workers were in the courtyard, peeling a mountain of fresh shrimps. The kitchen is a domain in which I have special interest, but when I asked an attendant if I could see it I was told unceremoniously, "Why? There is a garden across the street." She waved us to a table placed, as one might guess, right in front of Chairman Mao's portrait.

Though we had been unprepared for lunch at this hour, we were served large portions of a suggested menu, including piles of noodles with thin slices of pork and vegetables, and another dish of chicken sautéed with greens, all fresh and delicious. What was

* Chinese phonetic pronunciation.

left was carefully returned to the kitchen. We should have known better than to bring sandwiches to a culture whose equivalent for "How are you?" is "Have you eaten?"

As we were finishing our meal, the rest of the mob entered. Huge pots of steaming rice were placed on central service tables from which any person could help himself to as many bowls as desired, a custom we observed time and again throughout China. Attendants also brought chicken, prawns, meatballs, and soups to satisfy hearty appetites. Then we returned to the front seats of a fresh Benzie, with only 5,215 kilometers on its odometer. As we continued on the road to Canton, the driver turned his radio up to a screeching volume. The program described the terrible U.S. bombings of North Vietnam's helpless people. "The United States is anxious to be aggressors," said the commentary.

Above the din, the driver was an enthusiastic guide. Every worker gets one day off a week by rotation, he informed us, so that no business shuts down, and shops escape mobs. Rest periods are provided daily from 12:00 to 2:30 P.M. (I would like that.) Even the Canton Fair is closed during those hours. There was almost no other traffic on four wheels, a very few motorcycles, and some bicycles moving with us on the dirt-and-sand road, which was rated "sixth class," but was excellently maintained.

Green blades of rice were already six inches high in the fields, never possible "Before Liberation" until the summer monsoon. Now they were irrigated by pumps. Smokestacks and kilns showed that each commune was trying to be self-sufficient by firing its own building materials. For two and a half hours we drove through roads bordered on both sides with tall, fast-growing ironwood trees, and next to them glistened a never-ending network of canals which provided irrigation, fish-raising ponds, and transportation. If possible, the green vistas we passed were cleaner than Japan. There were even old ladies to spear fallen leaves. After we passed those rice paddies, the country changed as we approached my father's village. The ground was more rocky, and there were hilly contours. Here pine, palm, bananas, and bamboo had been planted for craft materials and for food. Here also were characteristic old Chinese gravesites, horseshoe shaped like half-retaining walls against the mountainside. I recalled my father's bedside pictures and my mother's lamentation when she heard about old graves being dug up and human bones used for fertilizer. She said that it was just as well my father had not lived to know about this disaster under the Communists. To the driver, I remarked on the many graves which were intact.

"Naturally, if a gravesite were in the middle of a field, it was moved after public notice," he explained, "but if the land isn't required, there is no reason to destroy graves." By the look of the monuments deteriorating in humid climate, I suddenly understood my father's mania for annual attention to grave maintenance.

Farther along our route were mulberry plants, a sure indication of silkworm culture. The driver told us that the mulberry fed the silkworm and fish ate the worm manure, completing an ecological cycle for the farmer who ate the fish. "Nothing is wasted in today's China," he impressed upon us. "The processing of sugar cane yields sugar, paper pulp, cloth fiber, shredded filler, coal, briquets, and finally, even the smoke from the briquets is diverted for heat." I also learned that the pagodas rising in the distant mountains, often associated with pictures of China, had been erected in olden days to satisfy the superstitious, as watchtowers for *fung-sui* (wind and water, natural elements also related to astrology and prophecy).

We arrived at the first of the crossings over the tributaries of the mighty Pearl River, which drains 420,000 square kilometers in China and a small basin of North Vietnam. As we waited for the barge to come from the other side, we got out of the minibus to stretch our legs. Women and children were selling hard-boiled eggs and tea for hungry travelers. A cluster of children gathered around to stare in amazement when Woody struck a match to light a cigarette. He gave his matchbook to one of them, and there was a scramble. I was sorry that all my candy supply had gone into that duffle bag of "unnecessaries," on its separate way by truck.

The barge was moored, and our full minibus drove onto the deck. It was a gorgeous sunshiny day, in the humid eighties, but I scarcely noticed that I was sticky or windblown, for I was elated by a soaring joy for myself and the memory of my father, of having crossed his "Third Water," that branch of the Pearl River which formed the boundary of Fragrant Mountains, now known as "Chung-Shan" (Central Mountain District).

Among the rows of houses we passed were occasional taller, architecturally handsome, three-story buildings. The driver told us they were built many years ago by retired overseas Chinese who returned after making money abroad. I wondered which among them might once have been the site of my ancestral stamping ground, or Second Uncle's home, or where Grandfather Wong's house had stood. For so many years, my mental map of Fragrant Mountains had been determined by those four sketches of Wong grave locations. I wondered beyond which rice fields I might be passing "Three-Cornered Pond" or "Large Golden Pagoda."

The driver pointed out a distant blue-tiled gateway. "That is Chung-Shan High School, famous for the high caliber of students it graduates. Sun Yat Sun went to school there. It is not far from his home." I could see the steps leading to the school buildings. No wonder my father had been Dr. Sun's sympathetic supporter. Their origins were the same in place and time.

After another half-hour, the driver announced that he would detour the Benzie in order to drive through the business section of my father's hometown. The ten-minute diversion took us through a district where buildings looked very old. Under old-fashioned veranda overhangs were stores selling cloth, food, herbs, fruits. They were dimly lit, as were most other stores and hotels in China, to save electricity. On this narrow street, ours was the only motor vehicle, but bicycles four to six abreast came toward us from the other direction. Our driver kept his hand on the horn defensively. Gesturing at the bicycles, he told us that the town was well known for its prosperity, for there were always more bicycles than pedestrians, and even the farmers used them to go to their fields.

It was not until we reached Cheung-Chow, the village across still another Pearl River tributary now spanned by a bridge connecting for the first time two towns on opposite sides of the river,*

* It is said that the people even spoke two different dialects because of the historical water separation.

and I learned that the local shipyard employed ten thousand persons, that I suddenly realized Fragrant Mountains, unlike my mental image, was no small village. The area ranked in population with Macau and Hong Kong. If it had indeed been small, perhaps my father and others like him and Dr. Sun would not have received the stimuli they did. News of revolt against foreign domination and domestic corruption and the seeds of discontent would not have reached a remote village so quickly, nor could its residents have sought such ready escape. But young people living at such a populated crossroads, hearing and seeing much—for instance, the first of those grand homes built by the returning newly rich compatriots from the United States—might well have been spurred to leave in order to better themselves. It was an illuminating lesson in geography.

With the fingers of water flowing at their doorstep, leading to the South China Sea, it was also easy for them to move north to Canton, one of only three ports which China had licensed for foreign ships. Some of the ships crossed the Pacific to the nearest American port of San Francisco, discharging both cargo and immigrants from Canton. Whether from Hong Kong or Canton, it was no wonder that California's history of Chinese immigration had been entirely Cantonese. Chinese immigrants to other countries—the Amoys to Malaysia, Fukienese to the Philippines—reflected other geographical factors, other periods of group migrations.

On a subsequent ferry crossing, we stood near the pilot cabin on the barge. A crew member came over, opened a box, took out a bull horn, and blared dutifully without emotion, "Down with U.S. schemes of invasion and down with their running dogs!" Then he put the bull horn away. Woody and I stared ahead as if we had heard nothing, but we dared not get our camera out of the bus for the balance of the ride, for none of our other Chinese traveling companions had cameras and we did not want to call attention to ourselves.

CHAPTER 23
CANTON

The ride was strenuous. Before we reached Canton a flat tire delayed us further, so that our journey stretched into eight hours. Even though we were dusty, hot, and exhausted, our joy and excitement carried us along euphorically until we arrived at the Overseas Chinese Hotel in Canton. The city was simply bursting with five thousand visitors to the just-opened Spring Fair. Woody and I lined up with the horde of new arrivals, so that we could register and turn in our travel documents for entry stamps. Since

"Mr." in Chinese is unisex (and often omitted), I signed "Mr. Jade Snow Wong." Woody filled in his form. The desk man looked at him and asked, "Sharing the same room?" We answered, "Yes."

He stared at us coldly. "What relation are you to each other?"

I was suddenly panic-stricken. Should I have brought our marriage certificate?

Our Benzie driver-friend had been observing on the fringe, and now he proclaimed, "Husband and wife!" to save the day. We were issued a key to our sixth-floor accommodation. When we opened the door to a two-room suite, my euphoria met indifferent reality.

The double bed was furnished with only a bottom sheet and a top quilt, and I groaned at the sight of a dusty white mosquito net hanging above. The cracked toilet looked unwashed and leaked noisily through the floor drain. I scrubbed the tub with a loofah sponge, but the stains would not come out. Woody got me a large chipped enamel basin, and I used it to improvise a shower of rinse water as I stood in the tub.

While this ritual was in progress, there was an insistent rapping at the door. Partially dry, I found my travel robe and opened the sitting room door to find a reception committee of three comrades, two women and a man, who had called to bid me welcome. They were smiling, shy, asked to come in, and forthrightly asked me what I was writing.

"I arrived only two hours ago, and I do not travel with preconceived ideas," I protested. "But I believe that a Chinese is going to see China differently from a non-Chinese. Have you suggestions as to what I should see?"

These visitors were now joined by an older man with greater authority, and I shall call him Comrade B. He made the standard suggestions: factories and acupuncture anesthesia. I firmly rejected them. I said I had enough personal experience of surgery and that it horrified me. Besides, I had seen the movie at the China Travel Service in Macau. As for factories, so many Western journalists had documented them that they did not need an overseas interpretation.

"What about the arts? That's my specialty." I gave them Chinese notes on special categories of wares produced at great kiln sites, around which they could plan an itinerary. In the meantime, we could visit the Canton Trade Fair and Fatshan (also known as Shekwaun), a famous local Cantonese kiln. Then they should get us to Peking as fast as possible.

In the hotel dining room, an oilcloth-covered table had been reserved with our room number. Our sweet waitress knew all about local foods and couldn't have been nicer. Our appetites were her serious concern. What did we feel like enjoying? Sautéed foods? Soup? After a discussion we had all the confidence that no matter what the conditions were in Room 630 upstairs, we would be served fine specialties in the celebrated Canton tradition. Soup was steamed duck with black mushrooms, pure flavors without herbs. Chicken came, with its skin fried to golden crackling crispness, surrounded by a white ruffle of shrimp chips. Plump straw mushrooms were in season, and they came alone, dressed in a rich brown oyster sauce. Two bottles of beer quenched our dusty thirst.

The waitress was delighted with the success of her suggestions. While we couldn't think of more food, she assured us tomorrow would come. In the morning breakfast was served from 6:30 to 8:00, including "Dim sum" (steamed tiny meat- or vegetable-stuffed pastries or buns, much like hot hors d'oeuvre) and rice soup, or "congee." From 9:00 to 11:00 A.M. was snack time, when noodles and wonton were available. Lunch, between 11:30 A.M. and 2:00 P.M., offered rice and various meats, vegetables, and fish dishes. Tea time from 3:00 to 5:00 P.M. featured Western pastries, ice cream, and soda fountain specials. Five thirty to 7:30 P.M. were dinner hours, with full course and à la carte offerings. And last came another snack time between 8:00 and 10:00 P.M. The government, which owns the dining facilities, provides generously for its visitors at prices they can enjoy. Two bowls of rice cost RB .06 (or less than three U.S. cents).

We perceived one reason for slowness in processing our visas. The hotels in Canton were jammed. The newer "Twenty-Seven Stories" opposite our Overseas Chinese Hotel was reserved for the Japanese, while the Friendship Hotel less than a mile away was reserved for Westerners. This segregation facilitated orderly services.

Every night, with cooling breezes and the close of work, local residents came to the huge grass oval in front of our hotel for diversion, to sit and watch a new era of visitors arrive and depart from the two Trade Fair buildings just across the grass oval from the two hotels. Spectators were so numerous that we could scarcely plow through the crowds, and they stared just as hard at Woody and me as they did at the foreign visitors. And I, of course, was equally curious about my first exposure to hordes of Chinese citizens. It is not true that men and women dress identically in China. It is true that women wear no makeup, and their outfits include a buttoned jacket and loose-fitting pants, normally of blue or gray cotton twill. But the collars on the women's coats are pointed Western shirt style, whereas the men's are the Mao Chinese stand-up type. Often the men wear dark blue. Higher-ranking older men wear better tailored clothing. In Canton, where the weather was warm and women did not require an outer jacket, they would wear simple white or printed cotton shirts or tops. To them, Woody in pants was not so conspicuous as I appeared, in a skirt and nylons. Moreover, the vast number of foreigners attending the fair were men, while those few Chinese women who were accredited to the fair looked similar to the local citizens. Each accredited buyer was identified with colored satin ribbons and badges.

Without these, Woody and I could not attend the fair. It was irrelevant how much cash we had; we did not have permission. Neither did we have permission to look into that other "Twenty-Seven Story Hotel," about which we were naturally curious. The guards at each hotel recognized their own guests, and no one else could enter. I asked Woody, the ex-Army man, if the long-barreled gun and bayonet held by each hotel guard were real. He answered, "If not, I'll bet it can still go through your stomach!"

We were finding the same restrictions to which the correspondents who had visited Peking with Nixon had objected. But I could see that from the Chinese point of view, in a country which had been through such wild disorder (the very oval where we were located was once the evil waterfront where unsuspecting Cantonese drunkards had been "Shanghaied" onto foreign ships), separation, procedures, and control were sensible. I was to learn over and over again that their government knew exactly where each person was, citizen or visitor, just as my parents used to know exactly where I was. One cannot be responsible for a guest's or child's well-being without knowing his whereabouts.

Comrade B contacted Trade Fair officials and obtained two visitors' passes with specific hours for our use the next day. We visited the Handicraft and Art Display Building in the morning and the Heavy Industries in the afternoon. Since it was five days after the fair had opened, activities were at their height. The entrance hall of the Handicraft Building displayed a huge slogan (conveniently in both English and Chinese for the benefit of foreign visitors): "Let a Hundred Flowers Blossom. Weed through the Old to Let the New Emerge." Antiques and jades (at very high prices) displayed fine workmanship, but the contemporary materials were of lower quality. We worked our way through each of five floors. Samples were in display cases, and behind them were discussion rooms, where interpreters, tea, tables, and chairs were on hand for negotiations. What a contrast to the pace of those semiannual wholesale gift shows I attended on the run in San Francisco! I would rush up to a display salesman, go rapidly down the line while he wrote the numbers of the items I wanted, sign his list, and leave! The buyers at this fair had to talk things over, go back to their hotel, think things over, return, and add to or subtract from their order. Some carried electronic calculators. Some spent the whole month of the fair negotiating. We heard that the Japanese buyers of art were the least particular. They would walk into a display and announce, "I'll take this whole roomful of furniture and accessories." It would disappoint the Chinese host to lose his exhibit so unceremoniously, but we noticed that more merchandise replacements were ready in the wings.

Most of the porcelain display was Western-style dinner ware, and only a small percentage traditional Chinese table settings. Within this group, the pattern was predominantly willow ware or the translucent rice pattern, both blue and white. I did not see those soft pastel porcelains with yellow and turquoise overglazes which so many Americans long to buy again.

The paintings and crafts were even more disappointing. Possibly produced in quantity for underdeveloped countries eager for "Chinese art," I presume they were planned to attract exchange rather than be applauded for taste. A shoulder-high vase appliquéd with kappa shells, superimposed with orange-dyed shell goldfish, is a specialized kind of craftsmanship, but not art.

In the afternoon, we went to the larger exhibition hall. The slogan here was: "If all nations cooperate, there will be victory for all." Gigantic slogans in red constitute the major decorative theme in buildings and outdoor spaces. They are dramatic media to rally the thoughts of people who may not be fully literate, and who are constantly reminded of the government's goals. We moved on to a rapid tour of such items as heavy machinery and medical equipment.

I was so depressed by the hotel when I first arrived in Canton that I had wished to get out as soon as possible. This decision had to be changed when cloudy skies grounded planes to Peking (instrument flight and landings were not used then). The only alternative to a four-hour flight was thirty-six hours by train, so Woody and I agreed to explore Canton further.

The next evening, Comrade B arranged reservations and car transportation to the Nam Yuen garden restaurant, 15 minutes away. What was once a thatched hut by a pond with an island in the middle had been reconstructed by the Communists into a series of dining rooms and pavilions, decorative courtyards and rock gardens. We arrived at 7:00 P.M., that lovely time of dusk when daylight lingers into evening. First we passed through a huge dining hall crowded with hundreds of men bare-chested or clad in undershirts. They sat in groups at round tables, consumed their food with relish, and tossed the bones to the floor as they ate. We crossed a bridge facing a waterfall and entered a courtyard sheltered by a huge banyan tree, under which at least another two hundred persons must have been seated at dozens of tables.

Surrounding the courtyard was a six-sided building. We could see diners through the wide-open windows of the rooms. Beyond, another small bridge led to a floating barge on the lake. Within the charming dining area of this barge, like a giant gazebo in bamboo pattern, Western visitors were accommodated. In a matter-of-fact way, segregation was again in order.

A table for two awaited us on a small, out-of-the way private balcony overlooking the lake, between the "better" Chinese section under the banyan and the foreigners on the barge, and perhaps this physical location indicated our status between those two worlds. Our fine white tablecloth was beautifully embroidered in multicolored clusters of tiny silken flowers. Matching cloth napkins, cut-glass stemmed liqueur glasses, and silver chopstick rests were other pretty touches which surprised us. Woody called for a "Mao Tai," which he had wanted to try since that potent colorless liqueur was publicized during President Nixon's visit. It was RMB 1.00 (40 cents U.S.) per glass. One sip was enough for me.

Dinner represented the best in Cantonese cuisine specially cooked for two. Fresh, just-in-season tiny points of bamboo (dug up like white asparagus) were sautéed with tiny frogs' legs. I thought of Ming Choy, who inherited his grandfather's passion for frogs' legs. Fillet of chicken was toss-fried with green vegetables. A light soup came, floating slices of fresh-water pike with broccoli tips. A dish of hot, fresh mushrooms was followed by fried rice. Something new was ground shrimp, deep-fried, presented in small almond shapes. We had an enchanting dinner hour, watching the fireflies, hearing the frogs, being alone again, and not able to do justice to all the food. A car was already waiting to bring us back. Woody said, "All our movements are accounted for." But it wasn't hard to accept their care. It was pointless to complain about supervision when we didn't know where to go or how to get there. We didn't know Canton; we didn't know China; how much could we manage on our own?

And so the next day we willingly followed the program arranged by Comrade B in lieu of factories and acupuncture. By minibus, we were conveyed to a former temple, followed by a tour to the present Chung-Shan University, renamed to honor Dr. Sun's birthplace (formerly Ling Nan, where Norman had gone to study).

The Temple of Six Banyans, more than a thousand years old, was named after the trees in its courtyard. Su Tung Po, the famous Sung poet, had been demoted and exiled to Canton, and this temple had been his refuge. Members of a Cultural Protection branch of the government, a committee of pretty young girls, led us up the hexagonal pagoda. Once there had been eighty-eight Buddhas placed in fourteen stories of this pagoda, but they are now gone. At the top of the tower we had a magnificent view of Canton, which is mostly flat land. We saw the gorgeous blue-tiled architecture of the Memorial Assembly Hall named after Dr. Sun, and outlines of twin spires of a once-great Western cathedral. I asked, "What are the cathedrals used for?" The girls replied, "Warehouses. People no longer indulge in religion but work for the good of the country." I asked, "Does anyone come here to worship?" "No, priests are now working in factories for the good of the country."

After we descended, we were led to a large altar niche, lit naturally, gently, and artistically by a clerestory window. On one of the most magnificent giant rosewood altar tables I have ever seen a great bronze Buddha looked down in benevolence. It was cast in hollow bronze and weighed about 1500 pounds. Unlike most other Buddhas I have seen, it looked human rather than stereotyped, with very fine details in the robe and ornaments. Also unlike most other Buddhas with the myriad of bumps on top of the heads (variously explained as either curls of hair or snails which had climbed up to shade the head of Buddha meditating under merciless sun), this one was bald. The girl custodians said that it was more than nine hundred years old. I asked why this image was bald, and they answered that his hair was supposed to have been burned off, as the devout did not feel pain.

As we left the tranquil shelter of the temple, noticing the handsome, simple grillwork of its tall exterior bronze gates, I compared this experience with countless other Buddhist temples I had visited from Japan to India. Many of them were elaborate centers teeming with visitors, and many were big business, generously supported by the devout who donated a substantial percentage of their wages, in the hope of eternal salvation. I remembered the silver sanctuary in the Phnom Penh Palace, the Reverend Kobori's temple in Kyoto, the Bien Hao temple in Saigon; each of them a different approach to Buddhism. Now here was a beautiful temple, a cultural relic where no one worshiped, in China where Buddhism had once been the source of inspiration.

After this exposure to revolutionary change in religion, we observed revolutionary change in education at Chung-Shan University. With us were an overseas Chinese Ling Nan alumnus from Florida and a Chinese IBM computer engineer and his wife from San Jose, California. Though these three, like ourselves, were residents of the United States, they had been born or educated in China. A staff executive and four professors welcomed us in a pleasant reception parlor, where we sat on easy chairs, with natural light from windows and French doors framed by pale green silk curtains.

An introductory talk by the college spokesman summarized changes made by the Cultural Revolution. "Even after the Communist Liberation of 1949, the students were lazy, privileged children of capitalists. They studied old history and other theories. Now Ling Nan has been reorganized with other schools into a group called the Chung-Shan University, with stress on the practical application of theory. If a farmer knows something of value, he is invited to lecture."

The student body now numbered five hundred, but eight hundred more were being selected from other parts of China, the government paying full costs. All graduates must make a contribution to society; their students, for example, had already worked out a new way to make hydroelectric power from small resources.

The visiting Florida alumnus spoke out, "I studied botany, but I couldn't grow a plant. I knew higher mathematics but couldn't add up the price of a dinner."

The San Jose engineer was asked for his impression. He remembered the suffering before Liberation in Hunan Province, where he was born, and was proud of the accomplishments he was seeing on this trip.

The alumnus added, "I had heard Sun Yat Sen speak at assembly here. I will always remember that he said, 'Let us not think of being great men; let us think of doing great things.'" Renaming the university complex after Dr. Sun's birthplace commemorated his part in initiating the revolution that has culminated in the People's Republic of China today.

The executive chairman asked Woody and me for our reactions. Woody underscored the San Jose engineer. Though he had not been born in China, he had seen the terrible conditions during World War II when he had fought with the U.S. Army in Kunming. As for me, I had not even been in China. "In China, where for centuries scholarly Asians have scorned to use their hands, this dichotomy is eliminated for your citizens who are developing new skills." I told a little of myself, and that ridicule expressed by the Chinese community, even within my own family, when I, a college graduate, started dirtying my hands publicly. "Perhaps in my way, I was a revolutionary," I said with a smile. The university personnel nodded agreeably.

We walked around the spacious, tree-studded residential campus, beautifully situated on the edge of the river. Students attend six days a week, eleven months a year, in two semesters. A day begins with four hours of classes in the morning. After a two-and-a-half-hour lunch break, afternoon classes last another two hours. Sunday is the day off. Tuition and room are free. A poor person is assisted by an allotment of RMB 21.00 per month (roughly half of a beginning worker's salary), of which RMB 15.00 covers food and RMB 6.00 pays personal expenses.

School was in session this Friday. We toured the Life Sciences Building, where zoology and botany were taught. In the basement experimental lab, a young man was working on the life cycle of a pest which could be controlled by a natural insect predator—not news to an American, but news for him. No one was in the Life Science Library. No one was in the chemistry lab. When we emerged, it was the noon recess, yet no more than fifty persons were walking around. It was a ghostlike atmosphere, and I wondered when it would resurge with life. Deadwood has been removed, but new growth will take time.

At lunch in the Overseas Chinese Hotel, Comrade B rushed up excitedly to tell us that though the Shekwaun Pottery at Fatshan which I wished to visit was closed that day—Friday being its regular day off—its manager had been located and consented to open up the factory for our visit. Comrade B acted as if this special privilege was for my benefit. To utilize the minibus to advantage, he also asked the San Jose couple and another couple from California to join us, as well as two reporters from Hong Kong and Macau who were in Canton covering the Trade Fair but were not averse to covering me. I was surprised to find the government was interested in publicity, which I had carefully avoided.

With Comrade B and a woman assistant as part of our party, we soon came to an English sign posted by the road: "Foreigners

Not Allowed." We were elated to drive right through, and began to see a variety of local traffic. Cloth, bales, pipes—it was surprising what bicycles could load or pull, and what even a pair of human shoulders could transport. Never in China would I see idleness or shirking. The lowest human common denominator, brawn, multiplied by millions of persons, would get required work done in the absence of machines.

At the pottery works, the manager welcomed us with tea at a conference table. Around us, cases displayed samples of their wares. The buff-colored stoneware clay, like terra-cotta, gives Shekwaun pieces a distinctive, earthy look. The area is so rich in clay that it has thrived on this industry for a thousand years. The material is not suitable for soft overglazes or delicate gold decorations, like the court porcelains of Ching-Te-Chen, but lends itself to a robust and sturdy look. Since the clay pits are at the river area, their material is extremely plastic.

At one time, local workers were loosely scattered in cottage industries, every man to himself, selling individually, working exhausting hours. The government made short work of dynamiting a mountain of clay to create a level area for a large factory facility. Now the workers have been communized into one huge cooperative enterprise, enjoying decent hours and working conditions, and the sale of their output is assured.

Talk about ceramics is meaningless, so I asked to visit the empty workrooms. The design and setting for the building were beautiful, surpassing any other I have seen. Neat rows of work tables were placed by huge windows for optimum natural working light. One looked up from tasks to glimpse a gorgeous courtyard, with huge crocks (made at the factory) filled with blooming lotus. Figures, animals, and fish were made in molds; there was no throwing. I examined baskets of tools and picked up some leftover clay. It felt very smooth. Clay work is naturally messy, but I have not visited any clay work area, from college classrooms to the famous porcelain factories of Europe, which could have claimed to be cleaner than those I now saw.

We went on to the firing room. The manager explained, "At one time, we used the downdraft kiln [successive chambers tunneled up a hillside heated by wood fuel fed at the opening on the lower end]. But to stack was backbreaking because the articles had to be carried upward into the kiln and the heat was stifling, for we were always in a rush to unstack and restack."

Now there is a continuous tunnel kiln, a tube which operates indoors with a conveyor belt moving articles from cold to warm to hot zones, then decreasing in warmth to cold again, so that an unfired object fed into one end emerges finished and cold on the other end. In continuous belt systems, objects are placed on the belt by workers and subject to the individual's speed, so empty spaces are unavoidable. Here in Shekwaun, instead of one conveyor belt, there were three layers of belts, and each layer was packed fully with trays which had been preloaded with articles to be fired. A hydraulic jack simultaneously transferred full trays onto all three layers at once as soon as space allowed. It was automation at its best. No one bent or reached. Four persons could keep every inch of the kiln fully utilized.

Another innovation was the huge metal chimney. To prevent its becoming terribly hot, it had been encased within another cylinder bathed by a steady supply of cold water, regulated to maintain a constant 100 degrees. Diesel fuel was piped through the warm water bath to ensure its instant volatilization. For thousands of years, Asian kiln designs had deviated very little, and I congratulated my escorts on a tremendous step forward. The manager said proudly, "Our workers did all this themselves, according to Chairman Mao's principles. Engineers came for consultation but we constructed the kiln and machinery."

We also inspected the material supply area, where red river stones were being mechanically pulverized, possibly for the calcium needed in clay and glazes.

The manager had been observing me. When we returned to the reception room he asked me about two small green flower vases on the table in front of us. I had noticed them at once, since they had a crystalline glaze normally used on porcelains, and differed from other pieces in the room. I had done that thirty years ago at Mills, but had gone on to other formulas. He asked if I knew how to make that glaze. "Yes," I answered casually.

He seemed startled. "Our master of that glaze has long since gone. How did you make it?"

"I can't tell you, because I only know the names of materials in English and I can't remember the formula; but I do know that zinc crystals form that characteristic natural flowerlike pattern."

The Cantonese manager couldn't understand until the IBM engineer translated "zinc" into Chinese. The manager shouted excitedly, "Dui-la dui-la [correct, correct]. Then why don't you make such glazes?"

I had to explain that this glaze required more than the twelve hours of firing which are the maximum number practical for me; it is a problem in a one-woman operation to watch a kiln around the clock.

The manager changed from formality to friendliness. "Please come back soon, for you can tell us a lot." I received some souvenirs: little bisque-fired white-clay fishes which I could bring back to San Francisco, apply my glazes and try firing, to present to Ming Choy. I was to carry those fishes all through the rest of my journey in China, since parcels could not be mailed to the United States.

An example of old-regime corruption, called in Chinese "cutting our flesh" (Chinese expressions are often graphic), was pointed out to us as we returned to town across a bridge of the Pearl River. Comrade B showed us a parallel row of concrete piers for a bridge which the Nationalist regime had never completed, despite having collected taxes for it. This government decided to erect an entirely new bridge, leaving the old foundation to remind the people of the empty promises of those who had deserted them.

Looking at those piers, I was reminded of 1945 echoes from disillusioned Chinatown residents who had been promised that every dollar of U.S. cash they deposited in China's official San Francisco branch bank would be exchanged for twenty Nationalist yuan (Chinese dollars). Returning to Canton after World War II to retire on their Nationalist yuan, those who had entrusted their lifelong U.S. dollar savings found that their San Francisco receipts were not honored. Moreover, because of inflation, "a sack full of Nationalist yuan could not buy a sack full of rice; no one would even take time to count the sack," Second Uncle's son-in-law recalled: "In anger, I dumped my yuan in the streets. I had lost my heart with my savings. It was no problem for the Communists to seize control."

The old International Settlement was nearby, on a delta island of the Pearl River. We got off our minibus for a look at the ambitious stone structures in classic European style. The once grand consular offices were now rooming houses for the Chinese, their spacious front gardens neglected, the pavements suffering from disrepair. Chickens and children roamed freely, and laundry hung from balconies where once well-dressed Caucasian ladies used to sit. When the rest of Canton was hot and humid, the foreigners on this island were cooled by the river breezes. Chinese were not allowed entry to this privileged bastion for the whites. Even Cantonese customs officials, no doubt pacified by bribery, stayed in their own territory on the other side of the bridge. Out of Chinese sight, foreign ships engaged in unlimited traffic on Pearl waters, using the docks and warehouses of this Island International Settlement without duty payment. That was part of the "free trade" forced upon China.

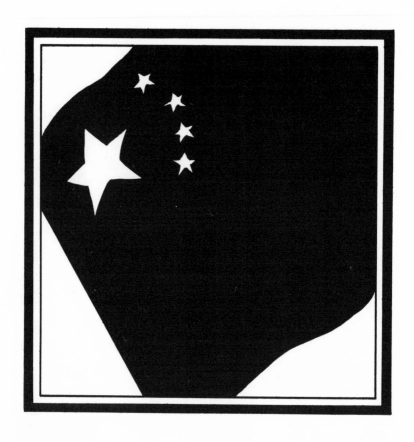

CHAPTER 24

"I CARRIED ON THE REVOLUTION FOR MY CHILDREN"

My request to visit the newer "Twenty-Seven Story" Hotel (formally named the Canton Guest Hotel) had been arranged for the following day. Comrade C, a gentle soft-spoken man with glasses and an altogether different personality from Comrade B, called on us. He became one of my favorite acquaintances in China. It had begun to pour, in that first burst of the monsoon which miraculously drops the temperature and humidity to a comfortable level; and it caught us unprepared. Pools of rain collected so rapidly on the balconies off our rooms that they could not drain through the gutters, and water began to pour onto the concrete floors within. I hopped around hastily, gathering up shoes and smaller flight bags, as Woody piled the large suitcases onto tabletops. A call to the floor steward was met with indifference. At this point Comrade C appeared. I told him that the hotel staff would not come to our aid.

Comrade C disappeared without a word, returning shortly with a bucket and mop. He worked to stem the tide of water, cleaning the dirty floor at the same time. I was embarrassed. "You shouldn't be doing that," I told him. "I thought you would have authority over the floor steward."

"If there is work to be done, it doesn't matter who does it," he answered.

In that instant, I understood one of the fundamental accomplishments of China's liberation. It had dignified physical labor. The floor mopper, no less than the doctor, was essential; hence expressions like "barefoot doctor" and "two-legged cart." Obviously this dedication without the motive of material gain, which is so enviable a quality of China today, is not total; there will always be that sixth-floor steward who doesn't want to move. But nowhere have Woody or I seen such willingness by a general populace to do whatever tasks are necessary, however lowly. I remember my cousin's telling me that as a doctor on a commune, one of his first problems was to teach sanitation. To this end he had to install, then teach the peasants to clean, toilet facilities. I think of other underdeveloped nations in Asia which are still backward, crying "Help" because their people will not use what they are born with—their hands. It is cause for wonder that China under Mao has succeeded in uniting hand with brain, theory with practice; for millions of Chinese had resisted change. The best resources of China, her people—women equally with men—are mobilized now to work with enthusiasm and pride.

Comrade C, having finished mopping, conducted us across the street, where Comrade D, the manager of the "Twenty-Seven Story" Foreigners' Hotel, whisked us by elevator to the penthouse. As we promenaded on the perimeter of the rooftop to enjoy the view, Comrade D indicated that three antiaircraft guns and some patrolling soldiers were prepared for defense. In the enclosure of the huge penthouse reception parlor, sunshine flooded in through all-around sparkling glass walls, as we began with small talk over tea which came in new-style large porcelain mugs with covers to keep contents hot. When Comrade D asked me what was life like in the United States, and looked expectant, I was caught unprepared. How would one make a quick synopsis of life today in the United States? Briefly I told them a little of our daily life in caring for our family and minding a combined travel and art business. I found myself telling them of our serious daily concern to meet the taxes that support civic, state, and national governments, and the insurance bills we paid to alleviate typical fears: fire, robbery, carelessness, accidents, vandalism, natural calamities, and sickness and death.

Comrades C and D paid only medical insurance. Comrade D stated that a Chinese worker who cannot make ends meet on his salary can apply to the government for a raise in wages. There were no salary deductions for retirement benefits, which commence at sixty, at 70 percent or more of normal wages, depending on number of years worked, or for taxes.

We talked of their Revolution. "Like immigration for your father, revolution is the desperate course when no other method has worked. Who wants to risk life in revolutions, or leave his home to immigrate?" Comrade D's tones were low-pitched and reasonable, but his eyes flashed in dead earnest at pain remembered.

In a land where, because of traditional reticence, no one I had met volunteered to talk of his family (no grandmother here would wear sweetheart bracelets!), this comrade with leathery skin and deeply sunken brown eyes, whose teeth and fingers were brown with tobacco stains, told me that he was a father of three. "I carried on the Revolution not for my life, which is brief—anything is endurable—but for the future life of my children."

He was younger than I, yet even in his generation, he had found his former life as hopeless as my father had, who had left China forty-six years before the 1949 Revolution. Responding to this theme, I said, "My father was going to make three thousand dollars and return to Fragrant Mountains to retire, but for the sake of his children's educations, he remained in the United States."

Comrade D took us downstairs to inspect hotel facilities. We stopped at the enormous dining room, where, as at our hotel, regular tables were assigned with room numbers. Unlike our hotel, menus were in English and Chinese. At their tables, guests could keep Western preferences: bottles of instant coffee, ketchup, opened whiskies, boxes of dry cereals—no one would disturb them, and no service charge was entailed.

Comrade D's conviction that children were the reason for revolution reminded me of the barber at the Chinese Hotel. I had found it difficult to find a turn at the unisex barber shop (no ladies' beauty parlors or permanent waves for Chinese women), and though when traveling I could improvise a way to wash my hair in nearly any bathroom, it was a challenge here with the very small basin and one thin small towel which was not changed the entire week. I mentioned to our waitress at lunch that I must hurry to the hotel's barber shop just before its reopening after the noon recess, because waiting in line might make me late for the afternoon visit to "Twenty-Seven Stories." She had looked thoughtful and returned a little later to say that she had found a friend, one of the senior barbers, who would take care of me privately at 1:30 P.M. before the shop opened. The waitress introduced me to Barber Mut ("Mut" means "honey"). Conversation in a barber shop is universal. I learned that he had had no formal education and, in the olden days, could not have hoped for any education for his children. Now they would finish high school without cost. The school provided both breakfast and lunch; his wife had only to cook dinner; and neither had to worry about child care while they worked during the day.

Revolution had not altered that special Chinese protective devotion to children for Barber Mut and Comrade D. Their form of sacrifice has changed, but there is no question that they prefer and would give up their lives if necessary for their present-day gains. Economic security has strengthened family values.

I had not been in pre-1949 China, but I can remember many years of my Chinese schoolroom teachers, 6,000 miles away in San Francisco, telling of floods, droughts, famines, and treeless horizons (bark having been eaten, wood chopped for fuel), of bandits, opium traffic, increasing foreign imperialist demands, and in the face of these accumulated disasters, the government's ineffectiveness and the citizens' lack of unity. We would listen to these weekly assembly lectures and then take brush in hand to compose endless essays on such themes as "The people of China are like a basin of loose sand; none will cooperate with another." Our twelve-year-old minds, unacquainted with our fathers' native land, were asked to dream up recommendations for handling problems so enormous that a quarter-century after the Revolution, 800 million people are still working out solutions. I could understand better now why our underprivileged parents left a rotten, hopeless China to struggle for pennies in a tenement basement in the United States. They cared about a better future for their children. Canton had been a staggering introduction to China.

As the weather cleared, we planned departure to Peking on a Sunday. We were to be ready by 2:00 P.M. for 3:05 P.M. plane time, but by 10:30 A.M. we were packed. We can never sleep late on a flight date, and Woody is the type who is at an airport two hours before departure. So before lunch we took a walk along the river, then deep into the people's residential district. The fact that China is cleaner than it ever used to be has been observed by many visitors, but I'd like to describe the unusually beautiful Cantonese garbage receptacles called "fruit peel boxes." They were waist-high, domed-top cylinders made of Shekwaun stoneware, with a hole near the top like a mailbox and another at the base for removing debris. The "boxes" were glazed a luminous jade green, with a design sculptured into the fragile clay, cast too heavy to lift, and were practical enough for what is normal street waste in China: fruit peels. There is no paper, metal, glass, or plastic refuse to discard, because people still go to the corner store with a home container and coins, to buy in bulk exactly what they need, just as my mother used to do seventy years ago. Four-page newspapers carry news without advertisements. There is no packaging industry with its attendant waste.

Our walk gave us a glimpse of neighborhood Sunday life. Outside their houses, people were washing vegetables, hanging up clothes, stringing salt fish to dry, chopping kindling. Some stores displayed food products and fruits, and the supplies seemed more than adequate to us. Cookies were unbroken circles neatly stacked in huge glass cylindrical containers, two feet high and eighteen inches in diameter. Children could buy one cookie or one apple, which the store attendant would obligingly peel without charge.

After lunch, we were off to the airport. But 3:05 P.M. came and went, and we recalled a rumor that planes did not leave until they could be fully occupied. When Comrade B said he had no idea how many stops the flight plan included, I looked at the schedule under the glass top of the check-in counter, and saw that it showed one stop. Mustering my Peking dialect, I asked where that would be. "Shanghai" was the answer.

"Shanghai," now only two hours away by air, evoked my thoughts northward to a China beyond the "third water," which even my father and mother had never known. Nothing in Canton matched what I had been told—not the temple, not the university, not the Communists. I wondered what I would now find a few hours away.

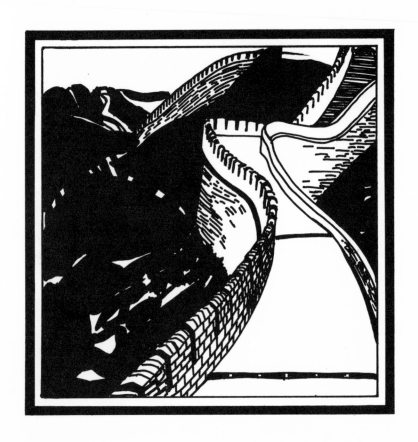

CHAPTER 25

PEKING, ANCHOR OF CHINA

We landed in misty Peking at 10:00 P.M. and looked in vain for someone to meet us. (We learned later that although we had paid Comrade B to cable Peking that we were coming, he had not mentioned which plane!) The concerned stewardess led us to a bus heading for town. There were practically no house lights. A dim glow was shed by the tall street lights; economically, only the lower tiers of globe clusters were lit and we saw that we were

248

traveling along a tremendously wide avenue. Trees lined both sides, and only an occasional figure was stirring.

At the Hotel of Nationalities, no room was ready for us, so we were seated in the cheerful lobby and served tea. It was quite large with high ceilings and natural wood columns and appeared spotlessly clean. In the center, facing the revolving entry doors, was a veritable indoor garden, featuring four huge pots of yellow forsythia and many bonsai pots of full-blooming double cherries set among twenty or thirty pots of greens. In Japan, one such flowering cherry would be the focus of a lobby centerpiece. The porcelain containers were glorious works of art, some as large as tubs, in every shape from flower petal to rectangular, flared or tall, flat or straight, their white backgrounds delicately decorated with scenery, bamboo, calligraphy, or colorful blossoms. They were characteristic horticultural props of Peking. Possibly in that climate of winter and summer extremes, potted plants were practical. Any one of those pots in the lobby would have commanded several hundred dollars in the American market.

Because the suite requested in our cable was not available that night, we were brought to a twin-bedded room. It was clean and pleasant, with freshly painted walls in soft robin's-egg blue, a white ceiling, and gray drapes. Under foot, the Peking rug was sheer luxury. Here, the attitude of the room attendants was vastly different from that in Canton. Northern Chinese are said to be more courteous than the contentious Southern Chinese, from whose territory revolutions have been launched. We were asked if we wanted a libation to soothe us after a long day of travel. On every floor, a station facing the elevator carried a stock of bottled alcoholic beverages. Woody accepted the servant's suggestion of grape "brandy," which came promptly in a very tall, narrow bottle, accompanied by two cut crystal stem glasses. The price was nominal, less than $2.00 U.S. We found it very sweet.

The next day, we were moved to a larger "suite"; actually, a twin-bedded sleeping-dressing alcove divided from a sitting room area by a full-width beige silk brocade curtain, an arrangement which permitted me to rise early and write without disturbing Woody. A huge walk-in storage closet, running shelves around the room, davenport, writing desk, numerous chairs, coffee table complete with covered tea mugs, and two half-gallon thermoses supplied with fresh boiling water twice a day, and a clean bathroom were truly all we needed to be comfortable for a long stay. Thus we began what I expected to be a leisurely ten days in Peking, a six-hundred-year-old city about which I knew little beyond reports of its physical beauties, its cultural depth, and its traditionally elegant way of life.

In the daylight of Monday morning, we saw that our hotel was located on the widest continuously straight main city street in the world. Six broad lanes were nearly free of vehicles and the 200-foot width was bordered on both sides by double rows of trees which sheltered pedestrian sidewalks. The din of Canton's river traffic and automobile horns, the sticky heat, the sight of humans straining under incredible loads, the pushing, staring crowds, were now replaced by calmness, politeness, style. Peking is the past and present anchor of China; it is also an anchor in time.

Away from the sea, inconvenient to foreign encroachments (though wars have been fought here), protected historically by the Great Wall, Peking stands as it has since the Ming Dynasty, handsomely massive, a reassuring and immobile backdrop for the decisions and plans made behind its façade. This is where the great personages of the past came and those of the present continue to come to seek audience. The "Forbidden City" was conceived to be the center of the Middle Kingdom, which existed in political isolation for thousands of years. "The People's Republic of China" in Chinese is, literally, "The Middle Kingdom People's Government."

That wide avenue from our hotel led straight to the heart of the city, Tien An Mien (Heavenly Peace) Square, which occupies 98 square acres and can take a gathering of nearly a million people (7 million live in Peking). On its perimeter stands the Great Hall of the People, built at the request of Chairman Mao to accommodate the First Congress of all of China's population base. It can hold in its banquet hall alone five thousand seated guests (as at the Nixon banquet) or ten thousand at a cocktail reception. This hall, engineered without one obstructing structural column, looks as big as a football field.

The Great Hall of the People is not generally open to the public, but we were invited to join a busload of other overseas Chinese visitors. Our interpreters spoke Peking dialect with the Hall custodians, then translated into Cantonese. We began the tour upstairs, which included twenty-nine enormous individual conference rooms representing China's twenty-one provinces, her five huge autonomous Western territories, and three general rooms allocated to Shanghai, Tientsin, and Peking, which are great metropolitan areas directly under Peking's control. The very best contemporary and old arts of each area had been sent to decorate their Great Hall headquarters. As we strolled, we noticed that nothing was stinted, from sparkling chandeliers to thick red carpets.

We visited the air-conditioned main auditorium where an audience of ten thousand seated on three levels can listen to speeches with individual microphones. The ceiling was lit with a magnificent canopy of lights in a sunflower and red star burst. Red, gold, and white are China's colors. It flabbergasted us to learn that this complex combination of art, engineering, and construction had been completed in exactly ten months by fourteen thousand laborers working around the clock. The cost had been less than a million dollars.

The architectural splendor of the present bordered on architectural splendor of the past. The gates to the 250-acre Forbidden City, containing nine thousand rooms in some seventy-five palaces, whose golden tiled roofs sheltered past Emperors, also opened on the Central Square area where those who would seek audience began their waiting. Not far away, Chairman Mao is in residence, and present-day power again emanates from this square, its vastness ironically cleared by Chiang's government. When the Nationalists planned to evacuate themselves to Taiwan, they laid an airstrip here to facilitate removal of some 25,000 crates full of Imperial Palace treasures. Today, four huge poster-faces dominate a scene of leisurely pedestrians and sightseers rather than a line-up of waiting caravans or planes: portraits of Mao, Stalin, Lenin, and Marx.

While we were sightseeing, the China Travel Service was working on our personal program "chart." Comrade E, a soft-spoken, mild man who had met us briefly after our late arrival, joined us again the next morning to note our special interests. Conveniently, their office was in our hotel: Suite 757 was going to be a familiar destination for me in the two weeks which followed. It was amazing how many persons worked out of those two rooms; each time

I called, I would see familiar faces and some unfamiliar ones, as field courier guides came and went after filing their reports. Personnel worked in shifts around the clock, using a bed in each room for sitting and resting. The phone at the desk of the office manager, an articulate woman comrade who kept tab of billings and handled cash, was in constant use.

Just as we had been included in other visitors' exploration of the Great Hall, so other Chinese visitors were included in areas of my interest. A full busload made the field trip to the Peihai (Northern Sea) Nursery School, close to the city center. Excitement was in the air when we disembarked at its entrance. Double rows of little girls and boys, bright-eyed, happy, healthy, dressed in clean clothes and colorful aprons, lined our path. The girls presented a rainbow look because of ribbon bows tied around their shiny black hair. Their mouths were wide open as they sing-songed at the top of their lungs, "Ai-yee-soo-soo" (Welcome beloved aunties, uncles). The children had of course been rehearsed, but it warmed our hearts to know that the rehearsal had told them we were "family."

The headmistress, like other women in executive positions in China, was straightforward and welcomed me by staying at my side through the next couple of hours. This boarding school was started in 1949, immediately after Liberation, for children three and a half to seven years old. A child stayed six weekdays and returned home to his parents for one day, at a monthly cost of RMB 20.20. He enjoyed three meals a day, with fruit for in-between snacks. The children awakened at 7:00 A.M., napped after lunch, and bedtime was at 8:30 P.M. A staff of forty-nine teachers (three teachers per class) and thirty-three other workers provided a high ratio of adults to the 364 children at the school. Its facilities included a medical clinic and hospital, and sick youngsters were immediately isolated.

A school barber cuts the hair of all, and all the boys had the same short crewcut. Clothes were provided by the parents, while the school furnished stationery and art supplies. The curriculum included arithmetic, reading, art, music, dance, and physical education. At five, a child began written Chinese.

Twenty-four children were cared for on a coeducational basis in each two-room, one-bath unit. One of the two rooms is the dormitory, where each child makes his own bed. One notices at once the gorgeous colors of silken quilts, neatly folded, no two alike. The adjacent bathroom was equipped with one large shower facility, hot and cold running water, a long trough for toilet use, low washbasins, and individual locker space for each child's cup, toothbrush, and towel. The children of each unit worked as a team to keep their bathroom clean, and it gleamed, as did the entire school.

By day the other room of each unit was used for classes and dining. Drawings and folded or cut-out paper designs decorated the walls. Particularly interested in the spontaneous artwork of children as a key to their intelligence, I was disappointed that most of the drawings looked alike. The teacher of this class of four-year-olds said that they had been given an example of a house to draw. Each of the ten little sheets of paper on the walls contained a house, all with the same roofline, a door in the middle, windows on both sides, and a tree to the right. A few had two trees. The young artists were now sitting quietly looking at lantern slides and listening to the story of a Canadian doctor, Dr. Norman Bethune, who served poor Chinese soldiers during the Revolution by reaching them on horseback.

In another classroom for five-and-a-half-year-olds, I saw a slogan of Chairman Mao's: "Practice very well; seek to do better daily." On the blackboard their teacher had drawn a sample composition: a palm tree, some birds, some Chinese ideographs, and a mandala pattern. I asked, "Does the teacher ever let the children draw as they please?"

The answer was, "Children can draw as they want."

"Do most of them copy the picture on the blackboard?"

The teacher replied, "No." I walked around for a better look. One child was drawing a tank, another a train, and another the sun (a mandala—a universal circular symbol in child art), and another, a ship. Two others were drawing sunflowers (mandala again). In another corner, children were drawing balloons in a random sky pattern.

I thought that the pictures showed tight organization; very different, for instance, from the exuberant scattering of Ming

Choy's drawings when he was the same age. If balloons were featured, the largest balloon was exactly in the middle, and small balloons were in an even line. The color distribution was excellent.

Five-year-olds were allowed two thirty-minute periods of play time daily for blocks or drawing. At other times they learned arithmetic, singing, reading. In the next classroom, they were engaged in block building, and I thought their three-dimensional achievements were more sophisticated than their drawings. One child was building a symmetrical pagoda, approached by a bridge complete with a gate. He worked in orderly fashion, alone.

I had expected that the class would be involved in one big cooperative venture, but perhaps because it was free time, each was absorbed in his own fantasy. Though girls and boys are certainly taught equally here, the girls had chosen colored blocks, and sat at tables making flat designs. The boys were at tables or on the floor, making intricate structures in-the-round. Both boys and girls were unusually quiet. Even when a table was accidentally pushed and all the blocks on it collapsed, no one made a sound. They were already disciplined.

Having to keep quiet in order not to be troublesome is only one type of discipline. At another class of six-year-olds learning arithmetic, I found in the making the articulateness of new China. Instead of the occasional practice in thinking and speaking on their feet that we encourage in our children, here daily work in public speaking was being accomplished. Girls volunteered more readily than boys to come forward to explain the lesson. They described numbers in vibrant tones, utilizing a display of real fruits and flowers. When I remarked with surprise on their use of Arabic numerals, the headmistress said, "But these are now universal symbols, understood everywhere."

The tour ended in the school auditorium, where a troupe of adorable children dressed in black velvet jackets and satin pants in a multitude of colors danced and sang for us. Leadership is encouraged and developed from childhood. If you saw the seven-year-old mistress of ceremonies of that group, with sparkling eyes and two saucy pigtails, addressing a hundred adults with ringing conviction and good-humored pride in her classmates' performance, a picture of positive confidence, you could multiply her by the millions coming up, and realize the formidable force developing today in China. Not only are women liberated; the children are. Girl babies who once would have been drowned, sold, or given away are now encouraged to develop their hands and brains to serve their country.

When I asked the headmistress if there were discipline or learning problems, she seemed to think the question inapplicable. "If a child cries or doesn't do his work, we simply talk to him," she replied. "And soon he understands. Education is subordinate to proletarian purposes. Therefore we teach cooperation, love of other races, cultivation of vegetables and fruits, practice of economy, and no waste in food. We start this program of self-sufficiency and cleanliness at three and a half years. By five, our children are trained."

Before leaving, I presented her with a bag of candy and fruits, and she gave me a batch of pictures, asking me to send them pictures from American children. "We have many weak points," she said, a statement I would hear again and again. "We welcome criticism."

Our exit path led us through an outdoor area with play equipment, but altogether there was less outdoor play space than in schools of comparable size in the United States. Still, no American setting could have been more beautiful or appropriate for a nursery school. With rust-red masonry walls, and roofs of green-glazed tile, this complex had once been the nursery of Imperial silkworms! We left to the high-pitched tones of the children's farewell chants, "Beloved Auntie, Uncle, see you again!" Again, they lined our departing path, an enchanting sea of waving arms.

In a rapidly changing country, one of the great unchanging symbols of China, representative of her past achievement and today, as for 2,500 years, either barrier or invitation for visitors, is the Great Wall. At the back door of Peking, it is really two parallel walls spaced apart for a walking corridor between them wide enough for six horses to patrol abreast, a gigantic curving spine of a dragon, going across six states, up mountain peaks and twisting over ravines for 6,000 kilometers, its bristling top ridge of bricks appearing like scales. Originally, it was built of packed earth; after the great Ming construction period it was fortified with bricks. My tape measured each brick to be 14½ inches long, 4 inches high, and 7 inches thick; if its density compares with common brick, each weighs almost 34 pounds. They were covered with golden lichen, black with age. The walking surface high up between the walls was repaved with gray stone.

On April 28 several busloads of visitors were scheduled to visit the Great Wall and the nearby Ming Tombs, and we gladly joined the all-day excursion. Four days before, I had worn what I had prepared for the Peking climate in April: my woolens, cashmere sweaters (made in China), and interlined coat. Woody had an all-weather padded nylon jacket specially tailored with inner deep pockets secured by zippers. April 24 must have been the last day of winter (which dips to 10 degrees Centigrade, or about 14 degrees below 0 Fahrenheit), for in the three days that followed, it turned into summer, and it felt 90 degrees the day of our Great Wall excursion. As our full bus jogged along the city street before 9:00 A.M., we could see that the people were preparing for the passing of winter. Padded winter coats were being hung out to air or to dry after washing. Energetic old women were spreading out piles of lime on sidewalks, to whitewash trees and discourage the new crop of spring insects. Our guide told us, "There were no trees before Liberation, but since 1949, we have planted thousands and thousands, some stands four to six deep, to act as baffles against desert sandstorms."

I saw a long line of people, perhaps a hundred, waiting at a store. "What are they waiting for?" I wondered. "There must be a new book out today, so they are waiting." (Books in China are either free or priced within anyone's means. Later, I understood that line: Not many new titles were being published.)

After we left the city limits and began to climb toward Pataling we transferred from our large buses to smaller minibuses. We passed fields of winter grain, and saw that reaffirmation of life which bursts forth with astonishing swiftness in response to warming weather. Pear orchards were in white blossom near the cherry pinks of dwarf double peaches. The mountainside between the Luliang Shan and Great Khingan mountain ranges was dry and rocky, not unlike the Sierra foothills of California in summer. Beyond lay the mammoth Gobi Desert of Inner Mongolia. The unfolding pale chartreuse leaves of saplings testified to the new Chinese mania for reforestation. Clusters of pale lavender lilacs and spears of yellow forsythia, the delicate pink-whites of plums, flowered alongside peonies so thick with bees that no one would dare sniff closely.

Motor traffic grew heavy, and we slowed to a crawl. The other vehicles were nearly all open Chinese-made trucks crowded with military personnel and workers packed in, standing up, on their way to a first spring outing. When we reached the parking area, we found dozens of trucks jammed in and thousands of people on foot, enjoying themselves, eating huge whole-wheat buns, drinking soda water (which costs RMB 1.20 per bottle as against RMB 48 cents for beer). Yellow pears and tangerines were sold at the snack stand, and man-high, stacked crates of empty soda water bottles testified to a brisk trade.

Our carload of tourists was told to follow our own schedules for climbing the Wall, but to return at noon for box lunches in the resthouse at its base. Woody and I went off together, among the crowds of leathery dark-skinned people of all ages and occupations (possibly the extremely low humidity of Peking caused the dry faces), testimony that the family units of China are alive and doing well. Children were chattering, giggling teenagers were taking pictures of each other (those with cameras are proud of possessing an article which costs about RMB 120.00), young couples were carrying their young and milk bottles, short old ladies were climbing on bound feet shod in black velvet slippers and thick white soles. They were perhaps sixty or seventy years old, the last in China to have been trapped by the slave-fad for bound feet because the revolution of Dr. Sun reached the North last. (More bound feet exist in Peking than in other cities.) Today the crowds were bubbling in the exhilaration of spring fever.

But Woody did not feel well because of a persistent dry cough, so rather than struggle upward against the wind, sun, and crowds, he waited at an intermediate height while I continued to climb and explore for another hour. The brick sides of the Wall were about 16 inches thick. Northward, facing the enemy, the Wall rises high with long, narrow, regular vertical slots set in to allow the discharge of weapons. Southward, facing home, its unbroken side was only 30 inches high. Square fortress towers sheltered observation posts, one of which I entered among a swarm of adventurous spectators, and descended with them down hand-hewn timber steps. A cell below provided for storage and sleeping space. The sturdy simplicity and honest construction did not differ from fortifications in other parts of the world, such as the Crusaders' forts on Rhodes; but the names visitors had chiseled here into the bricks were in Chinese.

The Great Wall of China, built before Christ, was not included in the Seven Ancient Wonders of the World, which were clustered around the Mediterranean area. Except for the Pyramids, most of those wonders are now remnants of tumbled-down stones or have vanished altogether. Perhaps this is fitting, for the Wall is a unique colossus. Built to carry out that centuries-old characteristic of Chinese psychology—to keep out unwanted foreign intruders, to protect domestic interests within—this Wall is affectionately nicknamed in Chinese "The Ancient Stopper." The Wall will no longer stop modern enemies, but the same psychology will.

While it builds in peace, the nation is prepared to resist aggression. She is wary of Western initiatives: Russia to the north and west, and the United States' record of relentless military flexing around her borders, as when bombs rained over adjacent North Vietnam. The China which long was ready victim of outside predators has been working these twenty-five years to prepare her defenses so that no enemy will penetrate; and when I say "China," I mean a determination that reaches down to each individual Chinese from the age he can talk, listen, and understand. All along city streets and country roads, classes of children march as "Little Red Soldiers." "The 'Sleeping Dragon' will awake someday!" was the vexed cry of the Chinese when they were humiliated by Western power. The lone Imperial Dragon Flag has been replaced by hundreds of millions of red flags and the children's red scarves, symbolizing a national dedication to their country's cause. In childhood calligraphy classes, I often brushed four ideographs: "Return my rivers and my mountains!"—never dreaming that I would indeed see those rivers and those mountains returned.

還	我	河	山
Return	My	Rivers	Mountains

We left the washed-out grays of the Great Wall to join the other tourists for our box-lunch break. Basins of warm washing water were brought into the attractive stone resthouse. We sipped welcome hot tea, ate generous portions of thick ham and beef sandwiches, roast chicken, fruit. Then we were on our way to the Ming Tombs.

Our young woman guide this day spoke Cantonese, in fact the dialect of Woody's Toi-Shan district. We approached the one Ming Tomb which has been opened. There were seventeen Ming Emperors, thirteen of whom are buried in the Peking amphitheater. (The other twelve tombs there have not been excavated, though they are well marked with handsome superstructures.) Against a backdrop of lavender hills, the avenue leading to the tomb is broad and flat, guarded by huge granite camels and elephants spaced at block-long distances. Our guide had told us at the Great Wall, "The workers sent to the Wall construction never returned." Now she said, "Of a thousand sent to work at the Ming Tombs, five hundred returned. This tomb has been created with the bones and flesh of the poor." The timbers, for example, are perfect, rare cedar tree trunks cut in a province so distant it took six years to transport them to the site. Two men with outstretched arms can barely encircle one of them.

Between strong marble retaining walls a wide avenue led us downward to a depth of 60 feet below the earth, where the "Quiet Tomb" or "Ting-Ling" was located, the tomb of Wan Li (1573–1620). The doors are solid marble, and each bronze beam weighs a ton. In the eerie darkness relieved somewhat by strings of electric lights, we were among hundreds of noisy visitors. (It must be a universal urge of children to yell in the dark.) The display of artifacts was documented with more object lessons of the economic and social oppression of the past. Long before foreign imperialism, Chinese land peasants had been raked over by their own ruling class. Their labor supported a hierarchy of nonproductive exploiters: petty magistrates, roving bandits, landlords and administrators answerable to the Emperor in Peking. Two buckets of harvested grain dramatized an object lesson: the great container went to the Emperor; one tenth of that amount, in a tiny container, was retained by the peasant's family.

Some objects yielded by this tomb had been transferred to

museums. Here we saw four solid gold vessels the size of washbasins, used by the Emperor, some decorated with the dragon symbol of his authority. His jade bowls and gold chopsticks were also displayed. His crown flashed royal blue with kingfisher feathers, shimmered with thousands of pearls and rubies, and weighed more than seven pounds. The elaborate craftsmanship testified to the innate genius of the uncelebrated artisan.

The "Middle Temple," a long stone vault with half-dome ceiling, contained the white marble sarcophagus of the Emperor, and jammed close behind it were the sarcophagi of his two Empresses. Immediately beyond were two crypt rooms intended to receive those sarcophagi, but when the time had come to use them, the entryways proved too small. I wish I could have been there when the stately funeral march ended in frustration! It was lucky that the Empresses were no longer able to mete out punishment.

From this underground area of five stone-lined halls, without a visible beam or column, we emerged into strong sunlight. It must have been about 100 degrees in the dry afternoon air. I walked through a distinctive feature of ancient Chinese architectural and landscape design: the approach to an important structure must be properly impressive and symmetrically balanced. Hence there would be four avenues leading to the front, back, and two sides. We came out a different way from our entry, along a broad path, through a small inner gateway of marble and glazed tile, and then through a thick, higher gateway covered with terra-cotta browns and yellows, topped by two tiers of green tiled roof and curving eaves. What the tomb lacked in color the gates provided.

It had been an unforgettable and exhausting day. We returned via a northeastern highway, into Peking city limits, eagerly expecting tomorrow.

CHAPTER 26
MAY DAY AT THE SUMMER PALACE

Knowing that the Temple of Heaven, worship center of Emperors, was in a southeastern direction two miles from the city center, I awoke Woody one morning at 6:30 A.M. after a sleepless night. A group of Americans, improbably singing "Down by the Old Mill Stream," had enlivened normally tranquil Peking until past 11:00 P.M. In early morning, we heard Chinese singing. May Day was in the air, and we had little remaining time for optional sightseeing.

At the dispatching desk outside of the lobby, we requested a car and driver. (Unless there is a special event, many cars are available for hotel guests. Each driver cares for his or her own car, and we preferred women drivers, who made a special effort to point out interesting city sights.) At the end of every ride, a passenger is given a receipt for the reasonable charges. To be on the streets of Peking before 7:00 A.M. was a novelty for us. Bicycles were four and five deep on the road, beeping horns; some were loaded for deliveries, others carried workers.

Peking is a gray city, hiding its houses behind long gray brick walls. Here and there, a vermilion door broke the monotone. We saw the use of latticed shojis (the forerunner of simpler Japanese adaptations) used high up in bands as clerestory windows. No building in central Peking is very tall, for the Imperial edict prohibited commoners from building any structure higher than the Imperial Palace. Color, too, was reserved for royalty. The old walls which had surrounded the city have been removed since Liberation to allow growth outward, but the old thick southern entry gates of gray, heavy stones were allowed to stand. Peking is laid out in rectilinear patterns, evenly and logically.

We walked from the outer gates through groves of pines and elms, up steps, along a properly humbling approach more extensive than any we had visited elsewhere, toward the Temple of Heaven, which was sacred to the Ming Emperor who had conceived it, for he had been trained by a Buddhist priest. Later, Ching Emperors also came each spring to make sacrificial offerings, to dedicate themselves, to ask for forgiveness for themselves and their subjects, and to request generous harvests for the forthcoming year. Such a solemn purpose dictated the properly humbling approach. We entered from the North Gate, which led to the first Temple-in-the-Round, the Hall of Prayer for Good Harvests. The area was virtually deserted, except for a few workmen engaged in reconstruction. Sweeping 125 feet high toward the sky were three tiers of sapphire glazed roofs, topped by a huge knob of gold, classically simple, copied nowhere else. They sheltered a cylindrical base 100 feet in diameter, within which the Emperor could pray in privacy. Not a single supporting beam within interrupted his view.

To the south beckoned the Imperial Vault of Heaven, with a single roof layer of glazed tile. As we walked, we could see the

East Gate and the West Gate in beautifully carved marble, surrounded by sculptured balustrades. There was at least a mile's walk between the Hall of Prayer and the Imperial Vault. The Vault is surrounded by a low stone wall, the famous Echo Wall, which is true to its name. Beyond was the Circular Sacrificial Altar. We continued along the path which had begun at the North Gate, leading straight through without deviation into the center of the site of the Hall of Prayer, then into the center of the Imperial Vault of Heaven and Sacrificial Altar, out through the South Gate. This path, once sacred to royalty, had brought the two of us into still another glimpse of the grand past of Peking.

Our hotel was now full of distinguished state visitors arriving for May Day. May Day is like America's Labor Day, symbolic of rest and privilege for the workers. After a week in dusty Peking (I could sit down at my desk to write a letter, and at the end of half an hour, the fine sand of the desert would have blown in all over the page), it was time to look for the barber shop again. Though it was already seven o'clock in the evening, one of the floor station men called upstairs and told me to go ahead. Those attendants had become our friends and knew all our comings and goings. If we pressed the "down" button at a meal hour, they would ask, "Eating rice?" and if we pressed "up" they knew it was to visit either the China Travel Service or the barber.

The barber shop was located past the billiard room, and its white tile-lined walls and floor appeared as clean as a surgery room. There were no trademark piles of cut hair here. For RMB 80 cents, Woody had his haircut and I my shampoo at the hands of a Shanghai expert, who kindly gave my scalp a few extra brisk rubs to relieve it of a headache. (Nowadays in China, massages are given only at hospitals if prescribed medically.) We did not talk much because we lacked a common language base. In the midst of hand-drying my long hair at 8:00 P.M., he and the other staff members lost their normal dignified calm and rushed to the window. So did we. The usual subdued night lighting of Peking had suddenly exploded into thousands of lights. The bulbs on both tiers of the street lamp clusters were now fully lit. Every building was framed by incandescent light globes. The City Gates, the important buildings, the squares which, like the rest of China, remained in darkness at night, all were luminously bordered, ablaze in extravagant joy, to celebrate the forthcoming day of the worker. "Wu-Yi, Wu-Yi" (Five-One, Five-One), the barber repeated as we stood at his window.

The great holiday dawned. With 7 million residents and a great number of visitors loose in Peking, even the huge Tien An Mien Square could not contain them all, and elaborate preparations had been made by the government to entertain and delight everyone. Woody and I were given color-coded tickets and instructed by the young and pleasant Cantonese-speaking China Travel Service guide, Comrade F, that we would be in Bus No. 11, group 31, leaving at 7:30 A.M. Each ticket admitted one to the Summer Palace festivities, and was good only from 9:00 A.M. to 12 noon. Comrade F divided our busload into three groups, each with a designated leader. We were to keep in sight of our own leader and were told that to avoid being lost or injured we should not climb any of the "mountains." By 12 noon we were to gather together for the first lunch seating. I asked Comrade F whether there was to be a military review at the Square, for I knew that May Days in Communist countries were often occasions for demonstrations of military power, but he said there would be no public parade. All activities were scheduled at parks.

For eight hundred years, the Summer Palace had been the gardens of Emperors, but in the latter nineteenth century, they were ruined by invaders. The last Empress of China, one of twenty-eight concubines to the last Emperor, rose to her reign by using every evil means to obtain power and loved to live in luxury. Seventeen million dollars had been collected from her people for national security and to provide for a navy. While her peasants starved, she diverted the funds to reconstruct the Summer Palace for her vacation resort, enlarged the Kunming Reservoir to provide cooling breezes, and built a stationary marble boat in lieu of the navy, along with a series of pavilions, palaces, and courtyards for amusement shows.

The pressure of crowds was obvious as soon as we arrived at the Main Gate of the Summer Palace, which includes acres and acres of extensive grounds intricately landscaped by man against a background of natural-looking hillsides. We strolled under long covered walkways, elaborately detailed with latticework. Neither rain nor sun would bother the fortunate visitors to these gardens.

Rock sculpture, trees, shrubs, and flowers covered every courtyard and terrace.

Entertainment was being presented simultaneously in a number of pavilions. Ethnic dancers, vividly costumed, represented united China's distant provinces. Dialogue skits, magic acts, and pantomime emphasized politically oriented themes. Female dancers and actresses had rolled up gray or khaki pants under their brilliant silken skirts. With stage makeup, the modern girl of China showed her femininity, grace, and beauty. When appropriate, the well-known Chinese instinct for color and decoration emerges. The music was lively and gay, the tempo of an energetic nation.

The organization and courtesy of the day were impressive. Booths with medical attendants were available, though I did not see a single incident in the hours spent among the thousands of visitors. When our group entered a courtyard, folding wooden seats awaited us in prime front-row locations. Already seated crowds would clap their hands to welcome us, and we could clap in response. After we listened in one area for fifteen or twenty minutes, Comrade F would signal and we would rise to move on. The crowd clapped a farewell, and again we clapped our thanks. Then on to another staging area and seats another group had just vacated. The feeling of being warmly received was positive and pleasant. It was an extraordinary combination of entertainment and national pride held in what was once exclusive domain of the Empress and her courtiers.

There were exquisitely restored buildings to enter and inspect in wonder. We toured through the Throne Room, gawking at cloisonné urns and candlesticks, ornately carved woods, and silken cushions. The Empress had an extensive collection of real gem "trees" arranged in jewellike enameled containers: solid gold trunks with white jade blossoms, others with hundreds of leaves in pure green Imperial jade (nowadays, even one leaf of Imperial jade is hard to find), as well as unbroken polished branches of coral.

We observed the winding mountain steps which we had been advised against climbing. But I could imagine the Empress being borne higher and higher in her sedan chair, up onto Longevity Hill (created by men with the earth excavated to form the lake), so that she could enjoy the cooling breezes, until she reached whichever one of the multicolored pagodas, temples, or pavilions she fancied at the moment. The northward course straight up would bring her first to the Tower for Offering Incense to Buddha, past the Temple of the Sea of Wisdom, the Chamber of Ancestral Seats at Fragrant Cliff, until she reached the Court of the Pines. Then, seated at this apex, she could engage her eyes with more architectural triumphs from the Porcelain Pagoda with Numerous Precious Things to the East, to the Temple for Clouds to Meet at the West. Scattered in between and around were the Headwaters of the Aromatic Sea, the High Foundation of Pure Ability, the Essential Location to Complete the Spirit, the Temple of Benevolent Revelation, the Pavilion to Rendezvous with Fragrance, the Pagoda of Cleanliness, the Elevation of Blessed Shade, and a hundred other spectacular sites to suit every mood, which would take days to visit.

On this May Day we had quite enough to content ourselves with the immediate features at the sparkling lake level. We could see the huge, handsome, immobile, and therefore infamous Marble Boat (the Empress's "battleship") and, across the lake, the seventeen symmetrical arches of the Marble Bridge. Starting at the point called "Welcome the Rising Sun," our group was rowed across to enjoy the cooling breezes. Our route along the willow-fringed shores bypassed the Jade Belt Bridge. We proceeded to the Pavilion of Fish and Seaweed, the Heavenly Canopy, Facing the Seagulls, Invite the Moon Gate, Fragrant Lotus area, Swimming Lagoon, Spring Perceiving area. How could one woman have indulged herself so selfishly (the Summer Palace was only one of her diversions) while her nation was toppling, her people in need? If she had spent the 17 million for the promised navy instead of these marvelous pleasures, would it have changed China's history?

In the Pavilion for Listening to the Orioles, a feast had been prepared. No box lunch today, but glorious celebration courses of Northern cuisine. Our group was motioned to a corner table overlooking the room, and as if by arrangement, I found myself seated next to Comrade G, a tall young man who was dressed in a well-tailored beige suit, cut in the Mao jacket style. I had noticed him, aloof but moving along with our group, and assumed that he was part of the personnel keeping us on schedule. He told me he was with the China Travel Service, his office was in our hotel, and his work involved the approval of visas. Comrade G said that the number of applications to visit China was overwhelming, but she lacked the facilities and services for a huge influx of Western visitors. China has other priorities, for the welfare of her people; so visitors would be accommodated only when possible. Spring and summer are peak periods for applications, which should be made at least six months in advance. Making a slight gesture with his hands, he complimented me: "I moved your application from the bottom of the pile to the top."

In that instant, I knew that Comrade G was no ordinary comrade. Classless though China may be, there is rank. I had not seen him with the working crew on my numerous calls at the China Travel Service office. Courteously, he helped me to a serving of fish; easily, we talked of writers we knew. It was the first time I shared rice with a Communist official, even though he was not introduced by title and simply referred to himself as "comrade"; but as it turned out, it was not going to be the last time.

Altogether it was a day above other days, about which I wished to think at length. As we left the Summer Palace grounds, my mind echoed the rousing, cheerful marching melody of "I Love Peking, Tien An Mien." I did not need another drop to feel that my cup runneth over, but nevertheless there were more drops that evening.

Back at the hotel, we learned that tickets were being provided for a basketball game at the Athletic Stadium. I had never seen a basketball game and moaned to Woody that the idea seemed preposterous on top of an already full day. "If it wasn't an important event, we wouldn't have been asked," Woody reasoned. "Well," I decided, "if I konk out, I'll sleep on your shoulder."

Comrade F, our escort to the Summer Palace, also accompanied our group to the Stadium. Eventually, he became our steady field guide. The eighteen thousand seats in the Stadium were inexpensive and virtually filled. After we were seated, the guests of honor entered the floor pit to sit at a long table on the same level where the athletes were to play. Official photographers for TV and the press surrounded them. The ranking official was the Minister for Foreign Affairs and his guests were Africans, but Comrade F was not certain of their country. It did not seem to matter to him. The American tendency to evaluate people by their origins, prominence, or occupation is not seen in China. During our month there, I was never questioned about where I was born, where I was educated, what my husband did, or where I lived. Friendship is enough in itself; it is a pleasing attitude.

Tonight's basketball game in honor of May Day exhibited the new physique of China's youth. "New physique" is meant literally, for the old mental disciplines that produced witty scholars of the literati class neglected the body; the revised attitude toward physical skills was demonstrated by teams of young men and women acrobats. A parade of children, girls in dark blue, boys in white tops and red trousers, also entered the arena to somersault over double bars. The way the crowds gasped when certain names were announced showed that they were stars of national reputation, and the stars included more women than men.

There was indisputable evidence of the natural difference between females and males. The girls could bend into elastic arches, while the boys were more powerful and stiffer. Lithe and strong, the beautiful figures showed us another discipline: after their acts, they cleared the pads and equipment; in one long row, the children quickly rolled up the huge central pad. They did not need stage hands.

The basketball game was played between the blue-uniformed Kiangsu Province team, and the National team dressed in red and black. It was close, but the latter won. The sport was fast and graceful, and I was too interested to konk out. On our way home, our bus detoured to the city center for a close look at the glorious light display.

The month of waiting was worth it; I would otherwise never have seen Peking as spring arrived, nor shared in its May Day festivities.

CHAPTER 27
NORMAN IS FOUND

During our first interview, Comrade E had asked us, "Is there any person you would like to see?" Woody said, "I'd like to see my brother Norman. My last communication from him listed an address at Yenching University in Peking, but I have not heard from him since 1957." And he gave Comrade E the envelope with Norman's last letter asking for books on basketball; he was an instructor in the Athletic Department of the university.

Comrade E told us Yenching was now part of Peking University, and he promised to make inquiries.

We were not sure whether Norman was still alive after the furor of the Cultural Revolution, but having listed his name and probable address in our visa application, it was logical to inquire here on the slim chance that we might find him. It was on a Monday that Comrade E gave us his promise. Though Peking is huge, communications are rapid, and the university would have kept records. By the time Wednesday came without a word, Woody said, "I have given up hope of hearing from Norman." Early Thursday evening, Comrade F came to our room to tell us about the plans for visiting the Great Wall the next day and then added casually, "By the way, they have found your brother."

Woody hardly could believe it. "Where is he?"

"He is at the university."

"Well, can I speak to him?"

"Do you want me to telephone?"

"Of course! Right now!"

Comrade F dialed while we waited in suspense. He talked for a few minutes in Peking dialect and then hung up. This is often the trouble with depending on translators. They take their own initiative, and one is left wondering what has actually been said.

"What is it?" Woody asked.

"You can't talk to your brother. He is moving and things are disorganized."

"Moving! At a time like this?" The report was totally unexpected. "Then when can I see him?"

"I don't know."

We were in agonizing uncertainty, but fortunately, the day at the Great Wall was an exciting distraction for another twenty-four hours. Returning that night, "eagerly expecting tomorrow," we received one of those understated calls with electrifying results. Comrade F was on the line. "We have made an appointment for you to meet your brother tomorrow morning at nine o'clock. We will leave the hotel at eight thirty to drive to the university."

That was the morning I woke Woody to rush through the Temple of Heaven, but even so we were half an hour late. We weren't much bothered; after twenty-five years, another thirty minutes couldn't be important. But when at the university we walked through a charming, tree-fringed garden to enter a courtyard, and found that an entire committee of university personnel as well as Norman, his wife, and two sons, had been standing at attention in a receiving line for half an hour, we realized that we should have been punctual. Norman's complexion had darkened and his crew-cut hair had grayed since San Francisco days. His figure remained trim—in fact, in all of China, I don't remember having seen one stout person.

I held my hand out to shake his, and so did Woody. "Hello, Norman," we said in English. That was all, an appropriately low-keyed greeting.

And his first words were, "You're late!"

We moved indoors to a reception hall and began to talk. "What's this about your moving?"

"Well, I was in Kiangsu Province," he explained matter-of-factly. "And my wife was in Honan Province with my sons." (Each of those provinces was 500 or more miles south of Peking, and the two provinces themselves are separated by the intervening province of Anhwei.)

We sat around both sides of a large conference table with mugs of hot tea, Norman, his wife, their two sons, ages nine and thirteen, a male staff administrative authority, the female head of the Literature Department, and an unintroduced man who looked on, all of them in their thirties or forties. The tea man hovered on the edges. Before we could talk further, a handsome young male Red Guard, a government representative attached to the university, rapped for attention. Clearly this was not going to be a simple family reunion; it was also an opportunity to introduce us to Peking University.

The institution dated back to 1898, in the Ching Dynasty, and the present facilities, which combined the former Yenching with Chingwa and Peita universities, were established in 1952. There are now seventeen departments devoted to the study of Literature, Reasoning, and Rhetoric, and ten associated Factories. The university had been closed during the Cultural Revolution between 1966 and 1970. It reopened in 1971 without its former students. Before the Cultural Revolution, high school graduates used to qualify for admission after taking examinations. The system today is different; a junior high graduate combines two or three years of high school and commune work and demonstrates his abilities in the field before qualifying for entry into the university.

"The leadership of Peita (Great Northern) University was old-fashioned thinking to preserve capitalism. It was changed after the Cultural Revolution of 1966, when teachers and students had to write compositions to criticize capitalistic defects. The college was divided—neither the Red Guards nor the administrative personnel could reconcile differences. But on August 19, 1968, peasants entered the controversy and persuaded them to lay down their differences. In September of 1969, a new Revolutionary Committee began educational changes. Chairman Mao has emphasized the importance of education at the village level, for old thinking did not meet the needs of peasant students. In 1970 two thousand peasant students were selected on a national basis. In 1971 three hundred were chosen to study foreign languages. The biggest difference between the old method and the new is practical. Some workers in factories may be paid a salary to work while studying.

"Our simplified curriculum, carried out on an intensive schedule, graduates students in three years. The objectives of education of character, spirit, and body are to glorify the nation, not the student, whose radio, chemical, pharmaceutical, or medical knowledge is improved in the factory, where he goes not so much to produce as to apply the theories he has been taught. There used to be only three elements to the old type of teaching: classroom, books, and teacher. The teacher taught the student by stuffing him with theory much as the confined Peking duck is fattened. That trio has been expanded by discussion study based on field experience.

"Departments are related, just as reading and science are related. Literature cannot be applied in the associated Factory, so society becomes its proving ground. The literature department organized thirty teams to go into society and come back to report. The students study past literature and foreign thinking to adapt the best recommendations for their purposes. A journalism major writes after he has visited a newspaper.

"The three-year curriculum is not determined by personal choice. Sometimes it involves a student's being gone for several months at a commune. The teacher also goes along to work with the students."

After the Red Guard's long serious explanation, I questioned, "Does a student ever change his major?"

He reiterated, "Since students are working for the country, not for themselves, there is no question of personal interest. In China, every occupation has a future."

Because of my interest, the head of the Literature Department took us to their library, which included both Western and Chinese books. In the stacks, the Western titles included a section of recent additions bought through a bookstore, as well as older ones. The Dewey system was used for cataloging these books, while the Chinese books were arranged by classification.

We passed the stack of Tang poetry bound in dark blue, cloth-covered volumes, fastened by the Asian hand-sewn method, just as I had made my own notebooks as a child. Row upon row was an extensive collection of the greatest Chinese poetry. In my junior high Chinese evening classes, I used to study "300 Selected Tang Poems." How could that lonely girl, confined by rigid tradition, by the poverty of the depression, and by her basement room, have known that thirty-five years later she would see all the Tang poems of her heritage, unabridged, in a university in Peking?*

As in the library at Canton's Chung-Shan University, we saw few users. Students were not allowed to roam the stacks and browse freely; they had to use the system once common in American libraries, requesting titles in writing after consulting the catalog. Thus there was a record of who read what.

We left the somber quiet of the library for the sunny, peaceful courtyard of ponds, willows, and elms, walking past long, low buildings designed with a special feature of Chinese architecture —lattice-decorated paneled doors which could open accordion style along a slotted track, so that in warmer weather occupants could fling open their rooms to the outdoors.

Woody's Polaroid camera aroused the interest of our university hosts, who were surprised and delighted by the instant colored prints he gave them. Naturally, we could not part with Norman when we still had a hundred personal questions, so we invited him and his family to lunch. His Shanghainese wife spoke only Peking

* Recently, enthusiastic Chinese of San Francisco have worked to purchase and install a collection of Chinese literature and records in the San Francisco Public Library's Chinatown branch.

dialect, so we communicated via Norman. She told us that their family had been separated for three years, their sons with her, meeting in Peking on their three weeks' annual leave. Suddenly she had been summoned back here, and Norman had been equally mystified by his unexpected orders. Neither had been told that Woody was waiting for them. They were all suffering from the series of rapid shocks: of being transferred, of finding each other, then of finding Woody and me (their first visitors from the United States). Nor had we been able to assimilate the reality.

Norman's wife had to excuse herself to take care of domestic arrangements. The oldest boy could not stay on with us because he had to familiarize himself with new lessons at his old school. Besides, he must practice for May Day festivities. His younger brother clung to his father after their long separation, reluctant even at nine to give up holding hands. Until I met Norman's son in Peking, I thought there could not be another child as actively unpredictable as my youngest, who was his age. But Woody soon dubbed him "Buster," and I jokingly added that if Ming Choy and he got together, they could shatter staid Peking. It was decided that Norman and Buster would come with us to our hotel for lunch, then spend the afternoon.

We asked our guests whether they preferred the dining room for Chinese food or the one for Western food, both of which we had used with enjoyment. Norman voted for the Western room. Its à la carte menu was international, including chicken Kiev, beef Stroganoff, tournedo steaks, tomato salad, fish à la pizza, and, at the very end, a painstakingly hand-written addition: "Hot Dog American Style—RMB 25 cents."

A manager of a fine hotel in Basel, Switzerland, once told me that American tourists were of two types: those who knew how to eat, and those who wanted steak or hamburger, then complained that its flavor was not like U.S. beef. (Few countries can equal the rangelands and aging facilities here, and beef in China may be water buffalo.) After trying fondue, they still wanted steak; with a delectable Swiss dinner, they ordered Coca-Cola. In Peking, in February, it must have been hot dogs that the Nixon group had wanted!

This noon we recommended caviar for a start. For RMB 1.65, a generous serving arrived on endive, garnished with chopped onion, hearts of lettuce, and toast points. Spaghetti and pork chops followed for Norman. Dessert was a treat for Buster—chocolate ice cream. We preferred local specialties in season: since refrigeration is limited, foods are supplied truly fresh. Perhaps this is why our parents always thought that foods in China tasted better, even though seasonal treats were limited. "When peaches ripened, we had to guard the orchard by night with bamboo sticks," we had heard. "In a week, they were overripe."

Without the strain of university personnel and protocol, we were free to talk about a variety of family intimacies, hardly knowing where to pick up the threads. We told Norman of his mother's recent death, and Woody rapidly described the various ways in which he and his brothers had provided her with twenty-four years of support and comfort from the time they had returned from the service. Norman looked thoughtful and made little comment. He asked about several of his friends, and what his brothers' occupations were. Most of his contemporaries were running gas stations, working as salesmen, or performing post office duties. His brothers were in banking or investments, and one had a law degree. Chinatown was home base for their careers.

We heard part of Norman's story. After he had returned to San Francisco from his tour of duty with the U.S. Army, he was awarded a year's scholarship to Stanford University, working as well to supplement his funds. (He had a brilliant mind and excellent study habits.) Wishing to advance his Chinese, he had left for Canton. Just at that time the winds of revolution from the North reached him. In answer to his mother's letter asking him to come home to safety, he had asked her to send him U.S. $100.00 for ship's passage.

"Ling Nan didn't have high standards, so I disobeyed Mom, took the hundred dollars and went to Peking," he told us. "Then when the U.S. Embassy asked American citizens to leave in 1948, I decided to remain, and moved into the college dormitory."

"But why?" I asked.

For a mild-mannered, soft-spoken man, Norman answered with unusual bitterness, "What future could I expect in San Francisco? Yes, I had a scholarship to Stanford. But weekends I had to run an elevator at a hospital and work at nights in a bar, to make a little money."

I knew the hospital—Norman probably got the job because some of his relatives worked in the kitchen. I also knew the Grant Avenue bar not far from their dark apartment, where day was no brighter than night. Norman was about the age of my younger brother and, like him, probably had suffered overt race prejudice. He continued his story.

"Besides, I knew that if I returned, Mom would never let me go again and I would be corrupted in my purpose."

How well I knew the subtle determination of his mother! He explained with rising intensity, "You never knew the old China I saw, how rotten was the regime and insecure were the people. The crime, the dirt, the suffering covered the face of the land. And when I saw what the Communists were trying to do, I volunteered. I saw my chance to work for what I believed in."

Here was the evolution of an American citizen by birth into a man who became a Chinese Communist by conviction. In Chinatown, he remained dissatisfied as one son in a family of boys in which he was neither the oldest nor the youngest, just one of many in-betweens. (As his mother put it, "One a year, sometimes two in three years.") Only within the Communist movement and at Yenching did he find double satisfaction: full realization of his Chinese identity, and the continuous growth of his personal self-image.

After China's Liberation, he decided to teach sports.* He had always liked athletics; hence the letter to his mother asking for the basketball books. He swam well from that YMCA beginning. In fact, during hot Peking Augusts, he and his sons swam at the Kunming Reservoir of the Summer Palace.

Norman was talking with the ardor of a missionary; he believed that Communism was unmistakably the greatest event in the history of China. For the welfare of a new nation, personal sacrifice was an expected price; not "I want," but "What does China need?" Ideals were translated into action; energy produced results. When the call came to relocate in Kiangsu, he had left with two thousand others from Peking University to live among the peasants. There they learned to build their own housing, hand-forge iron

* His Oldest Brother told me that when he had taken Norman to the 1932 Olympics in Los Angeles, they had been ashamed that there was only one Chinese delegate out of China's 400 million people.

tools, farm, and create a life of constructive interchange with the peasants, teaching them and learning from them.

"Oh, Norman, do you think it's worth it?"

He replied quietly, "I have no fear because there is no crime. I have no worry, because my sons will be educated at the university without cost. I pay no taxes."

"I hear, though, that the Chinese family unit has broken down," I said to him. "All these separations of husbands, wives, and children because of working for the country—don't they prevent you from forming strong family ties?"

Norman reached over and rubbed Buster's crewcut top. "Look at us; do you think we lack family affection?"

Obviously they were close, and as the days later proved, their interrelationship was typical of any affectionate family. They simply accepted their separations when assigned to wherever their country needed them, until the time when, together again, they picked up where they had left off.

He told me also that they paid RMB 1.40 per month for family rent at university housing. Regular meals were cooked for them in the dining hall at very little cost, which did not preclude them from cooking for themselves when they were inclined. Rent had been such a horror for the poor that the present government benevolently protects its people against excessive charges; "landlord" is a dirty word. As basketball coach, he was official referee for national games, so he traveled a lot within China. His salary was RMB 120.00 per month, and together with his wife, who made about half of that as a Revolutionary teacher, they could save at least RMB 30.00 per month. (From my 1972 observations, the purchasing power in China of one RMB was at least ten times that of our dollar for everyday necessities, excluding luxury goods. In addition, some items are undergoing deflation because of increased productivity. Prices are controlled to the split cent. Bargaining is a thing long past. Including utilities, they spend less than 5 percent of their income for residential expenses.)

Norman had no watch, but he had a bicycle. He did not need the watch, he said.* The only thing he missed about the United

---

* In Hong Kong I had heard the facetious remark, "Chinese in the Great Continent save for 'three wheels and a sound': the bicycle, the watch, the sewing machine, and the radio."

States was "the nickel cup of coffee." We were glad to offer him our travel supply of freeze-dried instant coffee. We wished we could have known what to bring him, and taken in a staggering variety of gifts, just like those other returning Chinese!

I thought over the implications of Norman's story. Was it just a trick of Fate which led to his choosing a drastically different life from his contemporaries?

He had always been the most altruistic of his family. It was easy to understand that a young idealist's hopes would be dulled in the huge bureaucracy of the United States and the maze of Chinatown politics. For entirely different reasons from my father's, Norman too had left his mother and birthplace forever.

How would he fit into San Francisco today? After the blacks, the Chinese are now the largest minority group, 9 percent of San Francisco's population, yet theirs is the meekest voice in community affairs and they struggle for social and economic equality. Except for modern architectural innovations, physical Chinatown hasn't changed much. Building profiles have extended skyward, but I was sure he could find his way around. On the other hand, would he find his way around psychologically? Since no private citizen in China possessed an automobile or a television set, could I in conscience make him envious of what I owned and enjoyed? Beyond the problems I had discussed with Comrade D, I left a San Francisco torn by different minority attitudes toward busing— the blacks wanting to be diffused and the Chinese wanting just the opposite; the streets unsafe at night (and sometimes even by day) for the innocent; homes and stores fair pickings for burglars during quiet hours; the schools a sales ground for dope and marijuana; the working middle class sagging under rising prices; the daily newspaper often a horror sheet balanced by persuasive ads for unnecessary luxuries.

I could not discuss our freedoms without discussing the financial and psychological price many responsible Americans pay for them, so I chose to tell him of other changes—like the disappearance of the nickel cup of coffee. "Remember Davis Schonwasser, Goldberg Bowen, the City of Paris, the White House, H. Liebes?" I asked. Norman nodded; they were prominent department stores within two blocks of one another, all family-owned quality enterprises. "Well," I told him, "they are all gone. You can't imagine how prices and costs of doing business have risen in the United States. Also traditional merchandising has been challenged by the growing chains of supermarkets and discount houses, and changes in people's habits. Even the Stetson hat has vanished." (Both our fathers always wore hats.)

Then it was natural to talk about our business and our problems. While we chatted in languages he didn't understand, Buster had remained remarkably controlled, though his quick eyes were never still a moment. I knew he would be the eager reporter to his mother and brother later. As we all left the hotel together, Norman stopped at the front desk on the way. "I had to sign in as a visitor," he explained, "and now I have to sign out."

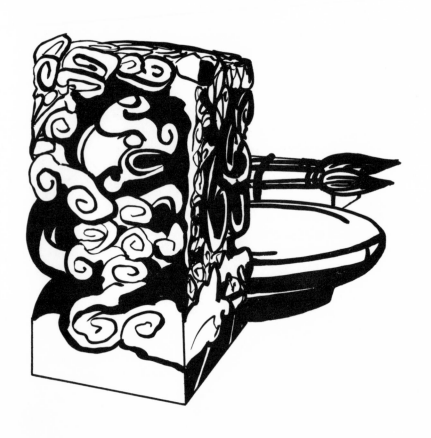

CHAPTER 28
SHOPPING IN PEKING

We were ready for the afternoon of shopping and errands which
we had previously planned, and with Norman along we could do
more than gesture. Our car brought us to an old street, still called
by its picturesque name, "Glass Factory Street." A crowd gathered
to stare as we parked at the main intersection and made our way
by foot into a narrow lane. Woody and I had done some pre-
liminary reconnaissance during our first days in Peking. Comrade
F, learning of our interest in art objects for our store, had brought

280

us to this street. Since stores were government owned, the merchants were not in competition with each other, and we found this refreshing.

All old objects had been inspected and each tagged accurately with date, condition, and type of article. Then they were affixed with official red sealing wax to indicate that they were released for export.

There was more we wanted to buy than we could carry with us, so Woody had to obtain an export license from the Chinese Customs Bureau at the railroad station. It was also necessary for him to arrange for packing and shipment, since stores were not permitted to do so. He had found the "Friendship Packer," managed by an excitable Shanghainese who was charged with packing for government guests, embassy officials, and shipments to the United Nations Chinese delegates. That day, with Norman's help, we wound up our purchases of porcelains, sculpture, and scrolls, most of which were fantastic finds.

I, of course, concentrated on the porcelains. It may be said that some Japanese porcelains closely resemble the Chinese, but when one sees an authentic Chinese piece it is indisputably and authoritatively the prototype. Other than vases and bowls, cups and plates, I was also drawn to hundred-year-old specialties: lavender-pink covered candy dishes with the inside compartments in turquoise, pear-wood boxes with nests of gray earthenware dishes fitted inside like jigsaw puzzles, white ginger jars decorated with orange peonies and little children at play, practical crocks used for steaming soups and poetic with calligraphy, teapots with a whimsical parade of ducks, even soap dishes with perforated covers shaped like butterflies. These were specialties because they were all items with the lids Peking residents needed to protect their contents from the omnipresent sand. (One of my requirements for completing a college pottery course was to make covered objects, for the cover completes a full form; open bowls are only half-forms.) This type of Peking ware, not shipped by Canton's exporters, is rarely seen in America.

The silver filigree settings for Peking jewelry reminded me of Balinese silverwork. Did these two prototypes go back to a common tradition, since Moslems came to the Mongol court of Kublai Khan and conquered South Pacific islands? I wished I knew more history. Excavated reproductions of Tang Dynasty horses and fanciful animals, white jade medallions stylizing many forms of nature, pewter objects, tiny ebony stands for precious small objects, coral strands, old cloisonné, stone brush rests, amber necklaces—I could not stop. Woody, Norman, and I worked. My hands were filthy from handling old stock, and my knees were weak from kneeling. In the end, our hired car transported our finds to the Friendship Packer.

While Woody was busy with forwarding instructions, I wandered on with Norman. Peking, for centuries the patron city of the arts, carries the best papers, ink sticks, brushes, chop marks (personal seals), and scrolls. We started at a spacious, seventy-year-old stationery store. The clerk was a large, balding man of sixty, dressed in a long gray robe, whose Peking dialect Norman translated. When I had seen Professor Chang in Singapore prior to coming into China, I had asked him about the best paper, and he had written down its specification, cautioning me that long length stock of 4 to 6 feet was superior. The clerk told us that Anhwei Province produced the short, native shrubgrass fiber specified by Professor Chang. Wet ink doesn't run or blur on its surface, and it doesn't wrinkle—both important to an artist. I bought a supply in five-foot lengths; when mounted on silk backing, a finished scroll would hang eight feet long.

I had thought brush bristles came from birds, but the shopkeeper informed me otherwise. They were hand-made in Soochow and Shanghai from a variety of animal sources: white hairs from a goat's chin, brown hair from a wolf (for stiffer brushes), yellow hair from a "rodent." The circular Chinese brush comes to a fine point that is held by a hollow bamboo handle. The huge ones are hung by a silken loop at one end so the tip will dry straight. An artist or calligrapher chooses the diameter of the brush (which determines the proportionate length of the bristles) according to the size and width of the ideographs he is planning. For small-character school copy work, children need a brush about ¼ inch in diameter. A calligrapher preparing for large characters, as in a hanging, may choose a ¾ inch brush. I once saw a nearly blind artist in Malaya hold a brush about two inches in diameter, and using all the strength of both hands, achieve fluid ideographs in the "Running Grass" abstract style.

I chose a supply of inexpensive white ones for Ming Choy, whose beginning work necessitates a high replacement rate. Larger ones were selected for Ming Tao and Reverend Kobori. Norman said, "I practically never use a brush since we write with the ball-point pen, and I didn't know about such differences."

This store also stocked other art necessities: ink sticks, and stones. The ink stick is ground slowly, lubricated by water, on a special type of flat stone shaped so that the ink will run into a reservoir at one end. Unusual old water droppers and grinding stones are collectors' items. Ink sticks, made from smoked pine pitch and compressed with glue, vary greatly in form and quality. The best are lightweight. Once, I made a gift to Reverend Kobori of a set of ten old, colorfully decorated ink sticks in flat rectangular form.

"This is not an evenly matched set," I remarked. "Some have been used and replaced." He took up stick by stick, then pointed to one, saying, "This is not so old as the rest; it is heavier."

Now, ink comes conveniently in liquid form that is suitable for students or business people, but the true artist always grinds his own to control the viscosity and intensity of the ink. Besides, as Reverend Kobori explained, "I only do calligraphy when I have time, and as I sit grinding the ink, my inspiration comes."

Affixed to a completed painting or contract, the "chop" or red seal is a person's or firm's official signature. Unlike a signature, the chop cannot be forged. Some scrolls are not only recognized by the artist's chop or chops, they have been made famous by the chops of successive distinguished owners. Chops are legally valid in modern-day Japan, where a business friend told me seriously, "I go to sleep each night with my safe-deposit key and chop-mark; they are my most precious possessions, not even the business of my wife."

Upon the death of the head of the family, the person who gains his chop is official heir to the estate; widows and sons have fought over chops. One of the scrolls I bought in Peking bore the chop "Successor to White Stone." Chi Liang was the only son whom his famous father, Chi Pai Shih (which means "White Stone"), designated as his successor.

When my first book was published, my father had ordered an ivory chop from Hong Kong. It was contained in its own ivory case with a compartment that held the red ink pad. I use it for autographs. Professor Chang had carved his own chops, like many Chinese artists, some of whom had a hundred or two hundred chops. Ming Tao, for whom drawing was second nature, had asked to have a Peking chop made. My search brought Norman and me to a small specialty shop in the heart of the shopping section of Peking, on the "Street of the People." Now I could learn the rationale for the use of different materials in chop-sticks (for seals, not for eating) such as tiger eye, jade, adventurine, agate, and horn, which came in various widths, heights, and proportions. Some were sculptured with lion or turtle heads; others were plain. Some were round, others oval, and most rectangular. Some nestled in silk-lined boxes and others in utilitarian metal containers.

The learning was fascinating. When I ordered the chops for our children and wrote down their names for the salesman, he asked if I wanted a positive or negative impression. (To carve the names meant that the face of the chop would make the impression and the name would be negative; to make the name positive, the entire background had to be carved out.) I chose the positive form. Lai Yee and Lai Wai would have red and white jade respectively, from Sinkiang. Ming Tao's was reddish granite with sculptured waves, from Fukien. Ming Choy's greenish granite from Chekiang was in the form of a lion cub looking up. Crystal, which cost nearly three times as much as stone, was the hardest substance and made the sharpest impression. It was used by banks. The clerk sent our names upstairs to the master carver who specialized in traditional designs, using the Chinese script of old picture-writing days.

One chose the stones, the imprint designs, the type of case— and finally a sufficient quantity of ink, deep red and oily, the consistency of paste and, at a cost of RMB 16.00 per ounce, as expensive as some chops. The ink was worked into silk fiber to make a moist pad, which was kept in a flat, round porcelain-covered jar, chosen to fit the outside perimeter of the chop. Some of the most beautiful porcelains of the past were made to hold brushes and chop-mark pads. The ink remains moist and indelible through the ages.

When we were nearly through, I asked about a curious yellow-

MING TAO'S CHOP: BRIGHT WAY

 LAI YEE'S CHOP: BEAUTIFUL VIRTUE

 LAI WAI'S CHOP: BEAUTIFUL WISDOM

 MING CHOY'S CHOP: BRIGHT TALENT

 "CULTURE IS A SHORT WAVE"

ish marble chop stone, with two mythical horned animals carved on its head. It did not carry anybody's name, an antique curiosity. The sample imprint was a satirical abstraction in four words, "Culture Is a Short Wave." I wondered what eccentric artist had taken the trouble to make such a chop and when he would have used it. I had to have it.*

We left our orders and walked down the Street of the People, looking at windows of yardgoods, books, clocks, and many portrait photography studios. Lining the lane approach to a department store were small booths where local residents were bringing clothes. The businesses did not look like cleaners; Norman explained that they were professional menders. I exclaimed, "Oh, if we only had that in the United States! I've spent hours patching children's trouser knees, sewing tears, letting down hems, when I could have done something else more creative. Their clothes were too good to throw out and not worth paying a professional tailor to fix."

Norman was surprised. "Charges for mending are very minimal," he told me. "The service is necessary if we are not to waste clothes."

Woody's cough had got worse; he had already gone to the Capital Hospital for medicine, and since we were near there, he returned for refills. Though he was not protected by their medical insurance, his bills were small. His examination and medicines for himself and for my Cantonese mosquito bites came to less than one American dollar. He reported that he had been treated with utmost courtesy.

We stopped at the Friendship Packer's, and the manager showed us to the back warehouse, where energetic workers were wrapping each piece in shredded wood excelsior, placing larger pieces in separate corrugated boxes and then carrying them out to the sidewalk, to fit them into a huge crate the size of a small room. I was confounded. "How are we ever going to handle this gigantic container?"

* An artist's chop may not bear his name at all; it may describe himself or represent a philosophy, a thought. For instance, Chi Pai Shih carved hundreds of modest to elaborate chops—including "Happy White Stone," "Master of Drawing," "Knowledgeable Old Man," "The gods and the devil don't work," "Flowers and trees may not be unemotional," "Nothing is impossible to do; some things cannot be"—to name only some.

The manager grinned. "Believe me"—he spoke English—"I have had plenty of experience. A box like this will require special handling equipment. No one can drop it; no one can steal it. It will be packed plenty well, for I know it has to go twelve hundred miles by train to Canton and then another six thousand miles by ship to San Francisco."

It was time to say goodbye to Norman and make a date to meet him again next week, when we were due to tour inner parts of the Forbidden Palace. I was sure that he and his family would be permitted to accompany our group, so that we would be able to visit together as we went through some of those nine thousand rooms.

CHAPTER 29
CHINESE PROTOCOL AND HOSPITALITY

Though we had not wished to seek out prominent figures, it didn't mean that they did not wish to see us. The evening of our busy May Day, we were told to be present at a meeting immediately following breakfast the next morning. When Woody and I arrived in the private small dining room of our hotel, officials were already seated at long tables which formed a hollow square. They were assisted by two language interpreters (Peking dialect and Cantonese) and four diligent recording secretaries. We found that the seventeen overseas Chinese who had been invited, including us, were all United States residents, some among them from Honolulu. The tables were covered with snowy linens, and at each person's seat were a tea cup, plate, napkin, and fruit knife. In a line down the center of the tables were plates of those juicy, crunchy, yellow Chinese winter pears which are a cross between pear flavor and apple texture, and choice tangerines. There were also bowls of freshly made potato chips, fried brown walnuts and pale peanuts, white shrimp chips, and red boxes containing cigarettes and matches. It was an inviting sight. Obviously the meeting was not going to be short.

The ranking officer was a sturdy man in his late forties with tousled black-gray hair, dressed in a dark blue wool suit with a Mao jacket, whom we shall call Comrade H. His right-hand man was Comrade G, with whom I had sat at the Summer Palace lunch. Comrade H was the director in charge of Overseas Chinese Affairs. He began by welcoming our group and told us the purpose of the meeting was to discuss, compare, and speak of one another's problems. It was refreshingly direct, without the flowery preludes used by some Chinese speakers to show off their erudition. He intended to ask each of us to state our respective geographical origins and present residence. Using a prepared list, he first called on a slight, elderly man from Hawaii, Mr. I. Mr. I had worked in the United States for thirty years and had retired fifteen years ago.

"How much do you receive in Social Security benefits?" asked Comrade H.

Mr. I replied, "Four hundred and five dollars."

"Per year?" continued Comrade H.

Mr. I was insulted. "No! Per month."

We all laughed. Comrade H said, "Older Chinese like you who have seen the China of the past will notice the changes for the better. This year, we have had many Chinese visitors from the United States."

The Chinese visitor from the San Francisco Peninsula, an insurance salesman, Mr. J, said that he had enjoyed remarkably good care in his travels in China, and thanked the chairman. He knew that many Chinese were impatient when they had to wait a long time for their visas.

Calling Woody by his Chinese name, Comrade H remarked, "The weather in Peking is changeable at this time of the year, being cool in the evening and early morning. You should take care of yourself by wearing warmer clothes at those hours, so that your cold will not get worse. But then, you look so healthy to me, I wish I could have a transfusion of your blood!"

Both of us were astonished. Obviously he had been informed by the Capital Hospital.

The wife of the IBM engineer, whom we met in Canton, is a grade school teacher in California. She asked for books to take back to her students. The answer was, "The books are still under change after the Cultural Revolution."

I had two questions when I was called on: (1) If all film had to be exposed before departure, what could we do about our Kodak color transparencies, since China could develop only Agfa and Fuji color film; and (2) I had also heard that censorship is rigid. I was apprehensive because of the copious notes I had taken. Would I be sitting around the border for days while they were examined? And what of the letters I was sending off to the United States? I had no way of receiving letters, so I could not determine whether my mail reached home unopened or if anyone wrote to me that I would get it without it being tampered with.

Comrade H replied that as for question 1, they would clear it with the customs department. As for question 2, it was ridiculous and showed how misinformed I had been by anti-Communist propaganda. There are more than 10 million Chinese overseas, at least 500,000 in the United States alone. If they were to check all the mails it would take an enormous staff, and they had more constructive concerns. I was assured my notes would not be censored upon departure.

Young Mr. J said that one of his most serious concerns was that his third-generation children living in the suburbs would grow up without a real knowledge of their Chinese heritage. What did Comrade H think of bringing Chinese-American children to study in China and what did he think of retired professionals who wished to contribute their services to China?

Comrade H had a ready answer.

"Most Chinese come to visit; few to work, and fewer to retire. Chairman Mao has said that there would be space in China for students, workers, and retired persons, but that space would be in agricultural areas. Why not in the city? Because this country is prepared for war, and is methodically decentralizing its population areas to frustrate the effectiveness of nuclear attacks and to simplify defense. One-sixth of the nation's population is now in rural villages, especially the youth working in communes. But most overseas Chinese are not prepared to adapt to living in the country because you have a higher standard of urban living. Sixty years here is retirement age.

"If where you are you have a problem of living or employment, you will always be welcome without restriction. There is no unemployment in China! Everyone has work to do under the leadership of Chairman Mao. That is the difference between our country and a capitalistic country. But some people can adapt and others cannot.

"The same thing applies to the child. He has to study in a small, decentralized area. If he returns to America, he has no way of making a living, not because of his having studied in China, but because he will find another way of life strange."

It was evident that except in rare cases, repatriation to China, that dream of so many overseas Chinese, is not encouraged, nor can China be a convenient "instant culture" course for children of parents who want to provide them with links to their heritage. Comrade H sobered daydreamers by his practical candor. He knew why immigrants had had to leave the hardships of their China: imperialism afflicted China from the Opium War of 1840 until after Dr. Sun's day. "Imperialism is literally invasion," Comrade H said. "The Communist party was established in 1921; our present government has *terminated the history of Chinese emigration*, since it is no longer necessary to go abroad to seek a future. We have no international debts. Employment, technical advance, and our agricultural base are all adequate. If an overseas Chinese has an heir within China, and he wishes to send for him to inherit the gain from his sweat, he can apply for special permission from this government, and such requests have been granted."

Mr. I inquired, "Taiwan is constantly appealing to us overseas Chinese for financial aid. If I give only one American dollar, I can have my name printed in the Taipei newspaper as a donor. Does China wish any monetary contribution from us?"

The answer was, "Few overseas Chinese are rich; most work for a living. Some who own newspapers have tried to help our cause. But as for money, this country doesn't need it. Please help your own Chinese fellow men abroad."

Then, as if he was afraid he might sound arrogant, he continued, "Humility and caution are also part of Chairman Mao's teaching. To overcome the deficits caused by robberies and humiliation, China had to unite to win the greater victory. Now China is strong; rice is heavy on our hands. We have been able to build only a foundation in twenty-three years, very short in the history of the world. Foreign imperialistic aspirations drained several hundred years from us. Our work begins with our high level of morale, and though everyone has work to do, our standard of living is really not very high. So we must continue to work harder. On the other hand, our people are not materialistic, not tense, not rushed, different from the Americans. You can see people at ease everywhere. In the stores, high-class merchandise is not plentiful, nor is there any TV for sale. These are facts, but they are unimportant. More important is to have a high morality. Some countries concentrate on acquiring cars. We do not. Bicycles are better for your health."

Then, changing the direction of his speech, he said, "Many Chinese have become naturalized United States citizens; yet they still love China. Others do not understand modern China and criticize the new government, but they will slowly change. Some are especially close to Taiwan—but few people flee to Taiwan, for there is no future in Taiwan. The United States has backed Taiwan—tell your Chinese friends that Taiwan trembled when Nixon visited China. Even the political big wheels of Taiwan sent their children away from their country, which shows that they lacked confidence in themselves. After Nixon's visit, a U.S. official was sent from Washington to 'show them old friendship.' But they might as well have sent a tape recording!"

Comrade H was grinning, making his little joke in a fine mood.

Yet he drove home his point firmly, passionately: "We are *determined* to liberate Taiwan. We will never change; Taiwan must rejoin China . . . there can be no 'Two-China' policy.

"China under Chiang did not experience anything good, only bad; and then he left. It is true that the war with Japan was partly responsible for our miseries. Once reunion with China is imminent, the Taiwan Chinese will be welcome here. As for the land, Taiwan has always been part of China and must be reunited."

And as he closed the meeting, he enjoined us, "Communicate to others what you have observed in China. Ask the overseas Chinese to work toward one China."

Late the next day, with very little notice, we were asked to prepare for an official dinner party and be ready to leave our hotel by 6:10 P.M. The invitation was in the name of the Consular Staff for the Department of Foreign Affairs. Only eight of the seventeen at the morning symposium were included, but the party at a Peking duck restaurant near the South Gate must have included more than fifty people in all. Our American group was seated in a very large parlor for tea and conversation with the Consul for Foreign Affairs, a genial soft-spoken man in his late fifties or early sixties. Obligingly, he wrote his name down in my notebook, and when I protested that I couldn't understand his shorthand, he rewrote it in exact script.

Soon we were joined by a large group of about twenty persons, overseas Chinese from Peru, including a little boy of three. Our Chinese hosts welcomed them in a manner which conveyed high esteem. The women were dressed informally in print blouses and pants. The older members appeared to be laborers. Others with them were a middle-aged woman editor and the publisher of their Chinese-language newspaper who had steadfastly attacked the Taiwan regime while supporting the Communists. I enjoyed talking with the publisher, Mr. K, who was from my father's area and spoke his dialect. It was his third visit, and he had seen conditions improve dramatically. Fragrant Mountains now produces two crops a year, thanks to irrigation. On Mr. K's first visit when mechanization was just starting, his friend, the mayor, had been very upset at a national irrigation scheme that would have inundated a valley and required massive relocation of the existing homes. The mayor hesitated to protest or suggest to the national government an alternate plan to pump via aqueduct. But fearless visitor Mr. K went to Peking, and saved the land and homes by obtaining approval for the alternate pumping plan.

He told me, "Now there are one hundred thousand residents at Fragrant Mountains, of whom ten thousand are employed by the shipyard that makes vessels of more than a thousand tons. More than four hundred factories are constructing essentials like bricks for self-sufficiency, which our town never enjoyed before."

"Didn't you find Canton very disappointing?" I asked.

"The hotel was worse in Fragrant Mountains," he replied. "But you have to understand the malady of the South. Bordering on Macau and Hong Kong, it is the area where Nationalists infiltrate and the avenue through which those dissatisfied with commune work will try to escape. In fact some Nationalists almost succeeded in bombing the present Canton Trade Fair by attempting to enter with identification papers they had purchased or had stolen from invalids in a hospital."

Mr. K was accompanied by his smiling Peruvian wife and the youngest of his four sons, perhaps seventeen years old. Neither of them spoke Chinese. Their son had injured his left shoulder playing soccer, and months of treatment in Peru could not restore shoulder movement. American medicine arranged by his oldest doctor-son in New York also proved ineffective, so Mr. K and his wife brought the boy to China. In Peking they would settle down as long as was necessary for medical treatment. "I expect that I can better afford the cost of treatment here," Mr. K commented. (Before we left Peking, I ran into him at the hotel, and he reported that the hospital routine had begun utilizing herb poultices and therapy practically around the clock. The prognosis was that in a few weeks, without surgery, the boy would recover. This ancient branch of Chinese medicine, "dieta"—literally meaning "fall treatment"—is distinctly different from acupuncture; it has worked quickly (without surgery) on those who have suffered minor accidents, when Western orthopedic techniques have proved to be much slower or unsuccessful.

It was fascinating to speak with Mr. K, whose idiomatic expressions and accent, love for his native village, and devotion to his son reminded me of my father. His wife and son had enough ear for Chinese to understand our conversations. It amused me to ask him a question and hear him answer, "Si." *

The folding doors at one side of the parlor were thrown open to a dining room with individual round tables. Woody and I were seated at a table for eight, together with Mr. and Mrs. J, the IBM engineer and his wife, whom we shall call Mr. and Mrs. L, and our hosts, Comrade H to my right and Comrade G to Woody's left. It was an intimate group. Mr. L, born and educated in Hunan, became our interpreter.

The consul made the welcome speech. "In the twenty-plus years of this regime, China has become great and raised herself to a level of international importance. Overseas Chinese must have had various imagined conceptions of new China; now I hope you will move around, and those of you who have known the old China will notice the changes. But I can say that though we have changed we are not satisfied. The Chinese people and the Communist party must still be led. We have firm faith in building a good future country, and if you people have any suggestion after your observations, contribute them for our revolutionary progress."

He repeated the familiar declaration that Taiwan must be liberated to China, and ended his speech, "Resist the two imperialist powers, and help the revolution of the world!"

The Chinese custom of speeches before dining had not changed with the revolution!

The weather had warmed this evening; the restaurant was not air-conditioned, and the room was crowded. Comrade H took off his coat and hung it on a stand, and waved to all the men around our table to do likewise. He beamed at us expansively. "Yesterday morning our meeting was to talk about mutual situations and problems. Tonight the purpose is to relax and enjoy friendship."

Our table settings included bowls, chopsticks and spoons, and three stem glasses at each place, one of which held colorless

* On Christmas Eve, 1973, Woody and I accepted Mr. K's invitation and arrived in Lima with our four children, who reported that his fully recovered son beat them at Ping-Pong. There I learned the bitter origin of Lima's large Chinese colony: from 1823 onward, Spanish expeditions conducted successive raids to capture Chinese males from the streets of Hong Kong and Macau by throwing sacks over them, a technique which procured thousands of slaves to work in Peru.

"Mao Tai," one, a tawny, milder, sweet wine, and the third, orange juice. The women stuck to the wine and fruit juice, but the men celebrated with Mao Tais. The evening wore on; the glasses were continually refilled as Comrades H and G proposed toasts. Mr. J and Mr. L gave up, as did the ladies, but Woody kept up each round with them, until after eight or nine refills all gave up trying to get anyone drunk!

I cannot count how many dinners we have attended with copious drinks, but the drinking at this dinner was different. Glasses were raised in the spirit of a joyous reunion, and like all Chinese dinners, the food was fine, with Comrades H and G busily helping us, their guests. The manners at table have not been revolutionized; Chinese politeness remains familiar.

Peking Duck Dinner as served in Peking wasted no part of the duck, and is not like its namesake served elsewhere. Soon after reaching this city, we had naturally wished to try this delicacy and had visited a smaller, famous establishment near the central "Wang Fu-Cheng" (the Street of the People) shopping street. Even there our identity had been no secret to the manager, polite Mr. Li, who greeted us and explained painstakingly what we were eating. The Peking duck is a special species; unlike squabs, which are killed at twenty-one days, it is force-fed a special grain for seventy or eighty days until young maturity. The chef used a long bamboo stick to rotate and roast the carcass inside a domed brick oven over charcoal fire. The duck had been dressed through a slit under one wing so that while cooking, its juices could not escape from the cavity. Rows of white birds hung in readiness, roasting was begun only after the guests had arrived, and they waited until the hot, crispy, brown duck was brought out smoking, to be shown to the diners before it was carved.

That explanation had prepared me to appreciate fully this banquet hosted by the consul. Tonight, while the ducks were roasting, we started with hors d'oeuvre of four cold duck dishes: boned webs of the feet (reminding me of that long-ago dinner with Daddy when we celebrated his home purchase); little shreds of duck meat captured in aspic molded into tiny stars; livers and gizzards cooked with soy; and hearts crisply deep-fried, served within a ring of shrimp chips. Each dish was a distinctly different texture. Every last part of the duck was relished.

When we had eaten at Mr. Li's, we had only duck parts and duck, but for this special occasion there was an expanded menu. Whole prawns in their shells, as large as baby lobsters, had been transported from the port near Tientsin; they were sautéed and dressed in tomato sauce. (An expert with chopsticks can remove the shells without using his fingers.) Next came sea cucumbers in a rich brown gravy. A clear soup had been brewed with the duck intestines, which have an exotic taste and are a delicacy seldom tasted, because it is so much work to slit and clean them. The carved duck course arrived and was served, as at Mr. Li's, with two kinds of breads. One was a small, flat whole-wheat bun, its crust studded with sesame seeds. The buns had been halved and the soft insides hollowed out, so that the crunchy aromatic crusts became wrappers for the duck meat. If one preferred a soft roll, there were four-inch-diameter unleavened white flour griddle cakes, much like crêpes but so thin as to be transparent. Shredded green onions and a sticky sauce of ground soy beans, laced with spices and lively with chili, always accompany Peking duck. To clean the palate, clear soup followed, with shreds of duck meat from the carcasses and green slices of baby cucumbers. Dessert was served on glorious blue and white porcelain compotes, piled high with tangerines.

The evening's outpouring of our hosts' best, their politeness without stiltedness, gave me a feeling of sincerity, honesty, and real warmth. When we made our farewells, Comrade H took my hand in both of his to wish me a good journey. Americans have the reputation for being physically demonstrative and the Chinese the reputation for restraint, but here in Peking I experienced the happy in-between: the Chinese accepted me as part of their family. It is a memory that stays with me.

CHAPTER 30
ACUPUNCTURE FOR TWO HUNDRED

The visitor to China doesn't find that maps are loosely handed around, as in other countries geared to tourism. The other item I should have brought besides my binoculars was a detailed map. Knowing by hearsay that Tientsin was an hour by train south-east from Peking, and that it was a city famous for its exports of preserved duck eggs and "Tientsin" rugs, but also having heard that it was largely industrial without the artistic fascination of Peking, we had planned only a one-day look at the "seaport."

298

Back in the United States there had also been talk in the travel trade that ships could anchor at Tientsin "harbor" and discharge sightseeing passengers for one-day looks at Peking.

If we had adhered to our original time schedule we would be leaving Peking about May 4. Our fellow overseas Chinese travelers had alerted us that departure from China required several days of work, so we had gone to see China Travel Service immediately after the May Day program. This usually frantic office was quiet on the holiday, but luckily, Comrade E was on duty. He told us that exit clearances would be delayed two days because of the general holiday, so we should instead plan on a May 6 departure from Peking. Since we needed to be in Hong Kong by May 16, we had only ten days to see the rest of the coastal area of China; we knew we could not see the interior as well in so short a time. To utilize the delay, he scheduled our excursion to Tientsin for a one-day morning departure, evening return, and picked Thursday, May 4. We asked him to purchase the train tickets and arrange for car and guide service at the other end. He verified that visitors had sometimes waited several days in Canton, usually the last stop of their itinerary, until the "red chop" of the government was affixed to their documents. I emphasized my aversion; "I have seen all I want in Canton, and the hotel isn't a pleasant place for waiting." Comrade E asked for our travel permits, partly to obtain authorization for our stops after Peking, and partly to ascertain alternative exit procedures.

"What about our bills here?" I asked. (Meals, room service, laundry charges, and other miscellaneous services had been paid for on the spot.)

"I will look them up," said Comrade E. "Your room rent and a few excursions like the Great Wall will be paid through this office."

So we assumed we would go to Tientsin on May 4 and did not check with China Travel Service again until the third. I was told that Comrade E was off for a couple of days to make up for working on the holidays. In the meantime, someone else had made arrangements for me to visit the Peking Deaf Mute School Number Three on May 4.

I waved my hand. "Call the school and change the date."

"No," was the reply. "It is easier to reissue the train tickets."

There was that un-American, Chinese way again! My hunch was that the school had been alerted and a group tour had been scheduled. I was right. It was also the first time a nonmedical group of visitors had been permitted. The train departure was delayed to 4:15 P.M. We would stay overnight in Tientsin, spend the next day sightseeing, and return to Peking.

At the school for the deaf, we were welcomed as usual in a reception building and seated with mugs of tea. Two Army men represented the school, one a doctor and the other the Revolutionary Committee representative, who was spokesman. Comrade F served as our Cantonese translator.

I recorded their information on my cassette. "This school has two hundred students and sixty teachers and other staff members. In the past, there was no medical effort to help deaf mutes. They were placed in special vocational classes and taught nonverbal skills such as handicrafts. In 1968 [two years after the Cultural Revolution] a young, inexperienced medical team visited the school, and were moved by the plight of the deaf. They traveled to Liu-ying to learn acupuncture techniques from Comrade Chao, who had been experimenting with acupuncture around his own ear. The old books had warned against penetrating beyond a certain depth in the brain area, but Comrade Chao deliberately probed deeper, until he felt a sensation.

"There are two types of deafness: that present at birth and that which develops through later illness. The former is caused by illness in the pregnant mother or her taking incorrect medication.

"Muteness is a result of deafness. One of the teachers at the school had become deaf when fifteen years old, and gradually he also became mute. Here the approach is first to cure the deafness, because children can't speak when they can't hear. Comrade Chao had learned the location of blood vessels and nerves affecting hearing. In turn, his acupuncture techniques have been taught to teachers, as there aren't enough doctors available. It seemed logical that teachers for the deaf should know how to treat as well as how to teach. Before the Cultural Revolution, this kind of combination was absolutely impossible.

"By 1969, only a year after the beginning of the program, most students had begun to hear, some quite clearly and some limited by the distance of the sound. *The minute they can hear, they are* *taught to speak. The importance of teaching speech cannot be overemphasized. Without speaking, they lose the effectiveness of their hearing.* But to learn to speak for the first time is extremely difficult. Some who learned to hear were still in the habit of communicating through hand signals, so we have now asked teachers to abolish the hand signal method of communication.* When the students hear, they are transferred to regular schools so that they are forced to speak with normal persons who do not use hand signals.

"In half a year, one of our students was able to speak normally. He joined the People's Liberation Army. Now he is in Shanghai and returned last year to visit our school. He has been featured in news articles.

"This practical application follows Chairman Mao's teaching." †

Then we visited a classroom in one of the low wooden buildings that formed a rectangle around a central play court. The teacher in the first classroom was an attractive young woman with bangs, pigtails, trousers, and a man's-style Mao jacket, who exuded enthusiasm as she led the class in an illustrated math lesson prepared on the blackboard. She enunciated her words clearly, and twenty teenage male and female students watched her lips and looked at the board. She asked for a volunteer, and asked him, "Do you understand the lesson?" "Yes," he replied tonelessly, and made a stab at the answer. "Wrong!" she corrected, and pointed out his error. The math would have challenged a class with normal hearing; the hard-of-hearing were being taught the same curriculum. Their hearing

* It was impressive to find that their concepts followed a procedure advocated by many professional audiologists in the United States. In order to move the deaf individual out of his isolation and into normal society, the "oralism" school teaches him (ideally, from childhood) communication by lip reading, speaking, and writing. The traditional manual method of sign language limits personality development. "Studies have shown . . . that out of 10,000 deaf people studied, those with the best paying jobs . . . job mobility . . . and rapid advancement were those who could speak the best and relied on lipreading." (Quotation from a report at the board meeting of the San Francisco Hearing and Speech Center, January 1973.)

† I am reporting what I heard. However, no statistics were offered which would satisfy the U.S. medical profession. Audiometers were not then in use, though China has now begun making them. The reader should not infer that a deaf person in the United States may expect to hear by taking acupuncture treatments offered here, which may be administered by unqualified as well as by qualified practitioners.

handicaps received special care, but their lessons assumed and demanded normal attention and intelligence.

In the second classroom, also taught by a woman, the slightly younger students, like the first class, clapped their hands in welcome. On the blackboard were profile illustrations of proper tongue positions for various sounds: "J" and "CH" combinations with "OO, UU, EN," were alphabetical phonetic guides placed above the Chinese characters. This teacher was equally dedicated, pronouncing the lesson with exaggerated lip movements; and the class articulated in unison. Then she called on individuals to recite, and promptly corrected any fumbling or off-notes. She coaxed and she reprimanded. She meant business, and the students strained to learn. Then the lesson was halted. It was time for acupuncture. The students cradled their heads with their hands, on their desks, as the teacher came around with a jar of sterilizing liquid and inserted the flexible fine shaft at the base of the skull near the spine. She twirled it a few seconds, removed the needle, swabbed the area with cotton, and was through. One student underwent two treatments: one for hearing, and a second needle insertion at the throat for his speech. Comrade F told us, "The students are always eager for their acupuncture treatments, which occur about every week or ten days, for they expect each treatment to improve them a little." *

The students in a third room were new to the school, and the male teacher used the hand-signal method. It seemed to me that neither the teacher nor the students in this class displayed the eagerness and intelligence of the first two. In none of these classes did we see any student with a hearing aid.

Most of the deaf-mute students live at the school, although there are some day students. Deaf adults can also visit the school after their working hours, or take acupuncture treatments at the community hospital, but the school is primarily for children. "In China, the concern for children is very great and special care is given to them."

This morning's visit fascinated the other Chinese overseas visitors as much as it did me. We had sensed at the school the com-

* Recommended further reading on this subject is *The Autobiography of Dr. Samuel Rosen* (New York: Knopf, 1973).

mitment of the People's Liberation Army to the welfare of these handicapped children. The soldiers we saw there acted like medical missionaries, and the teachers believed in their work with equal zeal. China is attentive to the problems of deaf mutes at every level. Premier Chou-En-Lai himself visited the school in 1971.

CHAPTER 31

WATER CONTROL: NEW POWER OF CHINA

When we arrived at Tientsin Station, our local guide, Comrade Kim, and her superior escorted us in a brand-new car to an old hotel. A ride through the streets of Tientsin paralleled the appearance and story of the International Settlement in Canton. The buildings were ornate stone structures in European style. Comrade Kim called attention to them with the familiar phrase, "You see the architectural remnants of foreign imperialists who inflicted surgery over weakened China."

And then she brightened. "But here is the street where Chou-En-Lai, a high school student in 1919, demonstrated against the traitorous compromise policies of Yuan-Shih-Kai" (who was president of new China from 1912 to 1916, after the child puppet Emperor's abdication). She pointed out the place where, in later years, Premier Chou and his wife had addressed a meeting in Tientsin.

Pleasant and bright Comrade Kim was our first personal guide. I asked her what I had wanted to ask in Peking, but had felt would sound too inquisitive: "I wonder if the Premier has any children?"

"I am not clear about that," she answered. "Not clear" is a frequent phrase in China.

"How about Chairman Mao?"

"I know he had an older son who was killed in action in the Korean War, but I am not clear how many other children he has."

In China, there is no prying into personal lives. But I was American enough to be curious about Comrade Kim, and learned that she was married, had a child, and though both she and her husband worked, they employed an "auntie" to look after the child, thus freeing her for the government work she enjoyed.

Woody said, "I have missed the sea in these weeks of travel, for in San Francisco we live in daily sight of water. Can we see the sea tomorrow?" It was agreed.

Tientsin, we found, was not at the edge of the ocean; we drove an hour over flat delta land to its port, Sinkiang (meaning "New Port" and not to be confused with the vast autonomous region of Sinkiang in the Northwest, which has a different Chinese name). We were received in a spacious Seaman's Hall by the port superintendent, Comrade L, who began with the usual introductory information as we sat over tea.

Tientsin was liberated in January 1949, even before Peking. When Nationalist troops were swept out of the city, they drove abandoned vehicles into the shallow bay, closing the port to shipping. To clean up their clutter took ten months of dredging. Until 1959, the Russians helped in harbor development, a project of national importance since earlier history; in 1939 (during the Japanese occupation), an estimated ten to twenty thousand Chinese had died in creating the harbor, and they were buried alongside the road on which we had driven.*

Now the goods of eighty nations pass through Sinkiang, carried by ships from fifty nations. An 18-kilometer-long breakwater has been constructed to protect a deep channel which can take five 10,000-ton ships or one 40,000-ton ship. Tonnage has increased 133 times since early days, 40 percent of it in trade with Japan.

Comrade L added modestly, "Please do not compare us with the progress of the United States. I heard that in San Francisco, you have a street called 'Street of the Tang People' which goes straight up into the air! [He was referring to steep Sacramento Street.] You have a famous harbor and we are eager for your criticism."

We walked out along the clean, litter-free piers. Dry cargo spillage this morning consisted of rock salt and wheat kernels. The brownish salt was a major export commodity, used by Japan for her chemical industry. It used to take 130 workers forty-eight hours to fill a 10,000-ton ship. Now, with the application of mechanical and engineering knowledge to practical problems, eighteen workers do the job in eight hours. The salt arrives in railroad cars. It used to take eight people an hour and a half to unload a 50-ton car. Now one person does it in nine minutes.

We watched the remarkable machinery at work: a crane operator steered her cab above the top of the rail car, scooped up salt, and dropped it onto a conveyor belt. Another crane relayed cargo from this belt to a narrower continuous belt that ran directly into the holds of the ships. Wheat from Canada was being removed from the hold of a Greek ship by four cranes which straddled waiting open railroad cars and unloaded it directly into them.

A total of six girls were loading and unloading all the ships scheduled for the morning's work. Each was paid RMB 40.00 per month (or U.S. $4.00 paid the dock crew for the day), about standard for an industrial worker's beginning salary. They had trained for two years.

Another ship from Poland was discharging a cargo of pipes.

* Sinkiang is on Pohai Gulf, which is the Inland Sea of China. It is one of the three largest harbors at river terminals, its river being the short Haiho, which extends 70 kilometers to Tientsin. The other two major ports are Shanghai, at the mouth of the Yangtze, and Canton, where several rivers merge into the Whampoa Harbor in the Pearl River delta.

Rows of bright red tractors awaited shipment to Albania. I wondered fleetingly about those tractors; surely China needed all she could produce for herself. Comrade L said, "We used to import many more larger machines from other countries, but now we can make smaller machines ourselves. Chairman Mao has taught us to use waste materials to make good deeds."

Then he turned to me and said, "Now tell me about how you do it in San Francisco!"

I could not begin to explain the intricacies of our city's unions of longshoremen, riggers, stevedores, and teamsters, and how they had battled bitterly against container shipping. I recalled long, violent strikes and the notorious pilferage. I could not imagine their letting six women load and unload for an entire dock! So I only said, "You people are commanding your resources splendidly and have found ways not possible in our city."

We walked in brilliant sunshine to the nearby tower of a dam which controls the outlet of the Haiho River system, the biggest of North China. The land of China may be said to slope from west to east, with her great rivers starting at headwaters in several extremely high mountain ranges which cover nearly half of her western land area, making their way east to the sea. Those mountains and deserts and high plateaus have protected and isolated China. (We shall talk about the other great rivers, the Yellow and the Yangtze, later on.) Several hundred tributaries from the provinces of Shensi, Hopei, and Shantung pour into five big waterways like the fingers of an outstretched palm, at the rate of 10,000 cubic meters per second, and they converged right here where we were standing. In the summer, waters historically roared to overflowing and ruined farmlands, since the Haiho could take little more than 1,000 cubic meters per second. In the winter, the shallow Pohai Sea (only about 20 meters deep because of the silt-mud fill) froze over and, with it, the water supply. In the spring there was drought before the rains. All the year around, sea water from the Pohai could flow inland, causing alkalinization of agricultural land. The big basin draining into the Haiho covered 265,000 square kilometers.

Under Communist planning, the people began to dig additional outlets, build more reservoirs, strengthen dikes; and in 1958 the gigantic planning and work of the present double project was begun—to prevent the inflow of the sea which affected the drinking water of Tientsin and land irrigation, and to control the volume of drainage in order to eliminate floods and drought.

Comrade M, the engineer in charge of the dam, led us to a scale model and pushed buttons; lights came on, real water flowed, and the gates went up and down. "Two of us operate this entire dam by electricity," he said. And he invited us to walk out for an inspection. Remembering how the salmon were aided over the falls at Bonneville Dam on the Columbia River, Woody and I inquired about conserving the local fish. "Don't you have a way to permit them to get back upriver to spawn?" Woody asked.

Comrade M shook his head. "We have plenty in the river, so we do not need to save them."

Though Comrade M's concern was with the dam at the mouth of the Haiho, upriver the people had undertaken an even more complicated task to control the flood of water, a task which has lasted seven years, almost to the present. Harnessing each of the five rivers involved half a million commune workers. Through summers and winters, in rain and storm, through mud, sand, and stone, they worked, inventing tools and machinery as they went along. New river outlets and large dikes extended 1,400 kilometers from the headwaters to the sea. Fourteen hundred reservoirs were also built to ensure against drought. Sufficient irrigation now enables Hopei Province, which had suffered the most since it occupies a large portion of the North China plain, to produce enough grain. In two of its cities, Peking and Tientsin, there are 12 million people. The drive of the people, down to the grass roots, excited our deepest admiration. The Haiho supplies the lifeblood of agriculture, and for the first time in China's history, it is not a symbol of disaster.

We joined crane operators and dock workers at the Seaman's Center for a bountiful lunch of fish and crustaceans. Afterward, we looked at the workers' housing village.

The newly constructed, long, one-story red brick buildings were divided into apartments, each with a separate entry to the street. When our car stopped, a number of people were already standing around expectantly, including the village Communist party worker. "All of these people are willing for you to visit their homes," said Comrade Kim, "and you can choose whomever you like." I looked around, hesitant and bewildered, but my mind was made up for me by a large-framed, tall, and sturdy woman in her sixties who took my arm and practically carried me with her.

Off her front hall was a combination sitting room-bedroom with a large, built-in, double-width bunk. The room sparkled, and the cheery sunshine which streamed in from a couple of windows caught the rainbow colors in dozens of hanging Mao Tse-tung buttons, ribbons, and pictures. You could tell who the hero of this family was. We sat on the bed and sipped tea. The man of the household, a dock sweeper, was home because of illness. He must have been in his mid-sixties, larger than his wife, unshaven, with a crooked natural front tooth and one gold one. I asked him for his history, the first time, he said, he had ever had such a request.

He spoke haltingly. "At the age of nine, I went to work in a foundry. My job was to pull the bellows to combust the heat for a forge. I was so tiny I had to stand on a pile of bricks. I lived on two bowls of corn gruel per day.

"When the Japanese occupied this city, the people had to live on wheat chaff or warehouse droppings. Some of us were constipated and some had diarrhea. If any were near to dying, the Japanese buried them alive. After the Kuo Min Tang [Nationalist] troops arrived, we expected that life would be better. Instead we suffered inflation and rationing. What would feed one person one and a half times per month had to feed my family of four, and all we had was grain.

"Now that we have been liberated, two of my children are married and three are working, and one son is a student. We have two grandchildren with us. All of us have shelter, are cool in the summer and warm in the winter, and pay RMB 1.00 per room each month."

His story explained the pictures of Chairman Mao that surrounded him. We took Polaroid shots and gave them to the couple as a memento. The rest of the villagers were eager to have us visit them too, but it was time for our train to Peking. They gathered around our car and clapped their hands in a friendly farewell.

On the hour's drive back to Tientsin, I asked Comrade Kim

another question which had been on my mind: "I know that you made many preparations for today's appointments. All the people we have met are enthusiastic supporters of the People's Republic. But it bothers me—do the people as a whole belong one hundred percent to the Communist party, and if they do not, do they suffer for it?"

Comrade Kim laughed. "Of course not. Take this driver, for instance. I do not know how many times we have had discussions about Communism, for he is not a registered Communist." As she rattled off in Peking dialect to him, we saw him nod.

"And you know that Madame Sun Yat Sen, who is vice-chairman of our People's Republic, is not a Communist party member. She represents China's Nationalist party. This was one of the reasons for the great People's congress called by Chairman Mao in Peking, so that all the people be represented democratically. Though ninety-five percent of the people of China are the Han race, about five percent in the huge autonomous districts are from a great many other racial minorities. Our People's Liberation Army has gone to help their regions in economic development, for they too are part of China. Chairman Mao said that the Hans must not be chauvinistic; we love all our Chinese brothers.*

"But," she added, "whether or not we belong to the Communist party, we must still work for the good of China."

Returning to our hotel, we used its old-fashioned open iron grille "lift." Our room was furnished with a gorgeous blue-patterned, garnet-background, thick Tientsin rug, and our bathroom was at least 11 by 14 feet, all lined in white tile. The tea set on the coffee table, comprised of pot and Western-style cups, was exquisite blue and white willow ware, but it was the tray holding it to which I was drawn. I have traveled enough not to be acquisitive about many things, but this round porcelain tray was unlike any other. Porcelain takes such a high temperature for maturity, and the Chinese paste is fired even higher, that an absolutely flat, thin bottom usually cracks from the strain of expansion and contraction. This tray was flat, with only a half-inch perpendicular rim. It was not just the perfect surface which attracted me. It had been decorated in the manner of a washed

* The symbolic union of the five-color Tung Meng Hui flag of Sun Yat Sen's time has now been realized.

ink panoramic landscape painting, with several tiny thatched-roof houses located on the bend of a dark river gorge, and three blue-figured fishermen, two on a shore, one on a boat, trying their luck, while two idle boats were tied up. A waiting wife dressed in bright red was silhouetted against one of the red houses. A delicate red fretwork bordered the scene, not unusual to a student of Chinese-Japanese art. What captivated me was that the season was winter, and the snow was crested with brushed white enameled relief which outlined the house, the mountains, the snow-covered boats, and every branch of a bare, gray winter tree. I had never seen three-dimensional white decoration brushed on white; it was a union of technique with artistry.

My fascination with ceramics is constantly renewed. Even though decorated porcelain is not my special interest, the unconscious genius of man who takes an ordinary piece of clay (or fabric, or wood, or paper) and experimentally creates a work of art that records forever his view of nature spoke to me strongly in the Tientsin hotel room: not in a scroll to be rolled away, but in a decorative and skillful accomplishment to be used and appreciated daily. Great or small, the artist communicates without having to explain his concept of truth. It is an unbearable pain to be mortal, but how marvelous to leave something worthwhile to the world!

The unglazed white clay underside of the tray carried no signature, no geographical or date identification. I asked Comrade Kim if we could buy another in Tientsin. She inquired of the hotel manager and told me, "This is an old accessory owned by the hotel, and they do not know where it was made nor do they think you can buy a duplicate. However, they would like to present it to you."

I was embarrassed, but not surprised. It is an old Chinese custom to give an admired object to an admiring friend. We carried the tray from Tientsin all the way home. There are thousands of more valuable, more ancient, and greater Chinese works in ceramics collected in the Western world, but I do not believe there is another one like that now on my dressing table. We have not begun to fathom the arts of China, nor have we begun to plumb the depths of her talents and energies.

CHAPTER 32
RELUCTANT FAREWELL

Our time with Norman and his family was not limited to our day together. They had come with our Cantonese group to see the Forbidden Palace. Taiwan Nationalists had taken most of the precious smaller objects with them, but in the tremendous court-yards there stood the huge bronze incense burners and other monumental sculptures which had been too impractical to remove. We saw the Ming yellow glazed tile walls and jade green tiled roofs and ramps of sculptured white marble laid between double parallel steps, over which Imperial Highnesses were carried in their sedan chairs, by bearers climbing the steps. Even today, no one sets foot on this marble. The record holiday crowds were enormous, and a guard with a bull horn had to clear the way for us. A woman comrade, who coincidentally was a Wong, was our guide.

The scale of the Forbidden Palace is monumental in comparison with the rest of Peking architecture, but it has been laid out in equally precise and harmonious geometry. As in our exploration of the Temple of Heaven, we could only follow a direct path through the heart of the grounds, leaving unexplored the maze of rooms to our left and right. Through the Tien An Mien gate of the Main Square we had started with the crowds down a long route, piercing through a succession of courtyards so enormous that I could picture the processions of callers paying tribute who once waited there with their gifts. We moved through the Tuan Gate, then through another courtyard to the Meridian Gate, on to the Taiho Gate (in the meantime observing other gates to the east and west out of each courtyard). After these four gates, another long courtyard stroll brought us to the Palace of Supreme Harmony, smaller courtyards, two more palaces, another inner gate, and finally the intimate inner Throne Palace. It would have been impossible for anyone to sneak up unnoticed!

In this ultimate palace stood a huge ceiling-high golden-marble-and-glass ornate clock that had been presented by France, and near it on a counter were a number of gigantic Imperial chops kept in individual cases. The symbols of past power, affixed to decrees which meant life or death, power or poverty, were now only historical anachronisms, like the clock. Finally we reached the courtyard which surrounded the private bedroom wing of the last Empress Dowager, and just as curiously as the crowds, we peered through her windows. She had a large sitting room filled with Western clocks of every design (they must have been her hobby), but if she collected exquisite art objects as well, they were no longer on display; we saw only some ornate cloisonnés. The sitting room led to her bedroom, where Her Highness slept in a huge raised bed, canopied and veiled by numerous layers of silk; partially opened folds in those faded pastels hinted of the dark privacy behind. Conniver that she was, she didn't have the confidence to sleep in fresh air, nor could anyone outside her intimate circle know how many persons actually slept within that curtained secrecy.

Norman's older son joined us to stare too. We had missed him, and he explained excitedly, "I was interested in what the people were saying about Uncle and Auntie, so I lost myself with the crowds. They said plenty. They think Uncle looks more or less like one of us, but Auntie is definitely different. They are very shocked at that girl in your group, with her Japanese mother and Chinese father, who is wearing a miniskirt!"

We ordinary Chinese had now satisfied our curiosity about the intimate sanctum of past Imperial dignity, penetrating areas closed even to the most illustrious visiting dignitaries in historical times. Once they had suffered through formal procedures, progressing through those courtyards, one at a time, making obeisance in one great palace after another. Today, though no authority emanates from that palace, Peking is once again the hub of China's cultural, communications, and political power. As always, people come to Peking; Peking does not go to them. It's not like a Chinese to want "in" at another's door—nor to open his own.

We spent our last afternoon with Norman and his family in Chung-Shan Park, actually an adjunct of the Forbidden Palace. In a brief week, the peonies were already past their prime, but the garden, which was smaller and more intimately enjoyable than the Summer Palace, was a gem. There were beautiful tiled court-yards and covered walkways, ice-cream pavilions and soda-water counters. In the hothouses, magnificent porcelain containers with exquisite overglazes in a multitude of colors and delicate floral designs, some bigger than my arms could span, once Imperial property, now were used for ordinary plants like calla lilies and geraniums, which grow neglected in California. Norman's wife was amused by my uninhibited gasps of wonder, and at my eagerness to photograph everything.

Then we returned to the hotel. With Norman along, we found it fun to take public buses. In a crowded bus, a girl rider offered her seat to me. I asked Norman, "Why do people stare at me?" And he answered, "Because they know you must be a guest of the government."

Knowing Buster's passion for ice cream, Woody had planned a short cocktail hour at our hotel room, where the boys could enjoy chocolate sundaes and the adults champagne. In comparison with the quality of the rest of the liquors, the champagne of Peking is uncommonly excellent. It has a very lively action and pleasant light fruitiness, not too puckery dry.

While we were enjoying ourselves, a series of hotel employees appeared suddenly to inquire what we wished. We wished nothing, and were mystified. "But someone has pressed all the buttons, in the bedroom, the sitting room and bathroom," they declared. Norman's wife looked immediately at Buster. He appeared the picture of innocence, but confessed. "Another Ming Choy," I thought again.

Since it was our last visit, I asked Norman to educate me as a member of the family. Now that I had seen something of China, I had a number of questions which I could not ask our official escorts. First, I wanted to know what had happened with the Soviet Union. I had not seen one Russian around, though the Western menu contained the echo of Russian influence, and so did some of the music we heard. When Stalin was alive, he told me, Russia had indeed been helpful. But after his death, Russia became a "socialist imperialist," the master state over a family of nations required to work and pay homage. Though China had first given in and relinquished some water rights in the Pacific, she wished to retain her autonomous self-sufficiency. If the price of aid was to be paid for by the surrender of her sovereignty and limitations on her economic progress, China did not find the bargain acceptable. In 1959, the Soviets abruptly withdrew their aid, leaving China unprepared for self-sufficiency. On top of this predicament, she suffered a period of unforeseen natural disasters, and the government told its people that they had to sacrifice in order to survive.

"What did you do then, Norman?"

"It was hard; it was grim; we just tightened our belts and did without."

"Oh," I said blithely, "to tighten our belts and keep on going without asking for help is familiar to every Chinese. We are patient—we have the long-term view of drawing upon the strength *within* ourselves." In San Francisco, the Chinese had been looked on as too passive at a time other minorities demonstrated, sometimes violently, for their rights or for support from *without*. "Face" is granted, not demanded. I felt that China must once again have depended on this traditional stamina.

But Norman disagreed. "Don't forget we had floods and disasters in China before this Revolution, and we never climbed out of them. The reason—a miracle—that we got out from under after suffering intensely for two or three years was because we had become *united!*"

I remarked that in order to unite the populace toward Marxist goals, the government utilized certain traditional Chinese virtues. Norman lost patience with me. "You say 'the Chinese this' and 'the Chinese that,'" he said indignantly. "Don't you know there is not just one kind of Chinese? What about the old landlords who squeezed the people, and the Taiwan Nationalists who exploited them? Can you say that those who culled the land and then fled exemplified the qualities you say 'the Chinese' have? Frugality, honesty, hard work, patience, sacrifice, acceptance, self-reliance? Those qualities are true only of the working Chinese people. It is their welfare which is the concern of the Communist leadership, who have depended on these qualities to carry out their far-sighted plans for our future. Chairman Mao is one of the great men of all time to be able to lead eight hundred million people by calling upon their initiative. He's smart and he's practical. As he says in his 'Red Book,' the past philosophical wisdom of China is being used to seize the hour of today."

Norman talked with intensity, sure of what he knew. "Remember that the class struggle of the exploiters and exploited has existed internally in China for thousands of years; we can't expect that the thinking of thousands of years could be changed in a few short years."

"What difference does it make what the people think?" I asked. "The government owns everything anyway; there is no chance for individual profit."

Norman discussed this with his wife, and then interpreted, "That is true, but a man running a government-owned business may still retain the old idea of personal gain. Does he serve the people if he continues to think of making more money? A few self-criticism meetings in commune gatherings are not enough to change such ways of thinking. It is a long process."

I turned to the question of the Cultural Revolution. What was the disagreement?

Generally, it was disagreement as to which way Chinese Socialism should go. "I heard there was bloodshed and open fighting," I said.

Norman answered, "Chairman Mao told the people not to fight, but one side continued to wage war." I repeated to him what Comrade Kim had told me, that Chairman Mao had traveled without escort, appearing unexpectedly all over the country, urging the people not to fight, urging them to unite.

He nodded. "But some people disagreed with Chairman Mao. Who are those people?" And he agreed with Comrade Kim's figure on the percentage of dissenters, and the existence of other political parties. "Chairman Mao has said that force cannot change people's minds, that reason must be used. No one is jailed for his point of view unless he incites violence. We do have laws and the death penalty." Indeed, for a man like Chairman Mao to have a following of 90 percent is remarkable at that. A living legend who has lived long enough to see the fruits of his revolution would naturally arouse controversy.

Norman's wife remarked, as if mind-reading, "Your brother's and sister-in-law's ability to visit with us is a triumph of Chairman Mao's foreign policy. China had not expected to get into the U.N. this year, but the small nations voted us in. That too was a victory of Chairman Mao's policy, a result of the friendships he built with those small Third World nations."

I was troubled by their contempt for the bourgeoisie. "Norman, you know that capital is by economic definition the accumulation of labor, or its conservation into capital goods that will ultimately save labor. The farmer saves his money to buy a machine which will save him hours of work. Now your brother and I have a small business, and a number of machines. Would you call us capitalists or bourgeoisie? We like to be independent; we do not wish to be employed by Westerners; yet we must make a profit to support ourselves and our family."

He explained, "If the tools are used by yourself or for the good of the country, and not to drive people to sweat for your profit, then you're not being bourgeois." The question did not bother him.

I changed the subject. "How do people get uprooted? The barber at this hotel is from Shanghai, and so is the manager of the Friendship Packer. When did it happen; why, and how?"

His answer was, "The real question is, do we put our interests first, or the interests of our country? *If our country did not exist neither would our interests.*

"The government calls a person for a conference to tell him his talent is needed somewhere, and he and the interviewer chat. If he has a reason for not being relocated, the government will ask somebody else. It also works another way; sometimes a person or a university student will ask to be assigned to another area."

Though the individual in China today has little personal freedom, a majority of them—as far as we could tell—do appear to believe in the concept of present sacrifice for the long-range good and security of all. Eight hundred million people cannot be harnessed toward a common goal without strong organization and tactics. Obviously some will have been assigned against their wills, but most of the people we saw were cheerful, grateful, soft-spoken, dignified, purposeful, courteous, confident, efficient. They like the results they see in this new country. They are the ones who remained to dike, canal, bridge, till, move, build, plant, think, innovate, clean and work, sacrificing and serving their country as its goals were set, changed, and expanded. Since those too lazy or cunning or rich or doubting have fled by now, the people in today's China are even more the stuff of which a united country must be made. Their reward is freedom from elementary wants. I had the feeling that they are confident that when there is more to go around, they will get their share. The friendliness in China has a tone of calm assurance. They never had that assurance before; then there were only fears of calamities.

As puritanical or unattractive as their present life may seem to us, the great psychologist and extraordinary poet Chairman Mao, who springs from peasant beginnings himself, a child when my father emigrated, has fired his people with identity and purpose. In conjunction with their traditional humility, they have found new pride. They have been stimulated by a new faith in "here and now" to experiment and reevaluate on every level of working and living. The *working* Chinese, who has had to win survival out of adversity (as Norman reminded me), has never been able to choose the easy way. It is uncomfortable not to be able to settle down and to live with ease on the fruits of one's labors, but by accepting discomfort and discipline, they are making visible progress; and most important, they remain dedicated.

I considered our freedoms in the United States. According to income, practicability, inclination, or responsibility, the Chinese minority here enjoys freedom in movement and choice in education, and—according to their degree of education—the chance to exercise freedom in creativeness, speech, communication, and politics. These are very precious rights. Members of our Chinese-American minority have been able to select from the wealth of options open to them. They can take for granted the "here and now"— and the future. And as Comrade H acknowledged, most overseas Chinese have become used to a standard of living which would preclude them from adapting to permanent living in rural China.

But neither minorities nor majorities are free from those fears and worries that I had discussed with Comrade D and Norman. It is easy to make comparisons between Norman's way of life and ours, and to say that there should be something that falls between their enthusiastic response and our need for cohesiveness in the United States, something between their passion not to waste and our corruption by commercial bombardment, something between the purposeful lives of their youth and the apathy of so many discontented American young, something between their positive community involvement out of which springs their image of self-respect, and the publicized search of many Americans for meaningful group and individual identity. In molding new China, her leaders utilized an ancient cultural base, for the necessity to accept authority had always been their way of life. America's socio-economic forces have been predicated on a different value of independent endeavor and the Western philosophy of individual expression. Perhaps the something in between is a dream which can never be.

Something else bothered me that I couldn't even discuss with Norman. If as he and his wife agreed, it will take a long time to retrain the thinking of the masses, as this is being worked at, what effect is it having on their literary and artistic creativeness? My hope is that their freedoms have been subordinated only temporarily to the service of their people. But this journey has shown me again that from one society to another, freedoms and restrictions are evaluated differently.

At dinner, we abandoned government and politics for the pleasure of Shantung cooking, in which Woody and I had been initiated by Mr. Li's recommendation. Originating a thousand miles north of Canton, the cuisine of Shantung Province had delighted and intrigued us with its understated, subtle flavors and surprises. Norman and his wife arranged a restaurant dinner, and China Travel Service helped them to reserve a private dining room of mammoth proportions, decorated with beautiful wall plaques and more of those gorgeous porcelain pots. I itched to water the plants, for their soil seemed quite dry, and Norman's wife laughed as I ran around doing this with pots of cool tea. A battery of gleaming Chinese-made electric floor fans with multiple speeds and revolving heads kept us comfortable until they stopped abruptly. We adults stopped talking and looked up: Buster stood there quietly, again the picture of innocence. But his mother knew better. Sternly she asked him in Peking dialect if he were responsible. Sure enough, he had pressed all the "off" buttons.

"I knew Woody would be the first of my brothers to visit me," said Norman on the interview we taped that evening for Woody to present to our San Francisco relatives. Eventually we played it at an Ong reunion when Woody described our meeting with their brother, distributed the gifts from Norman to each of them, showed the photographs of Norman and his family, and asked each to write to him in Peking. Significantly, Woody began the intimate report by requesting an observation of silence in memory of their mother, the one to whom the news would have meant the most had she lived.

The recording with Norman preceded our dinner. The Shantung Peninsula is in a corn and winter-wheat area. Bread, rather than steamed rice, is their staple. Rolls this evening were baked only after we arrived. They came burning hot: concealed within a thin crisp crust resembling a sweet-dough French roll were a hundred separate cozy strands of fragrant white bread. Pieces of cooked rice crust had been fried so hot that they sizzled when the waiter poured over them a sweet and sour sauce studded with fresh shrimps. True to its reputation for magic with seafoods, the kitchen prepared delicate fillets of sea bass rolled around thin slices of bamboo shoot, the whole bathed in a slightly sugary wine sauce. An entire browned fish in gravy made a picture in its elaborately decorated, begonia-petal-shaped, shallow bowl six inches deep, combining pleasure to the eye and the palate. With some other cold courses, soups, and fried chicken, there was of course too much to eat. We were glad that we had family with us and could urge them to take home the delicious leftovers.

We returned to the hotel for our suitcases and hand parcels. No less than a minibus was ready to transfer us. Somehow, the China Travel Service knew that the farewell party would include four additional passengers and more luggage than we had on arrival. The mellow glow of our dinner and the quiet melancholy which descended on us as we journeyed through the huge cavern of the Peking Train Station were suddenly shattered in my terror when I found that I had become separated from Woody. With his load of hand baggage, he had gone ahead as a matter of course to oversee the porter and to find our compartment; it would be overnight before we would arrive at the next stop. I dawdled behind with Comrade N from the China Travel Service, chatting with Norman, his wife, and his boys. Comrade N had been here and there during our several days in Peking, and was our interpreter at that morning group meeting with the Communist officials.

Approaching from behind, two security guards in blue uniforms and official red armbands stopped me to ask for my travel permit. I showed them the pink slip with my passport picture, given to me by Comrade E as a receipt for the original entry travel permit issued in Kung-pei. Comrade E had planned to have our exit formalities processed while we traveled through the rest of China, and on this temporary pink tissue each succeeding station would affix its seals as proof of our arrival and departure. But bureaucratic red tape and obtuseness exist in Peking too; never having seen pink receipts, the guards would not pass mine. Like criminals, Comrade N and I were herded into the security office with Norman and his family. Woody was gone, but all the rest of us were held.

Comrade N's perspiration poured down his face. He was caught between the obstinate security guards and his duty to get us on the train, scheduled to depart in five minutes. Norman and his family were bewildered. There followed a confusing, rapid-fire round of bilingual speech. "Tell Comrade N to call the China Travel Service at the hotel, Room 757, and get a verbal release!" I told Norman in English. "They work around the clock there." Norman relayed this in Chinese to Comrade N, who in his excitement forgot the telephone number of the hotel. Norman supplied it—he had been telephoning us so often. Norman's wife worried that Woody might be carried by train with the baggage but without me, and the two boys watched wide-eyed and silent while Norman furrowed his brow in anxiety, and I could not understand why of the thousands of people at the station, some even sleeping without disturbance, the two guards should so neatly pick me up from behind.

At last it was all unraveled and I was permitted to hurry on; the train actually waited ten minutes past its departure and pulled out at 11:15 P.M., five minutes after I boarded. Woody scolded me for being late! Our last view of Peking from the train window was also our last view of Norman. He stood alone, waving as the train began to pull out and then, in a final burst of longing, as the motion of the train gathered momentum, so did he, running parallel, waving, waving, until finally the train speeded us on our way.

CHAPTER 33
DISCOVERIES IN JI-NAN, SHANTUNG

We were so exuberant and fascinated by old and new China that if not for worry about how the children were faring and the expiration date on our air tickets, we could happily have gone on exploring the countryside for the duration of our visas. Ji-Nan, capital of Shantung and a city of 1,200,000, was conveniently on the railroad route running from north to south along the east coast of China. Woody had agreed with me that we should allocate one of our precious remaining days to look around there.

Disembarking at 7:15 A.M., we were met by the guide from another branch of the China Travel Service, called the "Luxingshe" (the international department), which handles foreigners. Comrade O had learned his English locally, and was teaching at the Shantung Teachers' College when the government asked him to become a local guide. As we drove toward our hotel for the day, he asked, "Have you eaten?"

"Yes, we have," we reassured him. (The train stewardess had overwhelmed us at breakfast with three eggs each, piles of toast, and noodles with greens.)

"When would you want lunch?"

"When we return from sightseeing."

"How much do you want to spend on lunch?"

I made a guess. "Well, RMB 4.00."

"For one or for both?"

"Oh, for both of us."

"For both meals or for one meal?"

"For one meal."

"The same amount for dinner?"

It was only 8:00 A.M., but we were pressed to decide so that the kitchen staff could plan ahead. There was only one other family dining there. That formality over, we went sightseeing.

Confucius was born 200 miles away from the city, and another great philosopher after him, Mencius, also came from Shantung, but we had come to see Ji-Nan, the famous "City of Springs" formed by water seeping through limestone and meeting the resistant granite of the mountains. It is located between the mighty Yellow River to the north and mountains to the south.

We expected a group of bubbling wells, and discovered instead an extensive network of beautiful garden parks which capitalized on the perpetual water supply and had been created by the Communist government in several years of work. Sturdy blocks of granite channeled the waters into an artistic pattern of canals which were the integral feature of the parks dominating the city. More abundant springs supplied ponds and lakes, which together with the canals formed connected, undulating patterns. They had poetic names; from the "Spring of Pearls," bubbles came up like white pearls. "Black Tiger Spring" resembled a tiger blowing water. "Leaping Spring" and "Gold Spring" were other names. In the pools, there were goldfish (long a Chinese hobby) of strange varieties with eyes on top of their heads so enormous they seemed near to bursting, or with topknots like pillow hats. They swam happily, testimony to the temperate and clean water. As we made our way through the parks under long covered walkways painted pleasingly in subdued browns with charcoal-colored tile roofs, the heavy rain did not bother us. In how many places on earth do we enjoy gardens in the rain?

The parks around the springs were different from any we had ever visited. There were few flowers, but many willows, and giant clusters of rock sculptures in twisted grotesque forms created handsome accents. They were all smoothly contoured; we were told that they had been placed under running water that had shaped the smooth flowing lines.

At the largest, "Great Bright Lake," a name derived from its smoothness like a mirror, a boatman was waiting to take us across in a most unusual vessel, big enough for twenty persons to enjoy a tea party on board. A long table, covered with an embroidered cloth and set with delicate old porcelain tea cups and carved trays, was enclosed within its cabin. Two huge, exquisite, drum-shaped, enameled porcelain garden stools—cool seats in summer—were provided together with a number of straight-back chairs. And so we drank tea and glided along through the soundless mist as if in a dream.

In the resting hall and gallery at an island stop, an unexpected treasure trove was casually scattered around: exquisite pottery of Sung and Tang periods, but unlike previously seen collections. A speckled, delicate apple-green glaze on a Tang ewer, covered urns of Sung, one in rare peacock blue, along with the usual celadons and Tzu-chou wares, and porcelains of later Yuan and Ming were in excellent condition. They had been recently excavated nearby under professional supervision. In old days, such finds would have been smuggled out to collectors. Two cases contained pottery from neolithic times (six thousand years old), including a large glazed urn, sculptured horses, and an unglazed white camel.*

* China's earliest civilization revolved around the Yellow River. The Shantung culture was called "Culture of the Dragon Mountain" and dated back to the late Stone Age. The first dynasty of China from 1450 to 1027 B.C. was Shang, a highly organized society with a political system based on class and an agricultural economy. Ji-Nan's history goes back 2,600 years, and a thousand years ago it was known for handicrafts.

At another very tiny island, an open pavilion sheltered a granite table and four matching stools hewn into lotus shapes. Comrade O told us, "Here is where the famous Tang poet To Fu composed poetry." From the stacks of finished works in Peking University, we had traveled to the spot where one of the legendary giants in Chinese literature had been nourished by the tranquil beauty.

After a delectable lunch of local specialties, Comrade O suggested, "Shantung Province is making progress in agriculture and reclamation of salty fields. Would you like to see the Hwang Ho?"

By now I had become most interested in the rivers of China. The Hwang Ho, or Yellow River, not only nourished China's earliest civilization; it has had a dramatic physical history. It begins at the northern part of the great Tibetan plateau, flowing west to east up and down across the face of northern China like a huge horizontal S, finally draining into the Pohai Gulf (south of the mouth of the Haiho, which I had seen at Sinkiang), which mingles with north Korea Bay waters before joining the Yellow Sea. Because of its course through soft loess lands and the Ordos desert, it is loaded with yellow silt, literally giving it its name. Longer than the Haiho, it has similarly plagued the inhabitants dependent on it.

The Hwang Ho is China's second longest river, of mammoth length and width (4,845 kilometers long, going through eight autonomous regions and provinces, covering a basin of 745,000 square kilometers); at its source it irrigated, but at its lower plain it brought flooding and soil erosion. With the repeated floodings, the river has changed course in the lowlands an estimated twenty-six times in the past two thousand years. Historically, dikes were inadequate to contain the river in flood, and it has been recorded that in 1938 when the Nationalists fled the Japanese, they deliberately broke the Yellow River dike near Chengchow in Honan Province to cover their retreat. Nearly 900,000 people died, and more than 12 million people suffered.

As at Sinkiang Harbor, the people had first to repair the sabotage. Millions of people, military and civilians side by side, moved millions of yards of soil and erected more millions of square feet of stonework. The control of the Hwang Ho since Liberation was less an accomplishment of expert engineers than of the people engaged in a twenty-four-year struggle.

Comrade O, Woody, and I climbed a huge dike outlook to gaze on this river which had been a curse since China's dawn. A sluice pumping project was operating automatically to draw water from which mud was separated for dike reinforcement and clear water yielded to irrigate adjoining farmland. "Everything divides into two" is an old Chinese concept.

Comrade O reminded me of a magician waving an obedient wand, for next he asked, "Would you like to see a museum?"

I had hoped for this the entire journey, but none had been open. In Peking, I was told that the museums were "under rearrangement" or "reclassification" and closed to the general public. Even at the Forbidden Palace, we had not seen the recent excavations displayed in the Palace Museum, because the May Day crowds were too great. I told the guide about this and wondered what museum was open.

"This museum is also closed to the public and is under rearrangement," Comrade O said. "But it will be specially opened for your inspection because you are interested in the arts."

"Oh," I guessed aloud, "Peking must have requested this when they made the arrangements for our visit here."

"No," Comrade O said. "I asked the director if he would do this for you because you are a returning Chinese."

Crossing a pretty garden court, we continued under the rounded contour of a high roof overhang and entered what looked as if it might once have been somebody's grand private mansion. We were met by a very tall gentleman and his assistant, a woman. They were both the directors-curators and the supervising archaeologists for the newly discovered old works of art which were so well diplayed that I could not see why "rearrangement" was needed.

I used to say that Chinese minds classified their arts differently from Western museum displays, as evidenced in the handsome and extensive collection in Taipei's Palace Museum. Now after seeing the Ji-Nan Museum for the Shantung Province, I will also say that one cannot appreciate Chinese art without seeing it arranged and documented by Chinese archaeologists.

Beside magnificent huge Shang bronzes * was a superb rarity

* Considered the world's finest technologically and artistically.

from the following Chou dynasty (1027 to 256 B.C.), used for ceremonies at funerals. It weighed 750 catties (just about half a ton) and had been carefully excavated; the site was noted, and a colored artist's map showed the visitor details of the location. A model of a tomb of the Han period (206 B.C. to A.D. 220), when local arts and trade with other countries flourished, showed the burial sacrifices of slaves, placed in layers according to their rank under their master's body. (The decapitated chief slave was alone in the layer next to him.) The master's tomb layer had been pilfered in the past, but the slave layers were intact.

There were more examples of six-thousand-year-old pottery items. Most neolithic pottery I have seen has been much the same the world over, with narrow bases and wide shoulders brought to a small mouth, usually decorated with encircling bands of red and black brushed border designs or incised textures. Unglazed, they were possibly water jars. But the Shantung pottery excavations were different, and so were the shapes of the bronzes.

Another case contained findings from the burial of the tenth son of a Ming Emperor, together with a scale model of the tomb, scale reproductions of all of the objects placed where found and, for comparison, examples of companion arts of their times were on display. An object classified by probable date and type of ware, isolated in a museum case, is less illuminating. The curator stressed that their work was continuous, and on the map he pointed out present excavation sites. It will be uniquely enriching to see the reopened, rearranged museums of China's past. Her soil is likely to yield undreamed-of treasures that will surpass what has already been collected, hit or miss, in present-day displays. For the present, as I had been told in Peking, China has other priorities. No one is in a hurry to make more art history.

Our tour was completed by documentation of one more legendary report about Shantung which I had heard in childhood, not only that the inhabitants were giants (as the over six-foot-tall hotel waitress and the museum personnel attested) but they used giant weapons in a unique "Huge Knives Force," moving silently and swiftly in the dark, lopping off legs and heads of the Japanese invaders. (The Shantung force was stripped. When they felt a clothed figure, it was the enemy.) Near the exit, I saw a display of shining knives with curving blades several feet long that ended in wicked points, and I told the director, "I have come seventy-five hundred miles to learn that my parents told me true stories about the height of your people and the use of those knives."

Back at the hotel room Woody and I were too stimulated by the events of the day to rest before dinner, and so we talked and talked, filled with exhilaration at China's accomplishments in so short a time, and our good fortune in being able to see some of them. Not only her residents, but immigrant Chinese all over the world who have suffered as second-class or lower-rated citizens can now take heart in their ancestry. The persecuted early immigrants to California, the overseas Chinese supporters of Dr. Sun's revolution, had not realized their longing for a new prestigious China to champion their rights. But their children, for whom they carried on the revolution, can see the strong China of their parents' dreams and take pride that their roots reach to the Middle Kingdom.

CHAPTER 34
SOUTH TO KIANGSU PROVINCE

We found Nanking in Kiangsu Province anticlimactic after Peking and Ji-Nan. It was ugly, except for carefully pruned quadruple rows of mature sycamores lining the main streets: their branches opened over the avenues like inverted umbrellas. Most of the buildings reminded us of Canton because they were badly in need of refurbishing. Even more here than in Canton, we saw human beings under harness, pulling incredibly huge loads balanced on two-wheel lorries.

For us, the high point of Nanking was that other great river, the Yangtze. Perhaps more than any single construction project, its new bridge symbolizes China's fruitful combination of engineering and manpower. It is pictured on many Chinese product labels from noodles to matches, for the river had never before been bridged; and we gazed in awe at the complex pattern of ramps which formed its long approaches. The lower deck is laid with train tracks, and the upper level carries motor traffic, at present sparse. Instead, pedestrians trotted across, arriving in Nanking with loads suspended from bamboo rods slung across their shoulders as Asians have done from time immemorial.

The Yangtze, or "Long River," also starts from headwaters in the Tibetan plateau, draining southward in a bend around Szechuan Province, tumbling sharply downward through mountain gorges and a series of lakes, into the huge Chianghan Plain in its middle reaches. Floods and periodic inundation over its dikes have also been part of its history, and after Liberation, efforts to widen channels, divert canals, increase the strength and height of dikes, and build thousands of water locks finally brought the waters under control. Now, by the time the flow—a flow of 1,800,000 square kilometers—reaches Nanking, it presents a calm surface. Alongside the great bridge, we saw cargoes of rocks still being loaded by hand labor onto sampans.

A little more time remained that day, and we decided to hire a car to see a mausoleum. Since I could not make a respectful pilgrimage to my family's ancestral graves, I could make a journey to the Father of new China. It was a visit my father might have wished for me, for the body of Dr. Sun Yat Sen, who had died in 1925, had been removed to Nanking three years later for permanent enshrinement in the vicinity of Nanking's two Ming Tombs. The approach along an avenue bordered by huge stone sculptures of beasts standing guard, as at the tombs near Peking, was in an area which had been left a natural wilderness, with branching evergreens against a background of mountains.

At the main granite gates, three arches had been formed by four carved pillars which must be 50 feet high. Hundreds of broad steps, periodically marked by huge bronze urns, continued onward and upward, reaching an intermediate gateway with tiled roofs much like the style of the Ming Tomb gates we had seen in

Peking, until at the top we reached a circular hall where the body was entombed in a white marble sarcophagus. Surprisingly, it resembled a European tomb with a sculpture of the full body covering the lid. Gray granite wall panels had been incised with the many words of Dr. Sun's famous declarations. The calligraphy was gilded and gleamed in the dim interior.

Outside, we faced the eternal hills and saw a group of hundreds of People's Liberation Army soldiers moving up the broad steps in waves. They had come to pay their respects. Woody and I were silent, profoundly stirred. Perhaps for no one else could Nanking have been so moving. I had recrossed Daddy's three waters and crossed three more northern waters than the fortuneteller could have foreseen. And I had visited the remains of the spirit who had sent that medal to Daddy.

Soochow, also in Kiangsu Province, was four hours eastward by train. On April 27, 1949, two weeks after Nanking was liberated, Soochow's turn came, on the Communists' sweep toward Shanghai, 100 kilometers away. Someday I would like a week in this ancient cultural capital of China, sometimes called her "Venice," where rich retirees used to enjoy their days. It is one of the most famous cities of China. Every Chinese has heard the four-part saying that starts with the desire to be born and to live in Soochow, eat in Canton, wear the silk clothing of Hangchow, and die in Luchow, where the wood is excellent for coffins. As soon as we arrived, we looked for the reason to be born and to live there—Woody was sure it meant that the women were the most beautiful. But our guide, Comrade Tsou, who spoke excellent English, assured us it meant that the climate was perfect, mild the year around. The fragile eave corners which curled upward into points and are characteristic of their roofs are never burdened by snow, for we were south of the Yangtze. The clean look of the town itself was different. There were long low white walls with black-tiled roofs, for centuries a local indigenous style.

Mr. Tsou described old Soochow with an English adjective I was to hear again in subsequent cities: "a consumer city." "Consumer" is a derogatory term for a life of pleasure without productivity. Soochow is also a very old city, begun 2,500 years ago during the period of the Warring States (after the Chou Dynasty, from 770 B.C. to 255 B.C.) when its location was the southern boundary of Chinese rule. The walls we saw were built at the very beginning to enclose what was a small city.

Its mild climate made it ideal for sericulture. Silk fabrication used to be in the hands of small entrepreneurs, but today there are four large factories, each with two thousand workers, plus four hundred new manufacturing industries both large and small. It is now a production city: iron, steel, coal, machinery, electronics, chemicals, instruments, and meters are being turned out even as the fine long history of arts and handicrafts, such as sandalwood fans, intricate embroideries, and the carving of jade and woods, is being maintained. Half a million people are busy. The most celebrated feature of Soochow may be said to be its gardens and pagodas (in the old days, there were more pagodas than chimneys). During feudal times, officials vied with each other to create exquisite homes and gardens, from half an acre to seventy acres in size. Soochow had other attributes—flourishing agriculture in fertile river delta soil, plenty of water, and convenient transportation along the Grand Canal which passed through.*

Since to her people, China was the only country on earth, Soochow became known as their "Paradise on Earth." With ideal conditions, it was also known as a land of fish and rice. (In fact, the Chinese character for "Soo" is composed of three radicals: grass, fish, and rice.)

The ten-year-old hotel, located in an area which was once a dumpyard, has been reclaimed into an elaborate garden setting where a hundred songbirds were to awaken me at five the next morning. Basketball backboards and badminton nets were for hotel staff members, whom we heard singing in the distance.

Through a spacious lobby decorated with beautiful pots of flowers on ebony stands, we walked to Number 106, a cool room overlooking the outdoors. Exquisite apple-green silk-covered quilts lay on the beds. One thing was missing, and Woody sent me to get our key. The Peking dialect word for "key" had been part of my first lesson, but after I asked for it at the front desk without

---

* The Grand Canal, built in the sixth century B.C., extended 8,000 square kilometers southward from Peking through eight states to Hangchow before flowing out to sea. Since China's major rivers all flowed west to east, this north-to-south connection was vital for communication and transport. After Liberation, the Grand Canal was enlarged.

producing the desired object, I thought my accent was bad. It turned out that my request was at fault. The clerk assured me that all the guests here were Chinese, so no one needed to lock up.

My temperature gauge read 72 degrees and 40 percent humidity. Perhaps Woody was right that the women might be more beautiful here, for they should find the climate more agreeable than Peking women, whose skin suffered from the dryness, sand storms, and extremes of temperature.

The local cuisine was simple, yet featured foods new to me: large roots somewhat like asparagus, long greens which looked like reeds, tiny fresh-water shrimps, new varieties of fish, a sweet red sticky rice, pastries of many sorts stuffed with meat or sweet fillings.

After lunch, we asked our driver to stop at an optical store in the main shopping center. I stayed in the car while Woody and the guide went inside to get a screw tightened on Woody's eyeglass frame. Immediately, the car was surrounded by some fifty spectators, standing four deep to stare at me in my white raincoat. When Woody returned (his glasses fixed), he said, "Why don't you stare back; they will go away!"

I asked our guide, "Haven't they ever seen overseas Chinese visit Soochow?"

"Some of the people are here from the country," he said, as if that should explain it.

Woody asked, "Can they tell if we are from the United States or Singapore or the Philippines?"

"No, they just see that you are different."

"But they know we're Chinese? They won't think we are Japanese?"

"No, they know a Chinese when they see one."

Five gardens in the city had been reconstructed by the present government; work on three more was in progress. (The Nationalists had stabled horses here, and the gardens had been ruined.) Some dated back as long as a thousand years and some to the Yuan (about A.D. 1300) and Ming dynasties (from A.D. 1368 to 1644). Each had its own distinctive character reflecting the idiosyncrasy of its owner. In general, a garden was subdivided into many connected areas, each a balance of plants, trees, grasses, mosses, water, bridges, and rocks, defined by walkways and accented by white walls, pergolas, or pavilions with patterned window cutouts which were cleverly designed to frame the views.

I took as many pictures of the geometric lattice trim and the patio pavings as I did of the gardens, for I had never seen such entrancing architectural detail in carvings and in patiently hand-laid floor patterns with different colors and textures of tiles and pebbles. I have seen wonderful flat mosaics in Greece and elsewhere, but these pavings used rounded black and white pebbles in neatly repeated flower patterns or bits of glazed tile in other designs. There were few flowers; I saw a stand of iris growing in an atrium, but otherwise pots of flowers gave accent colors wherever they were placed—sometimes in huge masses in a hall and sometimes just a pair in a corridor. The halls which had once been homes were high ceilinged with handsomely massive exposed beams, and were furnished with marvelously carved hardwood chairs and tables, more elegant and enormous than anything I have seen outside of China.

In Beverly Hills, California, Japanese bonsai experts are paid a hundred dollars a day to nurse private collections. In Soochow gardens, I saw hundreds of bonsai plants treated with utmost casualness. One man did all the work on a huge collection of bonsais of every size and shape. Comrade Tsou told me, "A garden to the Chinese is nature in miniature, and the bonsai is a big universe in a nutshell." The gardener pointed out a bonsai pomegranate that was two hundred years old, set in a rectangular dish about 15 inches by 30 inches, and 3 inches deep. It branched outward into two main trunks, perhaps 25 inches tall. "When the leaves fall in autumn, the red fruit hangs heavily, as large as fists," the gardener told us.

Our two days in Soochow were also partly spent exploring two famous handicrafts indigenous to her culture and synonymous with the arts of China's past—lacy, fragrant fans of sandalwood, and embroideries from gossamer fineness to ornate heaviness. Like other works of beauty that were once the unstandardized products of cottage industries, today these are cooperative achievements made in well-lit factories. Anybody who has loved old objects of beauty from China probably loves an object from Soochow.

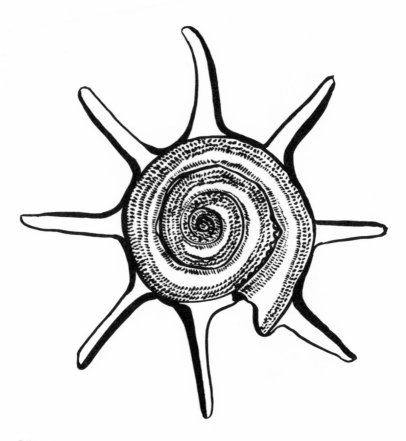

CHAPTER 35

SHANGHAI

If one could believe all that one heard of old Shanghai, it was a combination of extremes—from wickedness to splendor, squalor to sophistication—and though we had been told that the wickedness and squalor had been eliminated, we also knew that splendor and sophistication are not part of China's standards today and had no idea of what we should find. Woody had been here at the end of World War II, but didn't recognize the new street names. He did know that our Peace Hotel used to be the former gay

Cathay, but it was somber and almost empty now. Our suite was so huge that our four children could have slept in the sitting room. The décor seemed to have originated in the luxurious style of thirty-five years ago, with tiled bath, thick rugs, porcelain lamps, full-length mirrors, and large-scale furniture.

Shanghai is China's largest urban center, with 10 million people. Our guide was an earnest revolutionary who tried to learn English from me as I tried to learn about Shanghai from him. We passed the notorious lawn area which used to sport the offensive British Consulate sign: "Chinese and Dogs Not Allowed." The lawn is still there, but there are no more city dogs, for they are not needed to guard property; and the British Consulate is now the Friendship Store catering to visitors.

However, the broad walk and road along the waterfront, the famous Bund, is just as busy, with perpetual water commerce in the harbor. The Whampoo and Soochow rivers flow around Soochow and meet here, to course through Shanghai's heart and eventually unite with the much wider mouth of the Yangtze coming down from the north, finally to drain into the East China Sea. Water commerce coming from China's interior and out to the world, and inbound cargoes from other shores, have made Shanghai strategically important.

As we drove, the guide was telling me about books. After review by local revolutionary committees, manuscripts were printed for distribution. "Books are either in the class of 'Fragrant Flowers' or 'Poison Wheat,'" he explained. "If they express the ideas of the bourgeoisie, then they are 'Poison Wheat' and will not be printed. During the great proletarian revolution, the writers of 'poisonous' books were repudiated, but now, after they worked with the proletariat and realized the teachings of Chairman Mao, they are writing acceptable books." That all writing had to be classified as "either/or" depressed me. So much must fall in between and never see publication.

The next day, having convinced serious Comrade P that I would rather visit children than factories, we were on our way to the Children's Palace. Each class clapped us a welcome. This is an after-school vocational center that cares for seven- to thirteen-year-olds. Although the building was old, it little mattered to the enthusiastic children and dedicated teachers. All the activities were coeducational—girls were just as involved in modelmaking as boys, and boys as involved in dancing as girls. With the children's welcome committee and the headmistress, we toured a succession of classes: orchestra, with such Western instruments as accordions and violins, portrait painting, shadow-play dramatics, choral groups, classical Peking opera movements in stylized walk and hand-eye gestures, Chinese musical instruments, miniature ship building, cutout paper design work, and Morse code.

One of the activities which impressed me most was the reenactment of the famous 1934 Long March, when the Communist Army, under Mao's and Chou's leadership, traveled arduously by foot to escape annihilation by the Nationalists, who had driven them out of their Kiangsi base. After nearly a year, survivors found refuge north in Shensi. The Long March was simulated outdoors (we learned later that this takes place at other children's centers also), where the children got in line to crawl under barbed wire, scale a wall, fall into a sandpit, wiggle through a tunnel, cross a suspended wooden bridge, slide down a fireman's pole, climb up and down nearly perpendicular ladders, and glide on a suspended cable hanging by their hands. Fearlessly, they laughed and slid and climbed and dropped.

The second most impressive activity was the acupuncture and herb course taught by medical doctors to students who were only ten and eleven. It was incredible to see them poking needles into each other's fingers, arms, and legs. "What does acupuncture do?" I asked Comrade P.

"It reduces excitement and regulates the system," he told me.

"Ask the doctor whether, when they practice, it doesn't do them any harm." The doctor's reply was, "If you are ill, it will help, but if you are well, nothing will happen. This class has been taught for three months, and these children can cure simple illness."

"Like what?" I wanted to know.

"Headaches, throat pains, simple rheumatism."

The children went right on quietly poking each other, apparently feeling no discomfort.

A program had been planned in the auditorium, before an audience of about two hundred children. Eight musical numbers, each one brilliantly costumed, were performed to the accompaniment of appropriate Chinese or Western music. As in the Peking May Day presentations, the themes stressed friendship with the People's Army and minorities (Koreans, Mongolians), and militant victory for Communism (dramatized by skits with red flags, use of wooden guns and swords, adoration of Chairman Mao, and hard work in communes). The happy faces of the children wore stage makeup, and they danced smartly in gay colors: red ribbon bows, turquoise sashes, red scarves, black velvet jackets, slit apricot satin skirts over green pantaloons.

After the performance, we gathered for the exchange of critical views, and a little ten-year-old girl, a member of their welcome committee who had attached herself to me by clutching my hand, sat next to me. I was asked what I thought of their activities, and I told them I was impressed with the constructive nature of their program. From 3:00 P.M. to 6:00 P.M., while their parents were working, the children were occupied, obviously happy. It is my belief that delinquency begins when children are idle and unsupervised, for the unlawful can be fascinating when hands have nothing constructive to do. Seven- to thirteen-year-olds are not ready for long hours of aimless roaming.

I tried to grasp the astonishing implication of what I had seen. After seven years at a place such as this, a child could conceivably have learned music, acupuncture, how to survive a military march, how to operate the Morse code, paint, build models, and so on. What kind of a superyoungster may some day emerge? With the population of China predominantly young, how many energetic skills are going to be developed in them, agreeably and systematically?

"How many years do children attend this center?" I asked the headmistress.

"Children must attend in rotation, because there are eighty to ninety thousand of them in this district. Shanghai is a large metropolitan area; more social centers operate in the residential districts. We have older fourteen-year-olds who travel from one center to another to exchange ideas." One of the boys seated at the table was indeed one of these traveling emissaries. A girl spoke up, saying that this was important social training for them as future proletarians. (This was Comrade P's interpretation. We must remember his limited English and therefore his tendency to generalize or use political clichés.)

I asked how many types of skills a child actually learned here. The headmistress said that it was impossible for a child to be taught every subject, but he could learn at least two or three things well—for instance, acupuncture, the Morse code (as interpreted in Peking dialect), and modelmaking, including boats, airplanes, and motors.

She asked me for criticism or questions. I told her the guns and weapons bothered me. Did the children understand that they are to be used for defensive and not offensive purposes? At the Phoebe A. Hearst Pre-school Learning Center of San Francisco's Golden Gate Kindergarten Association, we do not allow impressionable two- to four-year-olds to have any toy weapons, for we deplore aggressive conflict, even in play. The headmistress was firm. "Our children do understand not to employ violence, for they regularly study Chairman Mao's teaching."

The ten-year-old girl who had been silently holding my hand looked at me with her big brown eyes and said, "We are for the struggle of the American people against their government. Please tell the American people that the children of China are their friends." (The Chinese words for children are "little friends." *) These serious, disciplined children, already trained into miniature adults, were psychologically secure and certainly not unhappy, even though they do not have the freedom of American children.

The family used to be the central focus of Chinese loyalty, for government benevolence was undependable. Yet despite the new opportunities for young and old, and China's strong central government today, the family has not disintegrated. Though physical separation occurs, family affection endures, as Norman's family proved to me. When I asked some of the children at the Children's Palace what they did on returning home, they answered much like my own children, "Do my lessons." "Help my younger

---

* The general Chinese good will for the American people is expressed from this child's level on up to government level. American people have reciprocated by forming U.S.-China People's Friendship Associations (which are nongovernment groups) in various cities in the United States; these were joined together on a national basis in September 1974 with headquarters in Los Angeles.

brother with his lessons." "Set the table and help my mother in the kitchen."

The next day I asked to visit a preschool group, for this was the age that most interested me. Children are conveniently cared for at a large housing project as close as possible to their parents' homes. The expectant youngsters had gathered outside and gave us a noisy welcome, rushing in a group to find our hands, practically pulling us into their classrooms. The ratio of adult supervisors to children was one to seven. Each class presented little skits, and though the children were so tiny that they faltered and were not well coordinated, we could understand them perfectly. One group grasped one another's bodies at the waist, pretending to be train cars on their way to Peking to visit Chairman Mao. Another group smilingly sang a song, "Chairman Mao's deeds on earth are as countless as the stars," in high-pitched baby tones. As soon as the performances were over, they broke off and came to us freely, surrounding us with adoring faces. My tape recorded their chirping voices, like songbirds.

Our tour brought us around to the kitchen, where the day's menu was being prepared. It was to include soybean curds, vegetable soup, and pork stew. A crew was laboriously hand-chopping the fresh pork for the smaller children. The blackboard listed the week's menu and showed that at 3:00 P.M., there would be a snack of soy milk and bread. Supper would be meat and cabbage. There was no sugar in this diet. The staff ate the same menu. Portions were weighed by scale.

"What do you serve them to drink?" I asked.

"They drink milk at home in the morning before coming to school, and will get milk again when they go home. This is a day school."

For a day school, the medical supervision was impressive. Four times a year, each child was examined and his weight progress noted. I remembered how often I had to stay home with a sick child; but here, if a child is sick, the mother simply tells the teacher when she brings him in, and goes on to her work. The child is taken to the clinic, given medical care, put to bed if necessary, and may even be kept there several days. Though the formal school hours are 7:00 A.M. to 6:00 P.M., a mother who must go to work earlier or is detained until later is sure someone will be there. Each of the three teachers for a class works eight hours, by rotation.

We could scarcely tear ourselves away, for the children literally clung to us in affectionate trust.

When we walked out of the school gates, Comrade P asked, "Would you like to go up into one of these housing projects and look at an apartment? Although it is one of the oldest, built just after Liberation, it is convenient to us just now."

We knocked on one door without reply, then walked up another flight where we found a family at home. Like the Tientsin dwelling, one large room was master bedroom and day sitting room, and these occupants possessed some beautiful ebony chairs and a table. The father of the household had retired from his job in a textile factory at sixty-two; since he had made RMB 100.00 per month, his 70 percent retirement pay was RMB 70.00.* Of his six children, only three had survived. His son and daughters worked, and one grandchild lived with them. Their pooled family income totaled RMB 200.00 per month, which they considered very good. Rent was RMB 5.40 per month.

We followed the couple to inspect their kitchen and bath. Three apartments on one floor shared a community kitchen, which was divided into three corner facilities, each with a two-burner unit, a sink, and a food preparation table. Just outside, there was an extra double sink. Each apartment had its own toilet. The tub was communal, since factories were equipped with showers or baths, and workers usually cleaned up before coming home.

One cannot compare the quality of this housing with American standards. What matters is that where once a Shanghai worker's family used to huddle under a lean-to between buildings, too poor to pay for an apartment, it now enjoys its own apartment for RMB 5.40 per month.

A cluster of housing units has its own cinema, general store, hospital unit, and other facilities.

Comrade P told me that each new mother had fifty days of maternity leave and subsequently kept her child at a factory nur-

---

* As previously noted, the percentage of retirement pay depends on number of years worked. Full pay is earned after twenty years of work.

sery until he was a year and a half;* then he was placed in a nursery for youngsters from one and a half to three and a half. From then until they were seven, the children attended a day-care unit similar to the one I had just seen.

I had described our Nanking visit to Dr. Sun's Memorial to our guide and explained its personal significance. He was impressed and offered to take us to Dr. Sun's home, where he had lived with his wife, Ching Ling, who is now China's vice-chairman in Peking.

The house was in a quiet district. A guard opened the gates and we came into a small courtyard, where pots of white azaleas filled the entry terrace. Two waiting Revolutionary Committee custodians bade us welcome. We passed through a living room and sat at Dr. Sun's former dining table, made of white marble set into a circular frame of ebony, with six matching stools, and as attractive today as it was fifty years ago. It was significant that it accommodated only six—huge dinner parties were not part of his life. It was also modest, resembling the table at Tao Yuan's basement restaurant where I used to dine with my father.

The home had been neglected during Japanese occupation of the city. The roof leaked and furnishings were ruined. A sword which had been Dr. Sun's was seized by the Japanese, but this had now been returned to its rightful place in this room. Under Mme. Sun's direction, the government has painstakingly restored the home's original appearance, for the building carries precious historical significance.

In August of 1922, Dr. Sun invited two Communist representatives here to confer with him. Subsequently he asked representatives from both the Kuo Min Tang and the new Communist organization to discuss mutual cooperation. Such a large group came to this little house that the overflow had to be accommodated out in the garden. Dr. Sun issued a joint communiqué in 1923, declaring the concern of the United Communist party for the working masses.

In 1924, Dr. Sun went to Peking to convince Congress to oppose military warlords and resist foreign imperialists. (The Republic of

* This fact fascinated me. The new Revolutionary equality has not changed Chinese working mothers, who continue to want their infants within reach. In my father's factory, his seamstresses used to bring their babies with them.

China had been established in 1911, but neither of these ills had been eliminated.) But his health was poor, and he died on March 12, 1925, before his mission could be accomplished. He was only fifty-eight.

In Dr. Sun's upstairs bedroom, a glass door to his brightly lit closet revealed his suits of clothes in suntan twill, cut in the style now known as the Mao jacket. He had not been a large man. On the desk were his surgical instruments and eyeglasses. The walls were lined with books in both English and Chinese, and more books were in the halls and along the staircase. We returned downstairs to walk through the garden, where tall poplars camouflaged the concrete walls. The pervasive feeling in house and garden was of tranquillity, quality, and simplicity. Beyond these intimate walls, 10,000 factories and 160 farm communes flourish today.

Our entire visit to Shanghai had been under rainy skies. Perhaps because of a particularly hard pillow, or perhaps because of the change in climate, I had awakened with a stiff neck on my second morning there, not a new problem for me. When the guide saw that I was not improving, he arranged for us to visit the Eastern Hospital. There is no private medical practice; all doctors work through hospitals. In the country, the scarcity of doctors is offset by corps of trained paramedics who are also part-time farm workers. Woody registered with me, for his Peking cough still troubled him. Never have I had medical care with less privacy. Soon three doctors appeared to join Woody, the guide, the nurse, and me, all in the same room. Comrade P described our problems—according to Chinese tradition, neither one of us undressed for examination—and the doctors conferred. One was Cantonese, with whom I could readily communicate. He identified himself as a surgeon, and introduced the others as an acupuncturist and a physical therapist.

Starting with Woody first, the surgeon took his blood pressure. It read 214 over 110, and he called in an internist and another nurse. Now nine of us were in one room.

The acupuncturist, a tall, dignified-looking man, asked me if I was afraid of acupuncture. "No, I have my reservations, but I am not afraid." The other doctors agreed that he should treat me. Besides my stiff neck, I was suffering from chronic low back pain.

I began to take off my suit jacket, the better for him to reach my neck, but instead, he asked me to peel off my knee-high socks. He inserted one needle above my right outer ankle bone, delicately twirling its gold handle. The needle was finer than any inoculation shaft and in itself was not painful.

"Do you feel anything?" he asked.

"I feel a weakness and vibrations."

Then he repeated the treatment on my left ankle, and asked, "Does your neck feel better?"

"No, but my back pain has disappeared."

"You will need another treatment tomorrow," he decided.

To treat Woody, he inserted and twirled the needles above each wrist. Prescriptions for Western cough medicine, a Western high-blood-pressure pill to be taken for a week to supplement his regular medications from home, and Chinese herbs were issued, which we filled at the hospital pharmacy. Each treatment cost us 63 *fen*, of which only 10 *fen* paid for the acupuncture; the rest was the cost of registration!

The next day we returned as instructed.

"Did you feel anything after yesterday's treatment?" the acupuncturist asked.

"My right foot was numb several hours until evening," I replied.

"That is as it should be. Is your neck better?"

"Only a little."

This time, he used the needles at my shoulders. He also gave me some advice: (1) always keep warm; ideally, I should wrap my neck in a scarf in cold weather, (2) never sleep on a high pillow, (3) get plenty of rest and do not permit myself to get too tired.

I asked him, "What about my headaches?"

He answered, "That is a matter of your temperament; it is a result of being in too much of a rush."

Since I still had some neck pain, he referred me to an acupuncture doctor at the hospital in Hangchow, our next destination.* Then, at Woody's request, the guide took us to a medical supply house, where we purchased a souvenir of Shanghai—an

---

* In recent years, many Western medical workers have made group and individual visits to observe facilities and techniques in different parts of China. One American committee reported: "By the end of the tour, it was clear that China's new society has developed a health care system which is unsurpassed by any nonindustrial nation, which excels the United States in the delivery of primary health care, and which has the potential for becoming the best in the world" (*San Francisco Examiner*, July 1972).

11-inch-high, soft white plastic acupuncture doll with muscle contours. On the front and back of the doll's left side, red (for "yang" or positive) and blue (for "yin" or negative) pathways were marked with needle insertion points; red dots prescribing frequently used places and blue dots indicating unusual, seldom-used places. These needle points do not correspond consistently with any nerve or artery pathway. The right half was cut away in front at the upper thigh, revealing the groin, the nerve in yellow, the artery in red, and the vein in blue. In the posterior view, cutouts at the upper arm, wrist, buttock, and the length of the leg revealed again the underlayers of nerve, artery, and vein. Ribcage and intestines were exposed on this half. An instruction booklet came with the doll. Its text began with a Chairman Mao quotation that good health should be enjoyed by everyone.

We also bought a set of acupuncture needles. These are made in many lengths, the longest ones for the abdominal area. Their flexibility reminded me of a steel guitar string. Anyone in China can equip himself with medical tools.

CHAPTER 36
HANGCHOW'S TEA

Three hours by train to the southwest, we reached Hangchow, famed for its West Lake and green tea. Three provinces converge here (Kiangsu, Anhwei, and Chekiang), and it was just enough south to be within a tea-rice growing zone. Its population is under a million.

Here we visited our first farm commune, in the company of a charming gentle lady, Comrade Chang, who enunciated English with clarity and knew Hangchow intimately. At last I saw tea grown in China, its country of origin. The tea specialty of this district is called Lung-Jing (Dragon Well). The director of the Tea Farming Production Brigade (one of fourteen Brigades forming the Commune) was a large, imposing woman who bore the marks of a life of hard work. She told us something of their history. "Workers on the land used to be tenants, but now we are released from landlord domination. We have been reclaiming waste land and terracing it; from 1965 until the present we have added 450 mous" (approximately 75 acres).

I learned something of the organizational structure of countryside and town. In the country, a family belongs to a Production Team that includes twenty or thirty households. As many as a hundred Production Teams are organized into a Brigade. A Commune is composed of many Brigades, which exchange knowledge and equipment and pool manpower as necessary. In the city, every household is part of a lane or street. One to eight lanes or streets—about two thousand persons, similar to the size of a Brigade—becomes a Residential Area. Multiple Areas comprise a city's Districts. Every person is accounted for; he belongs to a committee, and goes to its meetings. No one is a stranger. At each level of organization there is appropriate ownership and local autonomy. Thus, Brigades may control schools, but Communes control dams.

At this Brigade three pickings of tea are made annually, with the spring harvest yielding the premium quality. Income is distributed according to output, but if a family unit cannot muster enough manpower, it is still guaranteed an income. On reclaimed land, rice is a secondary crop, grown for the Brigade's own use.

We walked along the little village's main dirt road outside the Brigade meeting hall, and the Brigade leader invited us into one of the thatched-roof cottages. Bamboo slats covered the exterior wall, which must have been built years and years ago. Tea-branch faggots were piled high by the side of the entry. The huge front interior was very dark, but in the rear kitchen area, lit by electricity, we met a seventy-year-old lady who was taking care of her granddaughter. She had been born in this roomy house, and so had her children. Vivacious and neatly dressed in a white top and dark trousers, she welcomed us and told us that every day was better than the day before. She was pleased that her college-educated daughter now had the opportunity to leave the country and work in the city.

Down the hill was a Brigade nursery unit, caring for children from two to five. The teachers were in charge of about twenty-five children in one room, with a courtyard play area. It was not as well equipped as a city school, similar in character to the home we had just seen. It was only a few steps for working mothers to deposit their young for the day, but nothing prevented doting grandmothers from keeping company with their young at home.*

We reached a large concrete-paved clearing where the new tea processing plant had been built. Inside the two-story building, efficient machines dried large quantities of tea harvest. They were supplemented by hand toasters much like iron woks, which were tended by individuals who processed small loads. Hand-woven mats and baskets were everywhere. The first budding leaves of choice spring tea, which was being harvested now, command a higher price than the larger-leaf later yields. The Brigade chairman extracted a handful straight from the wok to present to me.

Hangchow also has Buddhist temples; we visited the "Cloud Forest Zen Temple" built during the Ching Dynasty on a site against a hillside carved with more than a hundred stone Buddhas in different poses, dating back to the older Yuan Dynasty. A pretty stream accented the natural rustic beauty of the ravine setting. We stopped to talk to a fisherman who was catching tiny fingerlings for his aquarium, using that international bait, the earthworm. His float intrigued me. It was a section of a quill.

Surrounded by mountains, on which 1,600-year-old pagodas still stand, the town was beautiful, full of groves of trees. Like a glistening jewel, the watery scenery of the shallow West Lake dominated the landscape. When we walked through the public park, it was being weeded by a long row of thirty children on their knees. Even a field trip was made productive.

* Readers interested in child care in China today can read Ruth Sidel's *Women and Child Care in China* (Hill and Wang, 1972). Mrs. Sidel made two trips to China in one year, and remarks that Chinese children display less aggressive tendencies than American children, that 80 percent of children from three to seven attend kindergarten, that half of those under three stay with grandparents, and that the sort of multiple mothering a child experiences in China doesn't hurt the children.

"To wear silk from Hangchow" had been one part of the famous Chinese ideal, so when Comrade Chang suggested that we visit a silk factory, we agreed to make it the last factory of this trip. Comrade Chen, its director, had been in the textile business since 1922, though she hardly looked old enough. Once she supervised seventeen looms and forty workers; following Liberation and the new leadership, she now has 330 electric looms and 1,700 workers on three shifts, in a factory covering 50,000 square meters. In 1958 the workers invented machines that could weave fifteen colors into fine artistic tapestries, long a specialty of Hangchow. During the Cultural Revolution, the air jet instead of the shuttle was utilized to shoot weft threads, and it increased production by 45 percent. By 1971, output had increased 500-fold compared to pre-Communist days, and quality was more dependable. Other factories making other products in China may match or exceed Comrade Chen's record, but by now the reader is familiar with the dramatic progress which all of them have experienced—all striving at improving techniques on the spot, and all crediting the symbolic inspiration of Chairman Mao.

In less dramatic figures, Woody and I can report on the follow-up acupuncture treatment at Hangchow's hospital. Woody's blood pressure had dropped to 170 over 80 (and has remained there since). He has of course continued his American medications. The doctor here had more than twenty-seven years of experience. He jabbed along my shoulders more deeply than the Shanghai doctor, and he cupped my flesh with vacuum domes. Thereafter, my stiff neck improved more rapidly than it normally did under treatment at home.

It was now May 15, and we worried that the flight from Hangchow to Canton, which operated only three days a week, might be canceled and affect our tight onward connections to Hong Kong. The previous week's flights had all been canceled. Luckily we departed that afternoon as scheduled, in a plane with a stripped-down interior of bare ribs and filled mostly with light cargo. Most of the nine passengers were Japanese. When we checked in at the airport we were not surprised to be asked how much dinner we would like to order for our one stop in Nan-Chong. Taking off, the slow plane traveled at about 2,700 feet and gave us a rare opportunity in our farewell to China to see many of her beautiful contours. The crust of our earth is spectacular in different ways, and here I was enthralled by the extensive flat lands with much water in snaky patterns as far as my eyes could see—from little ponds to big lakes, straight canals to winding rivers, narrow fingers and wide forks, blue lagoons and muddy sloughs, a maze for which there was no beginning and no ending, irrigating large square fields or tiny tiers of terraces clinging to hillsides. There were clusters of trees everywhere, outlining the black-tiled roofs of homes, or edges of pools, or long roadways. We saw all shades of green and tones of brown to red. Nothing looked barren across China's southern face; every inch was cultivated.

At the Nan-Chong airport, we enjoyed six marvelously cooked dishes including duck, but marvelous in an entirely different way were the framed tiled pictures on the walls. Who would expect that in this faraway simple place one would find examples of indigenous ceramic art fired in the nearby famous Ching-Te-Chen kilns? On a celadon background, traditional landscapes were accented by red-flag symbols of new China. Flat porcelain tiles are just as difficult to perfect as that flat tray I was carrying back with me from Tientsin.

Forty-five minutes later we were again airborne. It was twilight, and suddenly to my right through the plane window, I found that even the moon in China skies is different. The golden new crescent did not hang with points top and bottom as in San Francisco; it was suspended like an open smile, or a slice of cantaloupe on a plate, with points up on both sides. Then just above the center of the hollow, as golden as the moon, a star appeared. Sometimes long drifts of black clouds tantalizingly curtained the pair; at other times magic peepholes drifted open to frame their glow. I thought of what Reverend Kobori had said, "The cloud here is the same as the cloud there, but we see it differently."

And flying on, suspended between God and the affairs of man, I prayed that that star and that moon which have risen in eternity would see both the children of China and the children of America, those pure in heart in both countries, blessed with peace and love, within our lifetime.

CHAPTER 37

RECROSSING THE WATERS TO HONG KONG

Clearly, however, the affairs of man were not ready to bless me with peace. At the Canton airport, the immigration authorities duly released the Japanese passengers, but when they looked at our papers, a worse scene ensued than at Peking. Our guide, Comrade Q, was working for the Luxingshe Branch of China Travel Service. His intense eyes blazing, he was openly vexed with us for delaying him with an unaccustomed problem at that late hour. He asked for our U.S. passports, which we had been told in Macau not to show, and lectured us on having surrendered our original travel permits. "My other foreign travelers have no trouble getting out of Canton; I cannot understand why you left your papers in Peking."

It was my turn to be ungracious. "I was following orders in Peking. Can't you see the seal and signatures they affixed, and our pictures taken at the last minute in Tientsin? Do you think I forged these documents? Besides, Peking told me that my stamped exit papers would be waiting for me in Canton. Why don't you have them for me?"

We had no respect for one another and argued for an hour until the airport officer realized that this could go on all night. It was past time to close the airport (pointedly the drapes were drawn), so he released us, warning that we could enter Canton but couldn't leave it. We transferred to the Canton People's Hotel, which overlooked the Pearl River and was blessedly newer and cleaner than the Overseas Chinese Hotel where we had stayed. Since the Canton People's Hotel was used by Luxingshe, we concluded that the best of tourist amenities were reserved for Western guests—we were the only Chinese among the foreign visitors who remained after Canton had closed its Trade Fair on May 15. We had expected to leave the very next morning, but now I had to locate those missing documents. At 11:00 P.M. I placed a call to the familiar office in the Hotel of Nationalities in Peking. An hour later I got a return call from Comrade F, who happened to be on duty.

"Your papers were sent long ago," he told me.

"To whom? The Luxingshe guide knows nothing about them and we have had much difficulty."

"We sent them to the Overseas Chinese Reception Office. You go over to their hotel the first thing in the morning, and you may be able to get the seven-thirty A.M. bus departure for Macau."

Already irritated by Comrade Q, I was now angrier than ever, and the more I thought about it, the more overwrought I became. As I lay in bed, I tried to reason things out: either the mail was slow, or someone was inefficient in Canton, or someone was lying. I would not entertain that notion of my mother's—that I would have trouble getting out of China. But the sudden uncertainty conflicted with all the confidence I had acquired in this country, and I lay awake the rest of the night. At 5:00 A.M. I awakened Woody, and we proceeded to the Overseas Chinese Hotel.

There we found at least two hundred Chinese travelers on the street, fussing with their luggage and packages. They were the exodus from the Trade Fair, and most of the China Travel Service personnel was busy seeing them off. So we went inside to sit at the waiting room table. One by one, additional personnel arrived at the China Travel office. Many walked their bicycles in, parking them in the hallway. Then Comrade B showed up, just as officiously distracted as ever. When I explained our presence, he said, "Your papers have not been received by us, but there is one more person who handles passports and he hasn't shown up yet. Please wait." Off he went.

I sat there, not yet tired despite the all-night wait, for I was too excited by my one-woman war. Another hour passed. Comrade B reappeared. "The last worker has shown up and no one can locate your papers," he said, repeating smugly, "You shouldn't have surrendered your travel documents in Peking."

"Peking told me last night that they sent the proper documents long ago. I left them there more than ten days ago. Someone is certainly remiss. Will *you* be responsible if we cannot extend our air tickets, which call for our departure from Hong Kong tomorrow?"

"I'm telling you, we don't have the papers."

"I know what you're telling me," I said, ignoring the eavesdropping hotel guests. I denounced him angrily, for he seemed to me to symbolize all that was wrong with Canton's administration: "Because of you, I have lost my right to freedom!"

He looked visibly shocked. "No one is denying you your freedom; I am just saying you have to wait. Why don't you go into the dining room and have some breakfast rice soup?" He lowered his voice as if he were pacifying a child.

Woody reasoned with me. "There is nothing you can do now. Have something to eat, and then we'll go back to our hotel and check again with Peking."

This time I got Comrade E on the phone. It had been he who had initiated this strange and troublesome procedure. He assured me, "Your papers have been signed and exit clearance seals obtained, but I have to locate the person who was responsible for mailing them."

Waiting once again, I felt the exhaustion of letdown at last. I remembered that before surrendering those permits, I had asked Comrade F if I could have them photocopied somewhere in Peking. He had questioned me: "For what purpose?"

"Well ... ," I answered, "for a souvenir."

"Only documents concerning government affairs are important enough to photocopy," Comrade F had said reprovingly.

I called Peking again. They had found the person who *should* have, but had *not* yet, mailed our papers! There was no further explanation. When would they be mailed? Today, by air. Would it catch today's plane? Just rest and wait.

I sat in my room watching the Pearl River, the flying of quite inartistic white square kites, the fabrics stretched to dry across the other bank, the red and brown sailboats which came and went, the fishing net which was suspended to drop from time to time. The waiting was nervous; mercifully, the hotel was pleasant. In the next two days, all the other guests departed, and we ate alone in the dining room surrounded by dozens of friendly waiters. We wandered around the nearby streets to while away time. Now that Comrade P in Shanghai had explained that all manuscripts were criticized before publication, I scrutinized the bookstores. A blackboard listed new titles on politics and such technical subjects as *How to Fix Electricity at Home* and *How to Practice Medicine at Home*. There were two fiction titles, but I guessed that they probably dealt with acceptable political themes in order to qualify as "Fragrant Flowers."

We passed by the Fair Exhibition Halls. Although the buying had concluded, we saw parked truckloads of Army and Air Force personnel, and a thousand Chinese citizens on foot, patiently waiting in line at the doors to examine what visitors to their country had already seen. Up in Peking we had seen beige, gray, and blue coats worn with dark blue or brown trousers. In Shanghai, where it was still cold, we had seen heavily patched clothes; pants and coats on some workers were nothing but patches. Here in warm Canton, the people were in shirtsleeves of white and pale pastels, with some men in shorts, and women without stockings; adults wore sandals, and children were barefooted. But nowhere did I see women wearing the silks and embroideries that are being produced in the factories, nor did I see the brocaded robes which were currently popular U.S. fashions. Old jewelry and objects of art may be sold to the government. We saw such purchasing agencies in prime locations at shopping districts in the major cities.

We had waited to get into China, and now we were waiting to get out. I joked with Woody, "Remember how we would take the train from Hong Kong for an hour's ride, just to look at the Communist border? Wouldn't you like to see Hong Kong now?" He did not find it funny.

The next day, we called the Overseas Chinese Hotel again. No, nothing had come in yesterday afternoon's plane. Perhaps this afternoon . . . At 4:20 P.M., I called again and got Comrade B. Yes, the precious envelope was at the airport, but it was not "productive" to make a special trip there until he was escorting a group to the plane. Maybe by 7:00 P.M. . . . .

"But that will make it too late to reserve a seat on the next day's bus to Macau! There are so many people trying to get out from the fair!"

"Well, then maybe you can wait another day or so."

"Can't they send a messenger from the airport?"

"You don't understand. Important government pouch can't be handled by unauthorized messengers."

Angry again, I rushed downstairs to Luxingshe and found that other cold fish, Comrade Q. "You're not our business," he dismissed me. "You're the business of the Overseas Chinese Branch. In fact, we do not know why we were asked to take care of you. This entire hotel has to be kept operating because of you."

No wonder Norman had said that everybody's thinking had not changed! I wished I had known a Chairman Mao quotation to retort to Comrade Q!

Woody calmed me, "Well, if Comrade B said seven P.M., why don't we walk the mile it takes to get there and arrive a little before? We can ask in advance about seats to Macau, and can have dinner at the hotel there." Resignedly, we walked up to the China Travel Service public counter, where we had already experienced so many rebuffs, prepared to do battle once more. But, to our relief, we found the benevolent face of Comrade C, he who had mopped our floor during that long-ago rain flood. He already knew our circumstances, which must have been the talk of their office. "I think you must come back a little later," he regretted.

With Comrade C, I felt no need to argue. As we turned away, trying to decide what to do next, whom should we see rushing to us but Comrade Wong, the woman who had escorted us around the Forbidden Palace with Norman's family. I knew that personnel was mobile, but at that point I was really confused, not knowing why she was here. Nor did she explain. Which one of us was more excited I don't know, for she was just as surprised to see us.

"I have your permits here." She waved a brown envelope and spoke rapidly. "But I did not know which room you were in at the Canton People's Hotel. And just as I am trying to find out to send a messenger, I have found you."

It seemed unbelievable to us that the papers were indeed at hand.

"May I open the envelope?" Comrade Wong asked me politely.

"At your convenience." We were just as polite.

Inside were our original travel documents and a covering letter. Comrade Wong took the letter, saying, "It isn't important." I will always wonder what it said, for Peking isn't in the habit of writing unimportant letters. Had our documents been held until that letter was written?

I examined our exit seals. The documents had not been signed until May 14, not mailed until May 16, and it was now May 17.

The next morning we rode an uncrowded "Benzie" minibus to Macau. The driver was as eager to extend himself as the one who had driven us in. When we went back through Fragrant Mountains, he completed our geographical introductions to Dr. Sun's past. He detoured to take us to his birthplace, a simple two-story house of brick, now protected property of the People's Republic. Our fellow passengers were a Cantonese family of three, Mr. and Mrs. Pon, with their frail three-year-old daughter, who rode all the way alternating her perch on each parent's lap. They had been visiting Mr. Pon's family in a village near Canton. The Pons lived permanently in Birmingham, England, where they operated a fish and chips restaurant with good commercial success.

They had simply closed it up to come on this visit.

"There is great interest in Chinese cooking in the United States," I said, making light conversation. "Do you teach any cooking class in England? When we were in London, the Chinese food was terrible."

"No, I am asked, but of course I will not teach them, for then I would lose my bowl of rice," he replied.

"What is in those two brown earthenware jugs that you are carrying so carefully?"

"This is honey from my village. I am going to carry the jugs in my hand when I board BOAC in Hong Kong for London," he told me.

"Honey? Can't you get that in England?"

"Not the Chinese variety. In England there aren't many fresh vegetables or fruits, except expensive imports. If this little daughter doesn't get her Chinese honey daily, she becomes constipated."

At the Kung-Pei border checking facilities, Woody found that he could not take out with him about RMB 50.00 in currency, so he instructed the girl inspector to mail it to Norman. (After we returned home, a letter from Norman reported his receipt of the funds, with a rueful remark that Woody had pulled the "Big Brother" act by returning the cost of our farewell dinner.)

The lady customs inspector was in no hurry, starting first with my handbag and looking at each item therein. When she came to a picture of my mother, she asked who she was and her age. "She's seventy-two."

"Does she live with you and take care of you?"

"No, she is working as an inspector in a garment factory."

This surprised her. "In this country, she would have been retired for years. It is too bad, how hard the Chinese must work in the United States." Perhaps she decided that despite our coming from a rich country, we were not "bourgeoisie." Then she opened the first package in Woody's suitcase. It happened to be the chop marks with the receipted bills. She looked at our children's pictures and remarked on only one of them, as had many others in China: "Is that a boy or a girl?" It was Ming Tao, seventeen years old when the picture was taken, with collar-length hair. "It's my oldest son," I explained. This is generally the end of a polite conversation. And it proved to be the end of the customs inspection. Waiting through our turn for inspection and money return delayed our departure two precious hours. Woody had RMB 30 cents left, and I rushed to spend it on a porcelain fish for Ming Choy to put into his aquarium.

We reached Macau with only two hours to make the last hydrofoil to Hong Kong. At the China Travel Service, our friend Comrade A expedited the paperwork for Portuguese reentry and sent a messenger to purchase tickets to Hong Kong.

We could not leave Macau without saying "hello" and "good-bye" to Ninth Auntie. Cousin Tin Wai, who had been contacted at the hospital by Comrade A, appeared to drive us home. As we passed the knife stand at the alley entrance, I regretted aloud: "I meant to buy a cleaver when I returned, but now I don't have time." Predictably, Tin Wai called out to the owner of the stand, "Sharpen the one she wants and wrap it ready for her to pick up when she comes out, and I will take care of the bill."

Up the four flights we ran, to find Ninth Auntie, who, after the penetrating inspection which is the older generation's privilege, remarked briefly, "You are blacker and thinner." (To be called either is not complimentary.) Then reaching into her refrigerator, she brought out a large bag of ripe mangoes and thrust it into my arms for a farewell gift.

We did not need those mangoes on top of our nine pieces of miscellaneous net bags and luggage, but with true Chinese courtesy, the Macau China Travel Service was ready to help us onto the last scheduled hydrofoil. When we arrived at the Victoria Island–Macau ferry slip in Hong Kong, we had to get across the harbor to Kowloon. No one had known to meet us; no passer-by or vendor would change our money into a local payphone coin; and finally at 10:00 P.M., we arrived at the lobby of the Peninsula Hotel looking like haggard refugees, not even sure we would have a room. But the familiar receptionists gave us a warm welcome and a pile of letters from home.

We took our first showers in a month (only bathtubs in China), wrapped ourselves in the hotel robes, and settled to read without a word between us, until the last letter proved that all our children were well. A significant decision had been made by Ming Tao. He had decided to attend Occidental College, which had granted him generous scholarship aid as an art major.

At midnight, when we thought of food, we went down to the cozy Chesa Room. After a month of excellent Chinese food, I craved only dairy products. Swiss fondue was exactly right.

Fortunately, the airline honored our changed dates. As soon as we concluded business in Hong Kong, we were on our way to Osaka, for I sought the wise man of Kyoto, our friend, the Reverend Kobori.

CHAPTER 38
LOOKING BACK–LOOKING FORWARD

Woody and I sat on the mat with Reverend Kobori in his tiny upper corner study of the Ryoko-in, where a great number of bees, attracted by his blooming orchids, flew in to keep us company. We sipped the welcome brew of powdered green tea, prepared informally without ceremony. I had brought my Chinese map to review the path of our journey. I briefly summarized my experiences in today's China, and searched for the reason I had requested this audience: to consider the price her people paid in limitations of physical freedom, personal creativity, and certain intellectual pursuits. I sought the interpretation of a Japanese who knew both Chinese and American cultures. I told him that the former Buddhist temples were empty museums, for the priests and nuns have now gone to work in factories.

This fact was hard for Reverend Kobori to grasp; to work was not bad, but to lose home was. "They don't come home to their temples at night?" "No, they are no longer priests or nuns." I told him of mass movements of people—farther than a Tokyo man relocated to Kyushu. "Every single high school graduate does three years of service wherever the Chinese government sends him. Marriage is not encouraged until the ages of twenty-five to thirty, and afterward husbands and wives may be separated again. Children go along with their mothers."

Reverend Kobori asked Woody, "You have been in China before; how do you compare your two visits?"

Woody answered, "In the 1940s there was no unity, not enough food, no medication, no safety, no equality."

Reverend Kobori said, "Both China and the United States have merits and demerits. In the United States, freedom is too extreme, without restrictions. China practices economy while the United States practices wastefulness. In the United States, there is too much attention to luxuries but little attention to spiritual sufficiency. Consequently, Americans are materially full, but spiritually hungry. And other countries may be said to be suffering from the same condition."

I wondered, "Could they also be spiritually hungry in China without formal religion, or can the inspiration to build 'on earth as it is in heaven' substitute for spiritual faith? There is more to life than food, clothing, and housing. What will China want in the future?"

This question provoked Reverend Kobori to apply it closer to home and to the present. "I am thinking about Japan," he said.

I quoted to him the remark of an elderly Japanese Episcopalian that Japan was materially rich, but its young culturally poor. Reverend Kobori agreed with this. "Japan has a closer relation to the United States; but some Japanese prefer closer ties to Communist China. Why cannot Japan appreciate its own self? It is losing its identity!"

I returned to the subject of China. "It's the nonmonetary cost that bothers me. The people have no financial worries, but they have restrictions."

Reverend Kobori asked, "Doesn't this weaken the old family ties?"

"It eliminates that old family loyalty which used to take precedence over duties to the state. Little children expect to become little red soldiers and to be sent anywhere when they grow up. Older parents are loyal to this government because there is no class, no bribery, no tips; present alternatives are preferable to fear and starving. But still I am bothered."

I groped for understanding. I mentioned the Cultural Revolution. "The university professor who didn't know how to wash his own clothes now has to learn to operate a tractor. To an outside observer, the university at the commune is like scrambled eggs; no longer can the yolks be separated from the whites. Will both be improved? What will come of all this?"

Reverend Kobori was optimistic. "The Communist policy would not be suitable for us. But for the entire Chinese nation to become enriched and their workers educated—that is a very happy thing for all mankind. After common people are educated to a new level of self-sufficiency, they will know how to think, and when they have attained wisdom, they will be creative."

In the serenity of the Ryoko-in, good friends shared intimate thoughts. This audience we were enjoying could not have happened in priestless China. Zen, adapted from China, was a centuries-old answer to the Samurai's philosophical problems caused by political change. If dedication to the country is all-absorbing, is there a need for another philosophy? The Chinese have always been practical even when religious. Isn't it better to have dammed the rivers than to pray to the Heavens for comfort after disaster?

In lamenting the disappearance of artistic achievements which collectors would treasure, should we wish those achievements if the cost is to keep 95 percent of the people illiterate and poorly paid artisans? And can we not be grateful that a country that is on her way to a destiny of her own making is dedicated not to make war? When 95 percent of her people become literate, I agree with Reverend Kobori that "it is a very happy thing for all mankind." New China is a very happy thing for herself too.

As we left Kyoto, we had really only begun to consider new areas of questions and ideas. Woody's and my roots in China have proved long and strong. For centuries, like the roots of the remarkable banyan, which reach laterally through thin air to form perpendicular new trunks under the umbrella of the parent tree, those unsophisticated immigrant Chinese have rooted where they dropped, growing their own trees, sure of shared identity with their source and with other roots dropped elsewhere. In time, the inseparable roots, trunks, and leaves have formed a spectacular, impenetrable thicket.

I couldn't forget Comrade D's remark, "I carried on the revolution for my children." Mankind has always roamed. When my father disobeyed his mother to embark upon his separation, he set into motion revolutionary opportunities never dreamed of by his mother, for his children as well as for himself. We, his children, find in San Francisco the unique opportunity to choose between the magnetic pulls of Chinese and Western values. To make daily choices constitutes the rich dilemma facing Chinese in America. Even my father had to begin choosing, from his decision not to return to China to the decision fifty years later to attain United States citizenship.

My mother, having followed her husband and now her sons, is firmly uninterested in returning to China, where she has no living ties. She has achieved for herself independence and comforts in American life that she never conceived of as a girl. Her Chinese philosophy and Christian faith are her wellsprings in America.

Yet, these two who had made such dramatic breaks did not appreciate deviation when I tried to find my own independence. Though immigrants carry on revolution for their children, they seldom expect their young to engage in revolutionary experiments, but reward them instead for compliance.

This human impulse to conserve the status quo and to relax under it is the worry of China's present administration. A whole new urban generation, for whose security aging revolutionary leaders had sacrificed, was growing up unaware of the necessity to overcome hardship; yet there remain in China peasants without benefit of education and others, in other small nations of the world, who are struggling for self-determination. The Cultural Revolution's massive upheaval and reorganization altered doctrines and again imbued the young with the work ethic, forestalling a complacency which might have set the stage for power-grabbing and material corruption. Dissenting counterrevolutionaries were ultimately defeated, but since their principal leader had espoused certain Confucian analects, that ancient sage is being repudiated—specifically for advocating those relationships which protected the slave-owner class society of his day. (That day had produced the ceremonial bronze and slave burial in Ji-Nan.) Though years have passed since the Cultural Revolution, revolution in thinking continues to be actively fomented; and such national reeducation may continue in the form of other campaigns because Communist leaders believe that old thinking, if unchanged, will contaminate the new society and allow gains to revert back to old ills.

Do immigrants who are far from Communism and true to their tradition also have the courage to permit or to encourage their children to "carry on the revolution"? Having devoted a generation of work to provide for his children's welfare, having attained physical and economic liberation for himself and for us, my father had unwittingly given me a fifty-year head start toward mental liberation. Each Chinese-American like me has the opportunity to assess his talents, define his individual stature, and choose his personal balance of old and new, Chinese and Western ways, hopefully including the best of both. Father Wong's prize, more meaningful than gold, has also been the legacy he gave his children and grandchildren: he, and others like him, first gave us our cultural identity and then, by remaining in this country, permitted us the American freedom to attain individual self-images which ought to be constructive for the state but not subordinate to it. My own children may be potential revolutionaries who will throw their javelins earnestly and strongly; and I hope their targets will be the alleviation of mankind's miseries. When they drink water, as the old Chinese saying goes, I hope that they will think of its source, so that when they reach out to drop *their* aerial roots, their growth will bear the fruit of the banyan tree—wisdom.

While frequently enjoying the familiarity of Chinatown, I am grateful that my children can move on for intellectual headroom beyond the boundaries of a small community, and so can all other Americans, whatever background they represent. In my youth, prejudice was an obstacle to be circumvented by one's will, wits, and energies, so taken for granted that the insulted Normans, the tormented Younger and Youngest Brothers, and the worried Woodys delayed discussing a painful subject until years after they had made their compensatory adjustments. Perhaps these unarticulated obstacles had been the reason for Oldest Brother's pessimism about my choice of art as a profession; but perhaps first as a daughter, and now as a wife, I battle with race prejudice less often.

My future is in this land where Daddy and his progeny have sunk their roots around the rocks of prejudice, rather than closer to the shelter of the mother trunk. As I encourage my children's roots, I take heart from that "Foolish Old Man" in Ming Choy's lesson. With strong belief in our purpose, it may not be folly for the determined, with the hearts of children, to attack the high mountain of prejudice in our own way. When we die, our children and grandchildren will keep on working until, some day, the mountain will diminish. Then there will be no Chinese stranger.

For nearly all of us, our destinies are here, together and briefly, within this nation.